Organizing a Christian Mind

A Theology of Higher Education

Denise Lardner Carmody

TRINITY PRESS INTERNATIONAL
Valley Forge, Pennsylvania

Trinity Press International, P.O. Box 851, Valley Forge, PA 19482-0851
Trinity Press International is part of the Morehouse Publishing Group

Library of Congress Cataloging-in-Publication Data

Carmody, Denise Lardner, 1935-
    Organizing a Christian mind : a theology of higher education /
Denise Lardner Carmody.
        p.   cm.
    Includes index.
    ISBN 1-56338-165-6 (pbk. : alk. paper)
    1. Education (Christian theology) 2. Education, Higher – United
States.   I. Title.
BT738.17.C38   1996
207'.1'1 – dc20   96-24697
                                                                      CIP

Printed in the United States of America

96   97   98   99   00   01   10   9   8   7   6   5   4   3   2   1

In memory of
John Tully Carmody

In gratitude to
Paul Locatelli, S.J.

Contents

Preface

This book is a theological essay on education. I was stimulated to write it by moving to Santa Clara University in 1994 to become the chair of the Religious Studies Department. For it became apparent all too quickly that, under the influence of the papal document *Ex Corde Ecclesiae,* which lays out John Paul II's view of education, Roman Catholic schools such as Santa Clara University were bound to reconsider their sense of their identity and mission. Indeed, I found that a small body of literature centered on these issues had begun to accumulate — the fruits of a debate usually several-sided and sometimes passionate. However, familiarizing myself with the major voices in this debate gave me a telltale uneasiness. When I discussed my feelings with my husband, John Tully Carmody, who had fuller formal training as a theologian than I, I began to realize that I found unsatisfactory the theological vision implied in most of the analyses I was studying. This in turn led me to work out my own sense of the best way to think about education, which is what this book presents.

I leave it to others to judge how applicable my views are to primary and secondary levels of education. Let it be enough on that point to say that, though years ago I taught in Catholic grammar schools and high schools, my habitual frame of reference in this book is higher education, especially the college level. Sufficient for this day is the evil thereof.

On the question of the applicability of my views to Christian colleges run by mainline Protestant, Evangelical, and Orthodox churches, I assume that all of these groups could accept the fourfold delineation of reality that provides the framework for my basic curricular argument, and that each would have to enter the caveats, adaptations, and further developments that its particular historical and theological traditions suggested. At the end of the day, then, there is in my view and intention nothing essential about this theology of higher education that is "Roman Catholic" in a parochial let alone a triumphalistic sense. The theology and anthropology laid out here are far more ecumenical, common, than they are peculiar to the church to which I happen, and choose, to belong, and in whose cultural pale I now find myself working.

Introduction

Education: Teaching

Many activities bubble and hum at the typical American college, but the most important one, in my view, is teaching. Students go to a college for courses leading to a degree. They go to be taught — to learn under the guidance of professors. This is the assumption, the formality, that makes a college tick. In fact, a given student may go to a given college for fun, games, sex, beer, camaraderie. These are not, however, the activities by which any respectable college defines itself. The central focus of any respectable, representative American college is students' learning — most directly through the courses that professors teach and the studying that such courses entail. So, I begin my essay with some reflections on teaching.

Virtually all human beings teach and ask to be taught. Suppose that you are going on a trip, and that you have noticed that the tires of the car you plan to use seem soft. You take yourself to a service station near the freeway and ask the attendant how to fill your tires to the prescribed air pressure. He shows you the gauge in use at his station and you learn, through a little experimentation, first how to read its estimate of the current pressure of your tires and then how to introduce more air. The attendant has been your teacher. You have been his student. He has given you a little lecture. You have puzzled your way through it, listening, trying to get the appropriate pictures in your head, and then you have studied — experimented, worked over what he said, what you heard and imagined, pushing it this way and that, until you understood enough to make the little gauge work for you and get more air into your tires.

The assumption in all teaching situations is that one person knows more than another. A great deal of parenting is teaching, education, based on the fact that the mother or father knows more than the child. The parent knows that a hot stove burns. The child has to learn this fact — not through hands-on experimentation,

1

the parent hopes. What parents do, sometimes endlessly, older siblings, aunts, uncles, cousins, and friends also do — share what they know, what they have learned. Teaching is a natural, necessary part of human sociability, and one of the most crucial.

From the time that societies became large enough, complicated enough, to warrant if not require formal schooling, education has been a primary interest of local communities, and "education" has meant teaching, usually through oral instruction. Masters have taught apprentice carpenters, tailors, tinsmiths. Elder women have taught younger women cooking, sewing, medicinal arts. Moreover, religious teachers — gurus, roshis, mullahs, rabbis, catechists — have held places of considerable honor, because they have handed on the most sacred lore. To learn about the Vedas or the Buddhist sutras or the Koran or the Talmud or the Bible has been to enter the inner precincts, the most sacrosanct wisdom, of one's traditional religious culture. But the experienced people who taught the next generation, the inexperienced novices, what we now consider secular skills — how to hunt or farm or read or write or compute — were also people of substance in traditional communities. Along with the religious teachers, they contributed directly to both the practical survival of their people and the ongoing work of maintaining, developing, that people's traditions.

"Tradition" is what we hand on. The usual image is of the senior generation handing on to the junior generation the lore, the mores, the rituals through which the group to which both seniors and juniors belong has long defined itself. As such tradition became more extensive, and as it passed from being the lore of a particular people to being knowledge about the world as a whole, teaching became both more extensive and more specialized. For example, in European history, first natural science separated itself from philosophy and theology, then natural science itself divided into physics, chemistry, and biology, then these sciences developed dozens of subdivisions or specialties. Finally, many people involved in institutions of higher learning came to give the majority of their time to research rather than teaching (we reflect on the significance of research in the next section), but some form of teaching accompanied most moves of scientists into new specialties, because such scientists wanted students who would both help them with their work and, when the students had become competent, would extend the traditions the work carried forward.

One could sketch analogous histories for teaching and research in other fields, including theology. So, for instances, theologians began to specialize in scriptural studies, or doctrinal studies, or moral matters. These areas in turn gained subdivisions: the synoptic gospels, the prophets, Christology, medical ethics. Inasmuch as the physical sciences provided the model for modern research as a whole, specialization became the name of the game, even in theology. Yes, teaching remained the main preoccupation of college professors, who concentrated on undergraduates (in contrast to university professors, who might concentrate on graduate or even postgraduate students), but undergraduate teachers came under increasing pressure to do research and publish its results. Sometimes this improved undergraduate teaching in theology or the humanities at large by pushing professors to stay abreast of work in their fields and hand on to their students the latest findings. Sometimes this hegemony of the research model developed for the natural sciences hindered undergraduate teaching by causing many involved to lose perspective, wisdom, among the minutiae of specialization, and also by making some college professors resent the large amounts of time they had to spend on undergraduate students and long debilitatingly for more hours for research.

Furthermore, inasmuch as graduate work, indeed the Ph.D. degree, became the credential required even for teaching on the undergraduate, collegiate level, and this graduate work focused on research much more than on teaching, many college professors came to their work of teaching little prepared, even little enthused. The most prestigious form of "teaching" had shifted from the classroom to the laboratory or the specialized journal. What those considered knowledgeable knew, what they had to teach or pass on, tended to become narrower and narrower. As one rather bitter epigram put it, modern education became knowing more and more about less and less. In contrast, this perspective had it, traditional wisdom had reposed in knowing less and less about more and more. Unpacked, this epigrammatical judgment implied that specialization was endless — a verification of Zeno's paradox, according to which one can never get across a room because, analytically, the distance one has to go admits of infinite halving. In contrast, traditional wisdom headed in the direction of mysticism, where the seamless whole of ultimate reality defeated the mind. The more one dealt with God or nirvana, the less one knew, the more one realized that, when it comes to matters of ultimate import, ordinary, discrete human knowing is out of its league.

It is easy to describe how to teach specialized information, but often difficult to make the case that such information matters a great deal. It is easy to make the case that wisdom is precious and fascinating, but, in the measure that it becomes a mystical interaction with the Whole of what is truly real, difficult to describe how to teach wisdom well. Between these two poles, present-day academic teaching careens back and forth, at least in the humanities, my portion of the typical college curriculum. I have the impression that the physical sciences have largely given up on relating themselves to wisdom, and that the social sciences are not far behind. How it goes in the arts I cannot say, because there the quotients of practical matters (techniques) and emotion (related, presumably, to wider meaning) seem to vary considerably.

In the humanities, the prevailing pressure is for teachers to become more "academic" (that is, detached, concerned with supposedly objective data and analyses) and less concerned with personal meaning (that is, wisdom). Many scholars of religion, and some theologians, now think that this pressure is salutary, for reasons that I find both good and bad. (I distinguish theologians from scholars of religion on the basis of the former's necessarily having a commitment in faith and the latter's not necessarily having such a commitment, but not all members of either camp would accept this distinction.) The good reasons for becoming more academic reduce to professors' becoming better informed and more critical. The bad reasons reduce to professors' shirking the responsibility of showing students what their studies mean — the significance their studies can have for living fully realistically, in light of death and resurrection.

The fact that I have found it necessary to include research and scholarly specialization in my analysis of current undergraduate teaching suggests the pervasive influence of the educational model developed in the natural sciences. Research is now the most prestigious activity in most American institutions of higher learning. Even when professors spend most of their time on teaching undergraduates and receive most of their salary from their institution's offering such instruction, what such professors have to teach —

how they view their forwarding of tradition — stems in good part from their work in a specialty, a subset of their general discipline, and from their sense of what recent research has been turning up concerning the subject matter of their courses. In other words, few college courses now approximate the model of teaching and learning that prevailed for the first tens of thousands of years of human history, inasmuch as we can imagine how they went, when research was organized much less formally and the most revered portions of education dealt with wisdom (much of it focused on death, and so on how to live realistically).

Nowadays, most college curricula — orderings of the courses that undergraduates take, either as requirements or as electives — present only a wooly rationale for their structure and say nothing about wisdom or death. Nowadays it is not correct politically to say that human beings have an end (*telos*), a specific nature, an interior struggle between pulls toward reason and counterpulls toward sensuality, a more crucial struggle between their sinfulness and God's courting of them in grace. So, nowadays people reflecting on education theologically find themselves speaking from the margins. Still, as the theology of liberation has shown eloquently, the view from the margins can be extremely illuminating. Indeed, as the theology of the New Testament puts it, the poor, the marginal, have a special status. In the best of outcomes, I shall exploit this marginal, poor status to show how plain teaching can again hold its head high and concentrate on the heart of the educational, indeed of the human matter.

Education: Research and Publication

Although "education" entails teaching more directly than it entails research and publication, in present-day American higher education anyone reflecting on the state of the enterprise has to deal with research and publication. These are the two principal ways that educators, academics, think about "scholarship." Inasmuch as scholarship is extremely important in most departments, weighing at least as heavily as teaching when it comes to either hiring new faculty members or making decisions about tenuring or promoting experienced members, research and publication bulk large in the psyches of all the parties involved. Administrators, senior faculty members, and junior faculty members seeking tenure all worry about scholarly productivity. Much in this worry is helpful: an expression of a college's commitment to expanding or deepening knowledge. Some of it can become neurotic, a dark cloud blotting out the sun, but usually colleges manage to work out policies, and practices, that are both moderate and humane.

I start this reflection with the observation that teaching, research, and publication involve three different sets of skills. A given person may possess them all, but there is no guarantee that he or she will. The best of graduate trainings does not guarantee skills in teaching or, surprisingly, even in writing. It is hard to graduate from a solid program without having mastered the skills of a competent researcher, but nothing guarantees that the graduate will continue to be as industrious after securing an academic position as she or he was while being marched along a rigorous path to a Ph.D. Under the pressure of preparing classes, advising students, serving on committees, and, often, starting a family, many promising researchers wilt. Unless they are unusually good at managing their time, young faculty members can feel besieged. They need both to relax, contenting themselves with slow but steady progress through a faithful use of the limited time available to them for research, and to keep firm their commitment to studying, staying abreast of new work in their field, and making their own contribution to such work.

Teaching is mainly a matter of communication. Good teachers get across to their students what they are teaching. How they do this — through lectures, discussions, student projects, or other techniques — matters less than that they do it. On the whole, the skill of the good, rightly popular undergraduate teacher lies in being clear and interesting. Clarity — letting students see the logic of a given phenomenon or theory, showing the reasons, the antecedents and consequences — brings a note of rigor into the course. Undergraduates need this rigor, because most of them are not as disciplined in their thinking as we expect mature, educated adults to be. They are not critical — trained to evaluate arguments, to sift mere hypotheses from solid judgments yielding high probabilities. Relatedly, their language skills — range of vocabulary, ability to speak, read, and write fluently — are often poor.

Clarity relates to a teacher's being interesting through exemplification. We get our insights, our flashes of understanding, by grasping patterns of intelligibility in sensible data. Good examples, vivid illustrative instances, tend to rivet the hearer's attention. For example, I shall never forget Bernard Lonergan's illustrating the process of understanding by referring to Archimedes' discovery of specific gravity. To this day when I think of insight I see Archimedes lying back in his bath, relaxed, and then bemused by the floating of some objects in the water. When he realized that he could differentiate objects by the amount of water that they displaced, he was on his way to an important insight. His running from the bath (with a towel or without?) illustrates the power of insight — the excitement that understanding can bring. When he shouted "Eureka" ("I've found it"), he told the world that he had concluded a successful search, an arduous hunt, most successfully. One excellent example like this featuring a vivid image is worth a thousand words of unimaginative, pedestrian explication, either oral or written.

Now, there is something mysterious about the collation of the pedagogical skills that go into making a subject both clear and interesting. Teachers display their entire biographies in their classrooms, inasmuch as the ways that their minds work publicly flow from their upbringings, their educations, the circles of friends who have most influenced them, the books that they have read, and so on. Each good teacher is a unique success story, as is each good researcher or writer. We can speak of general precepts, as I have done in stressing clarity and imaginative ways of making a subject interesting, but now and then stellar teachers violate such precepts, substituting some other alluring traits that help students learn well. These include personal charisma, eloquence, suggestions of wisdom or courage or holiness. In those cases, the teacher may not be a model of clarity, may not even be unusually interesting as a lecturer on history or quantum mechanics, but the enthusiasm or depth, despite possible murkiness, or other distinctive quality (for example, skill at moderating discussion) of the regular performance makes the course a success.

Research entails, similarly, a combination of skills that finally can be quite idiosyncratic. Good researchers are patient, dogged even, possessing a keen intuition of the relevant datum, the salient document or previous study or defective traditional argument. They are alike in achieving a state that the desert fathers and mothers described (for different ascetical ends) as *apatheia:* passionlessness, detachment, indifference to the triumphing or losing of a given hypothesis. They want only what the fullest range of relevant data, the most cogent analyses, the most scrupulous criticism of assumptions and biases keeps saying is, at least for the present, the best reading, rendering, of the truth.

"Truth," and its correlative "reality," are words that make academic researchers uneasy, usually in the measure that their training and bent are empirical, but it is hard to dispense with these words. Scientists, and all other honest researchers, as indeed all people of integrity generally, want to deal with what is so. They want to describe it accurately and live by it faithfully. The alternative is a falsification that mottles, finally sickens, the self. After the dozen qualifications that psychologists and kind theologians offer rightly, the Johannine proposition (John 3:20) remains all too valid: Bad people hate the light, because their deeds are evil. Biased people hate the data that challenge their biases, often trying to suppress such data. Although we human beings cannot thrive in dishonesty, hypocrisy, prejudice, we succumb to them so often that the mystery of "original" sin remains as fascinating and relevant today as when the authors of Genesis first puzzled about Adam and Eve in the Garden.

Publication, the third item in our triad, used to mean virtually exclusively writing articles or books. With the advent of new technologies, it may expand its range in the future, either in the modest way of coming to include information made available through electronic mail or information networks, or more radically, by coming to include videos that present formal lectures — honed, scholarly presentations — as performances. For the near future, however, writing books and articles will probably remain the principal vehicle through which scholars "publish" their results, ideas, summaries of the present state of a question and suggestions about the most desirable trends for the future. This means that for the near future skill in writing will probably continue to be important to success in higher education.

Writing, like teaching and research, is a fascinating combination of things that others can teach us and things that remain mysteriously idiosyncratic. The good writer is usually grammatical, logical, able to weave examples and principles into a pleasing, persuasive flow of argumentation. Academic culture favors a high quotient of logical rigor, and often it encourages bad writing by favoring the passive voice, using nouns as adjectives, and fleeing from either ruthless editing or imaginative examples. That this occurs regularly among people who would subscribe overwhelmingly to the thesis that style and content, mind and mode of expression, run together inseparably is just a pertinent one of the many ironies that populate the cultures of higher education and suggest that it is not so long on fundamental self-criticism as it ought to be. Superficial criticism abounds, most of it negative. Academics are trained far better in destruction, slashing and burning, than in construction: building works novel and beautiful, helping other people improve *their* grasp of their scholarly convictions and presentation of them (in contrast to what the critic wishes the other person thought or chose as a literary level, genre, or style).

Productive writers, in this case academics who publish large quantities of work, have usually disciplined themselves to write on a regular basis: every morning, or evening, or at least weekend. On the whole, writing a little each day seems to work better than trying to write a lot occasionally. The regular, ideally daily contact with one's project makes it familiar, easily invited into one's inner self, so that one dreams about it, finds oneself constructing better examples or arguments while jogging or musing down the aisle of the supermarket or waiting in the doctor's office. Like sensitive friends or lovers, our projects seems to know when they are only occasional preoccupations, and they resent this, because they think it makes them marginal, second-class. Any legitimate rescue of such a personification of a book or article comes from the fact that it houses our muse — the quite personal part of ourselves that first conceived it. How legitimately we conceived a work can, by the way, become an issue affecting our enthusiasm for it. If it was a bastard, something we started more through lust than through love, we may be ashamed of it.

Our muse is our self, in part more or less important, and until we recognize this, coming to love our literary self, we will not go to our writing firing on all cylinders. As a result, we will not be as productive as we might have been, will not publish the full corpus that we might have published. I leave to others the practical matters of how to contact journals or book publishers, noting only that a little questioning of people who have been successful in publishing their work will reveal quickly the usual protocols in this business: What publishers want in a prospectus, how important it is to clarify what one's audience is, the utility of working out an outline that breaks a project down into realistic writing units (for example, sections of five pages). People with ordinary competence who discipline themselves and persevere will succeed, at least 85 percent of the time. There is much more reason for optimism than pessimism.

Last, it bears noting that through its sponsorship of research and publication, higher education serves as one of society's principal sources of new ideas, better ways not just to build mouse traps but to understand the general principles underlying them and our other feats of engineering. The same for our finding better ways of treating heart disease or cancer, for our dealing with differences in gender or race, even for our fashioning comprehensive worldviews that help us believe that our time under the sun is not futile: The research sponsored by universities is precious.

Any society needs such research, and the publication that makes the yield of the research available to others, if it is to advance the common good. Therefore, any healthy society nourishes skilled researchers and writers: laboratory scientists, investigators of social trends, historians, poets, artists, and theologians. My bias is that the more basic an area of research is, the more support it should receive. For example, the basic research in biochemistry that has led to our vastly expanded knowledge of genetics and so to new medical therapies based on replacing defective genes has opened entire new vistas for practice. Basic research in astrophysics and mathematics is having a similar influence in cosmology and economics. New ways of thinking about human interactions, many of them stemming from basic research in physical or cultural anthropology, have started to change the ways that philosophers and theologians think about the ecologies and politics of our social lives. And so it goes.

The more deeply we probe the basic structures of our bodies, our material environments, our social interactions, our patterns of thought, and our formulations of questions about ultimate reality, the more powerfully we equip our cultures to deal with the assaults of the painfully practical questions — how to slow pollution, how to replace war-making with negotiation, how to combat AIDS, how to deal with street people — that threaten to tear our commonwealths apart.

Theology: The Difference That God Makes

This book is a theological essay on education. Theology is the study of God. It is a peculiar study, because "God" is a peculiar reality. Indeed, if one probes the high theology of the theistic religions, one finds regularly the realization that what the word "God" names is a reality only comparable analogously to the tables and chairs, the trees and beavers, the men and women with whom we do most of our dealing day by day. God is more "ultimate reality," or Reality *simpliciter* — the source, goal, and ground of all that is, and so the most important aspect, cause, even stuff of all that is — than God is *a* reality in the sense of another thing, one more finite item in the general pile. So to be a working theologian is always to be dealing with a subject matter determined most crucially by a Someone or a Something that exceeds one's grasp, both physical and conceptual. It is always to be immersed in a mystery — a reality too full for limited human talent, capacity, to master. God is unlimited. A limited God is a contradiction in terms. Hence the theistic religious traditions are full of such teasing, paradoxical dicta as, "We can know that God is but not what God is," and "If you have understood, it is not God."

In the next section I take up the question of faith, both the general phenomenon that lies at the heart of all the major religions and has shaped the souls of the vast majority of men and women through the hundreds of millennia during which our species has existed, and the specific tradition of faith in which I locate myself, the Christian. Here I want to deal with the difference that God, whom most people reach through faith and all people must live with in faith if they are to deal with divinity successfully, can, probably should, make in one's view of education.

The difference is both enormous and humble. A well-known Zen saying captures this paradox: "Before enlightenment rocks are rocks and trees are trees. After enlightenment, rocks are rocks and trees are trees." The hidden middle premise is that during the search for enlightenment, and the process that brings it to climax, the world, reality can turn over, first shaking the searcher's consciousness to its foundations and then putting her back on her feet, newly upright. So, after enlightenment, when she looks out her kitchen window she sees the same cherry tree, but its significance, its place in the overall scheme of things, how she estimates what it "says" to her — all this has changed. The world is just what it was, yet it is completely new. By moving through enlightenment to the ultimate depths of reality (to what her culture probably calls nirvana or suchness or buddha-nature and to what a Western the-istic culture calls God), she has changed the ontology of meaning that gives any life its inmost significance, its personal (in contrast to simply physical) pulse.

To take another angle into this matter of the difference that God can make in how we estimate the human condition, and so, by quick inference, in how we ought to educate our young people, situate our teaching, think foundationally about our research and publication, let us reflect on what a leading theologian of the past generation, Paul Tillich, called "the Protestant Principle." This was the basic plank that Tillich found undergirding the best passions of the sixteenth-century Reformers and supporting the traditions that they engendered. It was a firm commitment to the soleness of God, and so a powerful determination to avoid idolatry. In light of the soleness of God on high, all human inventions, conceptual as well as political, occupied a much lower place in any religious practice or cultural milieu that Tillich considered healthy, realistic, faithful to the Christian message. No church, no liturgy, no theology, let alone any *Fortune* list of the five hundred leading corporations or any list from *People Magazine* of the foremost billionaires, mat-tered much, and so our practical tendency to invest ourselves in them or the images of "success" that they proffered to us proved often to be idolatrous. We were setting on the altar, in the center of our hearts, something less than the sole God. We were selling our birthright for a mess of pottage.

Our birthright is the freedom that a commitment to the primary reality and soleness of God entails. If we serve God, if God is our only surpassing passion and treasure, we are free of all the idols and tyrants that seem to rob most of our contemporaries of their peace, their joy, their maturity. Think of the drivenness to which so many of our executives are tempted. Study the impact of all the advertising that parades before us beautiful clothes, slim bod-ies free of pains and unpleasant odors, romantic holidays in exotic foreign lands, creature comforts such as sleek cars, washer-dryers and microwave ovens, stereo systems and VCRs. Collectively, they can amount to a summons to massive flight into distraction, a mad lemmings' rush. And from what do so many of our contemporaries, succumbing, run away? From the grim fact of their mortality, of the surety of their deaths, and from the vacuum of godlessness in their lives (or the silence in which divinity usually dwells).

The denial of death is no less powerful a cultural force in most of America nowadays, indeed in the entire developed world, than it was twenty odd years ago when Ernest Becker and Elisabeth Kübler-Ross exposed its malignant operations. Until people have death brought home to them in their own bodies or households, they usually fight tooth and nail to keep it at bay, beyond clear consciousness. Even when it gores their own oxen, they often shut the emotional doors through which death might bring them gifts of wisdom. For death calls into question, darkly and radically, the assumptions of most secular cultures. It says that what the advertisers and sports nuts and beauty saloneers promote as freeways to fun, even happiness, usually end in wretched little culs de sac. This situation tempts any serious, or simply literate, human being to wonder whether Albert Camus was not right: "People die and they are not happy."

Inasmuch as we seem constituted not to want to die, and to want to be happy, the harsh reality that we do all die, and that many of us spend many of our living days unhappy, produces a contradiction in the center of us that makes our human existence absurd. The root image of "absurd" is one of deafness — hearing no significant word. We cock our ears hopefully, then desperately, but reality does not speak, no word of solace or assurance that our lives finally make sense reaches us. For Camus this is our cruel human condition. We are like Sisyphus, pushing our rock up the hill, hoping to develop a work or a love or a religion that will make our pains bearable, our deaths acceptable, but always the rock rolls back down to the bottom, always the best we can do is start pushing it up again.

Related to this existential frustration and absurdity is the silence of God — how God seems to be before faith enables us to bear him. Certainly, the theistic religions speak of "revelation," the root image of which is a drawing aside of the veil behind which a reality or truth has been concealing itself, keeping silent. For example, the disclosures to the patriarchs and the prophets recorded in the Hebrew Bible amount to the Israelite Lord's taking away the veil in which he had usually enshrouded himself. For Christians the birth, ministerial life (healing, preaching, working of miracles), death, and resurrection of Jesus brought this biblical revelation to an incarnational climax. In the flesh of Jesus God showed all that human flesh can show of the divine reality. Nonetheless, Scripture itself says that God herself truly is hidden, silent, little concerned about human opinion. Relatedly, the regular testimony of faithful, even saintly Jews and Christians and Muslims through the centuries, the experience of those who have tried diligently to serve God through prayer and practical help for their neighbors, is that the revelations recorded in the Bible and the Koran, and still available there, do not remove the mysteriousness of God. God unveiled on Sinai or in Jesus is, experientially, still God veiled. When God gave to Moses the divine name (Exodus 3), it turned out to be nothing that human beings could grasp, no way that human beings could bring God under their control: "I am as I shall be with you." When God let Jesus go to an agonizing death and then resurrected Jesus to a strange new form of existence, before raising him to the divine "right hand," human beings gained precious new images around which to let their religious faith cluster, but these new images left the ways of God just where they had been in the time of the prophet Isaiah: as far from our human ways as the heavens are from the earth. And, finally, for Muslims, even fourteen centuries after Muhammad's reception of the Koran, Allah remains the exalted Lord of the Worlds that no human being can understand, before whom the first obligation of all human beings is to bow low without question.

The link between human mortality and the silent mysteriousness of God perhaps comes into clearest focus in Orthodox Christian theology, first Greek and then, through Greek influence, in the other Orthodox churches. There the first note of divinity, its most characteristic feature, is its deathlessness. We die. God lives. When God the Father resurrected Jesus, he took humanity into the divine deathlessness. Indeed, in the infancy narratives of Matthew and Luke we see the fruits of a movement in early Christianity to shift the crucial fusion of mortal humanity with deathless divinity from the resurrection of Jesus to the moment of the Incarnation, when the Son of God took flesh in the Virgin Mary. The climax of this movement to place such a fusion farther and farther back in the process by which God established Jesus as the deathless Lord of a new creation occurs in the Prologue of John, where it becomes clear that the One who took flesh in Mary was the eternal Word of God existing "in the bosom of the Father" from all eternity. Echoing the first words of Genesis, but altering their import in light of the event of Jesus the Christ, the Prologue says, "In the beginning was the Word, and the Word was with God." Thus, as soon as the Word took flesh, flesh gained immortality, deathlessness.

So, to admit the reality of God, and in consequence the legitimacy of theology, is to make all the difference in one's estimate of human nature and destiny, if not indeed of all creation. As the Zen proverb suggests, everything looks the same but now it carries a new meaning. As Tillich's "Protestant Principle" lays down, only God can lie at the center of a properly ordered human consciousness and living, while everything less than God threatens constantly to become an idol. Certainly, God remains fully mysterious, no thing or idea that we shall ever fit into a safety box at our bank, a corner of our consciences. Nonetheless, without God it is hard not to agree with Albert Camus that human existence is absurd, hard not to agree with Dostoevski's Ivan Karamazov that anything is permitted. The death camps of Hitler, and the Gulags of Stalin, and the chopsticks that Vietcong soldiers used to ram into the ears of the children of dissidents make this latter proposition so horribly pertinent to recent history that many of us can barely contemplate it.

Yet God is not only the dark divinity who may hold our lives now. God is also the splendor of our lives now — the beauty toward which our hearts fly, when we fall in love or gaze at a newborn child or watch the ocean on a perfect day or leave our work-station blessed by our muse — and the consummation of our lives "then," in what Christians call heaven. God is grace now, in space and time, glory then, in our deathless, ongoing fulfillment with God outside of space and time. How this can be we can only glimpse now and then, usually in moments that come unexpectedly. We are "surprised by joy," in the felicitous phrase of C. S. Lewis. We hear "rumors of angels," in the phrase of Peter Berger. If we are trained thinkers of an ontological bent, loving to contemplate the mysteries of being (beginning with the foundational question of why there is something rather than nothing), we may reason our way to the conclusion of Aquinas that we can know that God exists, though we cannot know what God is. In Aquinas's terminology, we can know the *esse* of God but not the divine *essentia)*. All this is wonderfully surprising and joyous.

One implication of this Thomistic conclusion that I shall exploit for my theology of education and realistic living boils down to accepting, indeed making paramount, the fact that we not only do not but *cannot* know, bring under conceptual control, the most basic and important things about ourselves and our world. We do not know where we came from, nor where we are going. We do not know how to bring ourselves or our societies into order, so that we would live justly, kindly, without hatred and slaughter. Any of these particular ignorances can lead us on to the final step: the constant relevance of our fundamental ignorance, of the nescience concomitant with our finitude and mortality. We are defined at least as much, probably more crucially, by what we do not know, our condemnation to live in the midst of mystery, as by what we do know. Indeed, for the deepest religious sages East and West, the best wisdom we can come to is knowing that we cannot know, with all its vast yet compactable implications. There is no end to the ramifications of our never being in charge of, masters or mistresses of, our world, both exterior and interior, both the physical universe and the human self. Yet we can compact all these ramifications into the simple, dense requirement that for true wisdom we need only to "unknow" what passes for wisdom in "the world," the secular cultures or godless zones of general cultures that mix secularism and religiosity.

Such intermediate or penultimate wisdom is finally idolatrous. It does not make primary the divine mysteriousness, the unknowability of God, and so it prevents us from practicing the simple contemplative adoration that Augustine implied when he said, "You have made us for yourself, O God, and our hearts are restless until they rest in You." Worldly wisdom does not let us define our human vocation as most radically a calling to cast off our narcissism, our crippling egocentricity, so that we may live eccentrically, ecstatically, outside ourselves in God.

The implications for education of admitting the reality of God, and so the exercise of religion and theology, into one's sense of reality, are both enormous and humble, as they are for our lives generally. Because God never comes under the control of any of the things that solicit our making them into idols or threaten to become our tyrants, we can be amazingly free. No boss or parent or pope or ethical code is our final master. There is no God but God. Therefore a prayer from a traditional Christian liturgy begins, "O God, to serve whom is to reign...." On the other hand, we remain humble creatures who have to eat, sleep, have sex, raise children, run businesses, fight crime, organize governments, and on and on. We continue to watch for the sun in the morning and plunge into our beds weary at night. Rocks are still rocks; trees are still trees. But now, with faith, all things are vestiges of God, and our fellow human beings may be images. We ourselves may be images, creatures whose intelligence and love, whose ability to make things creatively and form intentional communities through our searches for meaning reflects something at the heart of our Maker, something most revelatory.

From this status of our being images of God, as we come to a fractional understanding of it through biblical revelation, we can gain precious help for orienting our lives. In the summary orientation that Jesus adapted from the Hebrew Bible, we are to love the Lord, our God, with our whole minds, hearts, souls, and strength, and we are to love our neighbors as ourselves. Where Freud said, most helpfully, that the operative criteria for mental health are the abilities to love and to work, people formed by the difference that God makes in any adequate estimating of our human condition add the ability to pray. If we can love God and our neighbors through an effective life of prayer, a warm emotional life, and through works of practical help and mercy, we can be images of God in fact, action, not just potential. We can imitate the God who makes her sun to shine, her rain to fall, on just and unjust alike, providing the world with an ongoing presence of the benevolence from which she first made all that is, the full universe, in the beginning.

Theology: Christian Faith

This book is a theology of education. More specifically, it is a view of higher education worked out of Christian faith. Bernard Lonergan has described faith as the knowledge born of religious love. His description applies to more than Christian belief or trust in God. We can find that it illumines what Jews experience when dealing with their Lord through their Torah, what Muslims experience when dealing with their God through the Koran. Faith is a knowledge in the sense of a connatural familiarity with God, an intimacy like that which the best spouses, friends, parents, and children experience. We know God as we love God, by and in the process of loving God. We love God from the center of ourselves, as the known unknown that we seek from the first moment that our souls take flight after meaning. God is the term, the goal, of all our erotic quests for beauty. God is the great rightness inspiring our search for justice. When we revolt at the partiality of all the meanings that creatures can give us, feeling that we have been made for something more, for a simple whole that would suffer no defect and could quiet our restless minds, what we implore tacitly is God: "Take us where we need to go to slake our thirst, fulfill our longing. Take us to yourself, the light in whom there is no darkness at all." Finally, when we love something or, even more, someone to the point where our beloved becomes the other half of our soul, we experience an exodus from the fleshpots of selfishness into the comforting wilderness of God.

God is wild, fierce, as creative and destructive as the explosions of the suns, the eruptions of the volcanoes. Yet this very wildness, this very vastness and otherness into which we go when we desert Egypt and trudge toward first Sinai and then Sion, is also tender as a nursing mother, receptive as a father welcoming his prodigal child home. Love takes us into the divine creativity and so diversity as nothing else can. Love is our best clue to why God made the world in the beginning and how God lives internally, in his, her, its own life — what the divine community that Christians call the "Trinity" may be like.

This movement toward God from the characteristic drives, callings, ecstatic movements of the human spirit is one representative Christian theological way of expressing, working out, the implications of faith. It squares well not only with a description of faith as the knowledge born of religious love but also with the classical understanding of Christian theology as faith seeking understanding. Theologians ought to begin with faith. Faith is always their beginning and their end, something more primary, primitive, inclusive, and important than the understandings (determinations of facts and hypotheses about what the facts concerning traditional faith may mean — what coherence, *taxis,* they may possess in themselves). But despite all its limitations, its lesser importance than faith, theology remains precious, because what we have in our minds, the images and hypotheses that we use to make our way through life, have a loud say in what we experience and how we end up.

If I think that death is the gateway to God, I lie in my hospital bed with a different meaning than has the person next to me who thinks that death is the end. If I agree with the Christian fathers that the goods of the earth exist for all the earth's people, then I look at the disparities in the nations' standards of living differently than do the people who think with Hobbes that life is bound to be a warfare because human beings treat one another as wolves. And if I think that God is the end, the fulfillment of the human being, calling all of us to holiness (living most realistically, most wisely, most selflessly), then my evaluations of politics and economics and popular culture tend to vary significantly from those of people who think that human existence is an evolutionary accident and human beings have no intrinsic sacredness.

Where as a believer I am drawn to agree to the proposition that the needs of the poor ought to take priority over the wants of the rich, you as an unbeliever may find in this proposition nothing compelling. To you poverty or wealth is a matter of chance and hard work, genes and diligence and luck. There have always been many poor people and a few rich. Yes, it is unseemly, a lack of noblesse oblige, for the rich to trample on the poor, but in the final analysis neither riches nor poverty brings us enough meaning or dignity to justify a life and so one might as well eat, drink, and be merry. The poor we have with us always. It is unfortunate that the blighters live in cardboard shacks or on the streets, but we did not make this cruel, unfair, evolutionary world, so there is no point in our agonizing over its inequities.

Christian faith, trying to take to heart such evangelical high points as the sermon of Jesus on the mount (Matthew 5–7), cannot feel this way, think this way, in good conscience. Christian theology, trying to give rational order to such faith, probing the high points of both the gospels and such authoritative expressions of tradition as the decrees of the ecumenical councils, has to honor what Jesus said in the beatitudes, the high point of his sermon on the mount. There the poor and the other species of underclass people familiar to Jesus from the society of his day receive a special blessing from God. They have only God for their comfort and redress, and so God looks on them carefully, tenderly.

In his battles with the Pharisees, Jesus allies himself with the poor and those whom the Law calls sinners, arguing and behaving counterculturally. By sharing meals with people ritually unclean (tax collectors, whores), Jesus shows that the judgment of God, the Kingdom of God, is not pharisaic. The Law was made for human beings, not human beings for the Law. It is right to break the letter of the laws for keeping the Sabbath in order to heal human beings, because the spirit of the Law that God gave to Moses on Sinai is humanistic — meant to help people live full, free, blessed lives. The glory of God is human beings fully alive, while the life of human beings fully alive is the vision of God. The latter phrase of this sentence from Irenaeus carries a wonderful duplexity. Human beings come into their fullest vitality by seeing God. What God sees when he looks at the human beings that he has made is their flourishing. The medieval Christian conception of heaven as essentially the beatifying vision of God extends this duplexity. Human beings reach their unending fulfillment by contemplating God, who can never be exhausted. Yet heaven is also God's vision of human beings reaching their complete fulfillment — God's parental delight that the prodigals have come home and so the feasting can begin.

Theologians can never bring such a wealth of images, allusions, and implications under tidy control, but their labors to get enough organization to allow the gospel to be the basis for the humanistic vision that people require if they are to move well through the natural world, the social world, and the realms of their own psyches are precious beyond measure. For example, if God made the world in the beginning, then the world is godly. If the world is godly, then any ab-use of the world, any dire pollution, is an abuse of the gift of God, indeed of the presence of God in nature. Similarly, if God made human beings male and female, and if the divine image in human beings appears whenever an infant first squalls, then human beings are radically equal. No differentiation by sex or ethnic group or economic caste ought to mean more to the justice that human beings receive generally, the dignity that any person receives individually, than this radical equality based on a common origin in God and a common possession of the divine image.

Within the self, the realm of psychology, traditional Christian theology says that reason and love are more decisive than emotional and bodily concerns. There is a hierarchy in the self, though not a dualism. Matter and spirit go together inseparably. Matter is lower, in the sense that it is our fundament in nature. Through our bodies we are members of the realms that physicists, chemists, and biologists study. We despise our bodies or neglect them at our peril, to our imbalance. More Christian heresies about human nature have come from deprecating the body than from overvaluing it. If a faithful analysis of human beings as creatures and images of God did not make the dignity of the body, of human materiality, plain, certainly the central Christian doctrine that the divine Word took flesh from Mary, in Mary, ought to.

But the matter that gives us our animality does not make us human. The spirit that gives us reason and love does that. We are little lower than the angels, because with them we share spirituality. Ours is incarnate, and so social and symbolic through and through, while theirs is disembodied. But our spirituality is powerful enough to generate all the vast realms of human culture: the natural sciences and arts and political arrangements that make our species unique upon the earth. We have language from our spirits, and history, and music, and mathematics. Indeed, we have prayer and mysticism, clamoring liturgies and falls into the abysmal silence that we hope is God least mediated for us, most nakedly divine.

So our lives as human beings are constantly balancing acts. Constantly we strive to keep in harmony the below of our materiality and the above of our spirituality. We strive to keep our feet under us, on the ground, and our souls ecstatic for heaven. We fall off this balance, fall out of this harmony, again and again, yet we can do nothing else but try again. Thereby, painfully, we learn what it means for the wise to say that virtue lies in the middle, that there can be no easy absolutism on either side, no rightful repression or indulgence.

For instance, drugs can be good in a medicinal setting, helping the body or the mind, but they can be vicious in a "recreational" setting, a self-indulgent pursuit of euphoria. Wine can help to make a meal a work of art, a time of human warmth and joy. But wine can also put people out on the streets, sleeping in doorways or over registers. So too with work and sex and religious practice. We human beings can abuse anything, deal with any part of creation in a disordered fashion. The corruption of the best things — our bodies, our minds, our children, our churches, our art — brings about the worst things: slavery, pride, abortion and parricide, fanaticism, pornography. How fortunate we are, therefore, that the Wisdom of God took flesh to show us what we might become. How lucky we are that a few saints and sages have shown us better ways: lives in balance and harmony, bodies and souls grown beautiful in grace. These are the models we should take to heart. These are the human torches from which we ought to take our light as either theologians or educators.

This Book

When I think about offering students an education shaped by a solid Christian theology — one faithful to the mainstream of traditional faith, alert to the movements of the Holy Spirit in our own time, controlled by the central image of the Incarnation, and enlightened by the example of the saints and sages who have been the best images of God, the best "imitators" of Christ — what emerges is a comprehensive, systematic sketch of reality. For the sake of our work here, this sketch covers four principal areas, which we shall treat consecutively in the next four chapters.

My sketch begins with a theological reflection on human nature: what we educators and students are, where we stand in the universe, how we ought to think about our makeup, the goal of our lives, the most important tasks that we face. What are the educational implications of saying, for instance, that our goal is grace now and glory later, is meaning and healing now and visionary fulfillment later? These are simply elaborations or translations of such phrases in the Christian creed as "the forgiveness of sins, the resurrection of the body, and the life of the world to come." However, when one makes them bear on the task of estimating where all the parties to any educational venture are headed, such creedal phrases become less tame and customary, more dynamic and radical.

For then the students rushing themselves into shorts and halters because the temperature has hit seventy in sunny California in February may be more than simple sybarites. Then we can interpret the glow that they seek as a prod that God has put in their natures one day to seek a fuller light and warmth. The same with such staples of our human condition, of what we have to do and want to, as work, human love, and ritual. On the other hand, if we examine our human condition from the standpoint of a mature Christian faith, we can see that ignorance and sin mottle so much of what we do, of how we live both as individuals and collectively, and so that optimism is foolish, realism is sober, any responsible hopes repose more in God than in our human selves.

What practical implications do theological analyses, interpretations, exegeses of the human condition such as these carry for higher education? What do they say about a proper theoretical outlook on what our educational efforts ought to have in mind, consider realistic, adopt as a wise psychology? I think that a view of education shaped by a Christian theology such as mine is far more radical in its implications, both practical and theoretical, than most churchpeople or secular analysts realize. I think that here we meet a pertinent instance of the axiom that passing "relevance" doesn't hold a candle to deep tradition.

Chapter 2 deals with physical nature — the material world, the universe, creation. In fact, creation will be our first topic: where the material world comes from, what makes it be, when, it seems clear, it need not be. Our other topics will be the ecosphere, physical science, a sustainable lifestyle, practical implications of Christian theological interpretations of these topics for education, and finally theoretical implications. If chapter 1, on human nature, writes a license, a solid legitimation, for the academic disciplines that study the self in all its dimensions, social as much as private, then chapter 2 writes a legitimation for natural scientists to explore creation freely, boldly, with all the genius and patience and verve that they can muster.

This is not to assume that many such scientists have been standing back, waiting for such a legitimation. It is not to say that self-doubt seems their overriding characteristic. Finally, it is not an apology after the fact of Galileo and his restoration to good standing by the Vatican in its own glacial time. It is simply a paying of the debt that speculative theologians owe to nature when they take up the task of explicating a comprehensive vision of reality. Since the occasion for my taking up this task is the current debate among Roman Catholics about the distinctiveness that Christian faith ought to bestow on their institutions of higher learning, I feel the need to ground theologically the full humaneness and legitimacy of natural science. Whether any physicists or chemists or biologists themselves share this feeling is secondary. If their delight in scientific exploration, the joy that they find in scientific understanding, is stable enough, then perhaps they will not take it amiss for someone like me to link this delight and joy with the image of God that emerges when human intelligence is fully alive, human passion flames forth to understand what believers think is the great gift that God has made in creating so vast and beautiful a universe.

Chapter 3 focuses on politics, meaning by this word both how human beings should make their social arrangements and how they actually do. The subtopics through which we shall move are the common good, the church, governance, ministry, law, persuasion, practical implications for education, and theoretical implications for education. As in the other chapters, these subtopics are foci for theological reflections — movements from a faith seeking to understand its concrete implications for education into a given sector of reality, human experience, what all students and teachers have to contend with. The social dimension or sector of reality is no less real, no less imperative in the demands that it makes on all of us, theologians emphatically included, to think hard about its ways and means than are the dimensions or sectors of the physical nature that spreads itself throughout the universe and the human nature that we all possess as our own, the makeup of our personal self. Physical nature, the personal self, and the social aggregate of us human beings overlap, interact, and clash constantly, but any analysts worth their salt show the value of dealing with each of them separately, theologians included again. The separation is artificial, and the reality of the constant mutual influence of the realms returns as soon as one leaves the rooms of the university or the rooms of the mind where such separation took place. But one can leave enriched by having considered politics apart from biology and psychology. One's prescriptions for higher education can be the better for one's having drawn aside from the hurly-burly to contemplate a given sector peacefully.

Chapter 4, in which I deal with divinity, returns us to theology proper. Divinity is the fourth of the ineluctable components of our human situation for which any sketch comprehensive enough to orient a venture in higher education profitably has to provide. Yet, as we have already seen, divinity is not just another component, will not just submit itself inertly to be shaded into a sketch alongside human nature, physical nature, and politics as their equal.

Divinity is a realm of its own, yes, but one far more independent than any of the other three. In fact, a Christian theology has to make divinity the source of everything that is, as it has to make Jesus the savior. There is no parity between the three dimensions of reality that we treat in chapters 1–3 and what we consider in chapter 4.

On the other hand, theology has become a discipline housed in our common academic office buildings, sometimes on top of history or below sociology or to the side of fine arts. Scholars of religion have talked their way into the university by arguing that religion is as fascinating a portion of human experience, and so as worthy of serious study, as art or sport or medicine. This means that theologians dealing with divinity have to account for world religions and "religious studies" along with God, Christ, and salvation. It means that after we have dealt with the divine transcendence, the divine immanence, how divinity heals human nature, what "grace" brings into the world, the best ways to think about suffering (crucifixion), and the best ways to think about hope (resurrection), we ought again to imagine the practical and theoretical consequences that such thoughts carry for the work of higher education. The difference that the Christian God makes in a person's sense of reality has enormous implications for how that person conceives of the task of educating the next generation. The omnirelevance of divinity as the creative source in which all creatures live and move and have their being makes chapter 4 crucial.

In chapter 5 we revisit education, to see how it looks after our crucial enlightenment — from the vantage point to which I hope our theological passage has carried us. This is the view of a person with two feet on the ground, a firm grasp of the complexities of the human constitution, the natural world, and politics but also with a mystical appreciation of the prevenience and priority and finality of the divinity revealed in Jesus the Christ. If ever we needed delicacy and balance, here is the time, this is the place. When we look in this chapter at students, community service, academic freedom, arts and sciences, the heart of the educational matter, higher education as a creative moratorium in the life cycle, and how administrators can move higher education forward best, we ought to bring to these representative topics, these perennial concerns of all those involved in higher education, a more sophisticated appreci-

ation of their potential holiness than we could have brought at
the outset, before our enlightenment. Rocks are still rocks. Students are still students. But the rocks take a shine from the inner
lightsomeness that wisdom finds in their being, while the students
seem more pathetic — more significantly bound to suffer — than
we realized before we thought theologically, ultimately, about the
so complex and conflicted comprehensive reality with which they
will have to contend, to say nothing of the so simple, gracious, yet
utterly demanding divinity.

I am using this word "enlightenment" lightly, of course, with
the fun of play, as often I shall use the word "wisdom." Yet, in a
playful, properly humble way this book is about enlightenment and
wisdom, about what we ought to see when we gaze at students,
what we ought to think when we do our best to educate them for
the realities with which they will have to contend, in contrast to
the rootless dreams now dominating many of them.

Our Conclusion begins with the problem of vision (how to get
people to see where education ought to head, how it ought to as-
semble itself), which entails as a subproblem the tendency of some,
perhaps many parties to the educational venture, to assume that
there can be no consensus about vision, or that there is no "university," only an ad hoc collection of disparate studies. Next we
take up the problem of public support for higher education — basic research, teaching that is rigorous and more than vocational
(oriented to the marketplace). One advantage of choosing to base
an educational venture on a Christian theology is that this choice
makes education (*a*) intrinsically liberal and (*b*) opposed inimically
to a purely vocational or applied understanding of what "training"
after high school ought to be. While I shall argue repeatedly that a
proper theology of education legitimates all human inquiry and establishes academic freedom as an inalienable right flowing from the
nature of the human mind that God has made, I shall also argue
that a proper theology will not settle for a view of human destiny determined by money and banking, pleasure and power, works
that refuse to rise beyond this-worldly horizons. Our third topic,
lifelong learning, merely extends liberal education to the full course
of a person's time, reminding us that higher education should be a
mainsail for a voyage that has no end.

The last three topics that we consider in concluding bring the
theology of education that we have elaborated back to the prob-

lematic from which it began. These three topics are education and church control, theology and church control, and wisdom and dying. In all three the watchword is freedom, because the yield of our theological passage has been grace. Overwhelmed by the grace of God, the love poured forth in Christ Jesus his Lord, the apostle Paul told the Galatians, "For freedom Christ has set us free." The function of those who watch over ventures in higher education sponsored by the Catholic Church ought to be first to encourage such freedom and second to serve its flourishing ministerially. Education can thrive only in freedom, and free inquiry itself is the best way to achieve the sobriety about human nature, the convictions about the asceticism that human prospering requires, entailed in the Christian gospel.

These matters gain a further acuity when we take up the topic of theology and church control, but nothing changes in my essential outlook, because the church remains far less important than God. Theologians place themselves under ecclesiastical discipline if they understand their venture properly, but this discipline is not properly legalistic. Rather it is ideally the harmonious cooperation of the institutional and charismatic aspects of the Christian community, the cordial give and take of brothers and sisters focused on the common good of handing on well, faithfully and in line with the signs of their times, the good news that they themselves received from their teachers and love as their pearl of great price. Our last consideration wisdom and dying, ought to make where we end the good earth — into which Jesus himself descended and from which Jesus himself returned — wholly enlightened and divinized.

Chapter 1

On Human Nature

Our End

Could anything be more abstract, more apparently otiose, than a discussion of human nature beginning with the end, the *telos,* that we women and men are made, constituted, to seek? Is not such a discussion "classical," "scholastic," in the pejorative senses of those words, where the implication is that analysts are prescinding from historical changes, geographical and cultural variations, that give human beings enormous variety? Have we learned so little from anthropology and sociology that we can dare to talk about an end, a goal, that all people share simply by being people — human beings, incarnate spirits, featherless bipeds with brains? If you take your traditional Christian theological affinity for reflecting on why we human beings have been made into the flow of some recent liberal-to-separatist feminist discourse, for example, you will come away largely mocked for your affinity, abused for your troubles.

In such discourse, "genderedness" weighs more heavily than any analysis of the orientations that human beings receive from such characteristics (common to both sexes) as intelligence, mortality, and passion. Most contributors are fascinated by the insights that they discover when studying how women (and to a lesser extent men) gain their senses of themselves, of their roles and images. If you object that such studying does little to illumine what is the wisest response to the universal fact that we all die, or to the often seemingly equally universal fact that we all sin, you will probably find your objection brushed aside. This largely secular intellectual movement, or fad, will make it clear that it has little sympathy for grand reflections such as yours. If your experience and view match mine, you will conclude that the princess-bishops of this movement lust for the rush of self-recognition, the boiling awareness of victimhood, that a quite political, vested study of genderedness can generate over a weekend, even in two hours of circular discussion.

So I do not expect the avant-garde, as they think of themselves, of any of our currently influential secular schools working to interpret human nature to have great sympathy for my traditional starting point in this chapter. Yet I fail to see how social studies obviate philosophical and theological ones — why better appreciations of how our cultures feed us our ideas about ourselves as women and men, children and elderly people, minority or majority members of our population render questions about why we are here on earth, for what we ought to strive, and how we relate best to God beside the point. It is not a question of either/or, as though we could not understand better the dynamics of gender or race without calling Aristotle a ninny for making our final cause, our end, the first in the series of explanations that we ought to seek, if we are to understand what it means to be human. Obviously, we can chew gum and punch a computer at the same time. It is rather a question of our tendency to become bemused with what is new, become high on fresh ideas, and so to lose ourselves for more years or fewer in interesting but secondary, relatively trivial considerations.

If you die differently as a woman than as a man, you present a phenomenon worth investigating. How do doctors and nurses treat you differently at the end than they would a male lying in your bed, afflicted by a similar cancer of the stomach? Why do they treat you differently (if, in fact, they do)? Whatever enlightening answers we can get to questions such as these are worthwhile, perhaps even precious (if they can lead us to reforms that make our care of the dying significantly better). But the dying still goes on, the mortality continues to embrace women as exhaustively as men. To stop one's analysis at the level of differences in gender is to opt for the life only partially examined. What does it mean for any of us to know from the age of reason that we are sure to die? How ought we to think about our lives, where they are carrying us, in light of this most stubborn, enormous fact, and what implications should we transfer from how we ought to think to how we ought to educate the next generation?

I am not surprised that the mass media labor mightily to keep their audiences from contemplating mortality and the proper end of a human life. Such contemplation shows quickly that what most people concern themselves with most of the time is not serious, weighty, able to hoist much of the load that we have to carry if we are to find our lives meaningful. The general, popular response to the challenge to make our lives meaningful seems to be flight. People run away, distract themselves, make their routines at work and recreation into air-tight corridors where no virus of reflection can survive. Certainly, some such people become bored and feel ill-used. Perhaps many wish that their jobs and family lives were simpler, deeper, more beautiful. But the inertia of their culture at large, the grand forces of economics and the various social forces shaping our self-images, keep most people from examining their lives carefully, fruitfully. Amish, we grow too soon old and too late smart. Platonic, we content ourselves with living in a cave, avoiding the painful passage that might bring us to the light.

A Christian theology of education such as mine has to cut through the chases after distraction that characterize present-day mass culture in the United States and get to the traditional end. No matter how long we run away, the clock is ticking, the pages of the calendar are turning, we are losing cells in our brain by the thousands. Where is time taking us? What does our inevitable physical breakdown portend? For an orthodox Christian, one who thinks well of God and prays acceptably, time is taking us to death and resurrection. We illumine the implications of our time decisively by drawing on the paradigms of biblical Israel and our Lord, Jesus the Christ.

Biblical Israel left slavery in Egypt, wandered in the desert, and finally came to its promised land. Exodus, pilgrimage, and establishment in blessing gave its formative period its decisive pattern. Christians' Lord Jesus went through a similar passage, passover, the climax of which was his dying on the cross and God's raising him in the resurrection. In both biblical cases, the end of human existence, social and individual, is the promise and person of God — the promise that is the person of God.

So, in any responsible Christian theology of education, the first thing to mark about all the people involved — teachers, students, administrators, staff, and other human beings studied — is their mortality, while the second is the presence of God at their end. Such a marking does not imply that there is no God at their beginning or in their midst, but for the moment let us restrict our focus to the end. How can we educate people well if we place their mortality in brackets, as though it had no bearing on how they ought to think about their work, their marrying and raising children, their responsibilities to their local communities and the natural environment, their debts to God? In what significant way can our education call itself Christian if we do not shape it in virtue of the resurrection of the body and the life of the world to come that the classical creeds confess?

Certainly, one can say that everyone knows that human beings are mortal, and so that higher education, like corporate business and normal military affairs, simply, reasonably, places this fact in the background, the better to get on with the more novel, pressing matters that hog the foreground and spotlight. One can also say that all orthodox, right-thinking and right-praying, Christians assume the relevance of the resurrection of the body, when it comes to explicating the creedal views of human destiny, but that this assumption bakes little bread in the ovens where students turn up the heat to gain academic credits and forge satisfying friendships, so it makes sense for us to disregard it in everyday education.

In other words, few sensible people are going to deny that death is a crucial existential force in human existence, or that a Christian analysis of the human situation has to take much of its orientation from the resurrection of Jesus, but many people thinking themselves very sensible — realistic, sophisticated, experienced — in fact ignore human mortality when it comes to educational practice and act in virtually total disregard of the resurrection.

So a radically Christian educator shaped decisively by these two concerns is hard to find. Few of us live at the roots of our human condition, where death and resurrection intertwine. Most of us are deracinated — people trying to make do without the support, the vital tethering, that a clear, ruthless estimate of human finality as paschal (a passover that we may frame as moving us from death, or through death, to resurrection) offers us, indeed forces us to make our foundation.

I want to think about reorienting higher education by becoming more radical in these senses. I want to imagine, reason my way forward about, the changes that come when one assumes that the students shuffling their feet on the rainy day need more than anything else a solid orientation to death and resurrection. What I have in mind is not a transformation of the classroom into the chapel. It is nothing pious in the offensive sense of that term. It is in fact stark and sober. A student who concentrates on accounting is as mortal as a student who concentrates on zoology. A major in religious studies gives one no greater immunity to heart disease or cancer than a major in ballet or government. Similarly, in traditional, longstanding Christian perspective we can make any honest occupation a service of our fellow human beings and a demonstration of the grace of God in our souls, which entitles us to hope that we are pleasing our God, doing what we can to make ourselves fit for resurrection. Yes, what we can do is limited, because we cannot guarantee our salvation. But thinking of our destiny as a resurrection on the model of that of Jesus, and thinking of our work in terms of what qualities it would have to have to qualify us for such a resurrection, can make a great difference in how we feel about accounting or zoology, religious studies or ballet or government.

If we are concerning ourselves with a given study or work because we think that it comports well with our human end, that it bids fair to make us people who can deal well with death and resurrection, then our lives possess what clarity, what moral and religious logic, they can. If we simply bumble into our studies and jobs, with no concern for how they relate to what our lives are for, where our time is taking us, then we have not given ourselves much chance to feel that our days are unfolding with considerable meaning, that what we are doing with our time makes some sense. In the latter case we are like sheep without a shepherd, like students abandoned by their masters and so sent off little better than when they arrived. The fact that most students are like sheep without a shepherd, and that most teachers and administrators in higher education do little to give such students a ruthlessly clear sense of their end, does not mean that a Christian theology of higher education could not change this situation. Usually it simply means that in recent memory a Christian theology of education has not been tried.

Work

From Christian faith, as it takes its structure primarily from the experiences of Jesus recorded in the New Testament, educators can look upon the nature of the human beings with whom they deal as disclosed most decisively by death and resurrection. In Heidegge-rian parlance, they can realize that human being is a being unto death, while in theological parlance they can say that Christian faith offers people the chance to live gracefully now, on the way to death, and to enter into glory "then," at the eschatological mo-ment of the resurrection of their bodies. Granted some appropriate version of this Christian reading of human finality or destiny, what should we think about work, the first of the three "median" con-cerns (work, love, ritual) that I shall use to muse about how we should view the concerns of our students in particular, of our race at large, while they are on pilgrimage to their end, goal, final term? Ought work to be the most important focus when we ask how we can use best our limited time? Or ought we to deprecate work, making it a matter of little ultimate significance, because all works and workers wither: The grass withers, the flowers fade, and we and our works with them? Between these two unacceptable options let us try to stake out an acceptable middle way.

We ought not to define ourselves through our work, though the better (more creative, more personal) our work is the more we have to make what we do an important part of our sense of who we are. We ought rather to define ourselves first through our end, what we have been made to achieve by working, playing, praying, making love, and all our other human possibilities. The end is more im-portant than the means. If the end in fact rules and is noble, right, reasonable, it justifies many means that could otherwise be indif-ferent in their value, even dangerous because tending to make us idolatrous. In light of our ending at death and resurrection, how-ever, whether we work as attorneys or shoemakers becomes a free decision, something that does not matter ultimately. Either work can conduce to our ending our lives well — with meaning, gained by our having labored conscientiously and for the common good. Either work can also distract us from our proper sense of our pil-grimage, from where we are headed, as either can become boring or focused on making money more than making beauty, sense, or service. In proper Christian perspective, it means less to say that we are so and so the writer, or the teacher, or the medico than to say that we view our given work as the best way for us to come to our end rich in experiences that have prepared us well to undergo death and resurrection.

This is not to deny that being a writer will shape us differently from being a physician or a football coach. It is simply to deny that any such shaping goes to the heart of our matter, our makeup and destiny, more than our mortality and God's promise of our resurrection do. We can be successful doctors or writers or coaches, as the average estimate of success in such professions sees things, without being successful human beings. We can arrive at our end wealthy in money, disciplined, with a great fund of stories but still ill-prepared to call it all straw and let ourselves fall into the abysmal divine silence hoping for a resurrection like that of Jesus.

On the other hand, so radical and traditional a Christian view of human destiny and so of human work as this relativizing one ought not to make us deprecate what human beings do, as though our earthly lives, what we experience in space and time, were only a trek through a valley of tears or a parade field exercise having no final significance. No, a better Christian understanding of human destiny, time, and so work can look positively on what we do to earn our living and contribute to the common good, seeing it as a major way that we develop who we become by our end. Relatedly, such an understanding can underscore the many positive forces at hand in the work of physicians and musicians and coaches — the many ways in which, day after day, excellence in their profession requires intelligence, detachment, sensitivity to others, patience, and long-suffering.

My theological justification for a positive evaluation of human time and work stems from the conviction of Christian believers that the Jesus who died on the cross and rose to the right hand of the Father was a full human being. He was not merely a divinity in human garb, a Logos dressed up for a Punch and Judy show. It would be as heretical to say that Jesus lacked a human understanding and will, a human "personality" as we understand this word today, as it would be to deny that the final bearer of his existence, the final "person" in the Chalcedonian sense of that term, was only the divine Word. Focusing on the humanity of Jesus, we can say that the assumption of human nature by the Logos in the Incarnation assured that human time became not less significant but more. What Jesus experienced was not an instrument of the divine purposes in the depreciated sense of an inert, ultimately rather insignificant tool. What happened to Jesus through his experience, including his work — first, for pious Christian imagination, his labors as a carpenter, and then his preaching, healing, and wonder-working to announce the Reign of God — was the means, the operational lever and focus, of what Christians believe was God's definitive accomplishment of salvation. In the flesh and history of Jesus — his being and time, his work and prayer — God his Father (or the entire Trinity) made present to humanity on our own turf, in our own mode of creaturely living, the offer we need if we are to know that we can be saved and how.

Salvation is healing, restoration to health and integrity, gaining the strengths necessary to reach the destiny imprinted in us, placed before us, at our origination. To know that we can be saved, we human beings need to find in space and time, our natural milieu, an offer of deathlessness stronger than our surety that we shall die physically. This acute, paradoxical, terrible need calls for a solid, historical, irrevocable act of God, work of God, that eventuates in a resurrection. It implies the manifest defeat of death, with the further implication that, once and for all, God has pledged to be God-for-us — a good divinity willing to, desirous of, taking us to itself, where death will be no more. Come to be with divinity, which is different from us by being deathless, we can become other than what we are alone, without divinity. We can become deathless, and so divinized, and so not only saved but glorified — taken beyond healing into a fulfillment to which we have no natural right, on which we can make no forensic claim.

Inasmuch as a lengthy exegesis of this reading of the human experience of Jesus would justify or establish or habilitate his full history and experience, including his work, and so would give our full histories and rounds of experience, including our work, the most solid of authentications or justifications, a Christian theology of education such as mine comes equipped to believe that educators should prepare students to work well. A high Christology that makes the flesh of Jesus the precise site of eschatological salvation creates a radical humanism: what human beings do is the material cause of eternal fulfillment or frustration. We do not have to say that any human beings have in fact ever fouled their being or time so badly that they have gone to hell — definitive, irrevocable separation of themselves from God. We do have to maintain that such a horrible use of human freedom is possible, that human freedom is really free, not just a charade.

For such a radical humanism, the work that people do, and so the preparation for that work through higher education, is a holy business. A holy business can be boring at times, demanding more often than not, but it cannot be trivial, lightweight, insignificant. That teachers do good work in the classroom, and students do good work in the library, is crucial to making their interaction, the compact at the center of higher education, a help to the success of us all (by ending at death and resurrection well), rather than a hindrance.

What I take to be a balanced Christian theological view of higher education therefore is neither "vocational" or "professional," in the sense of geared primarily toward preparing students to assume (lucrative) slots in the work force, nor is it idealistic or "liberal" in the sense that it despises the world of work, is only a contemplative venture fit for the leisured. Between these two poles lies a humanistic view of work that sees it as both subordinate to the end for which we human beings have been made and fully important to our getting there well.

Though fully important to our getting to death and resurrection well, the work that we do, both in school and after we have graduated, is more than utilitarian. We do not work only to come to our end stripped and wise, though through good work we ought to mature in such a fashion. What we do has an integrity in its own right. How we argue in court, operate in the surgery, teach in the classroom, construct buildings or clean streets or raise children is a material cause of salvation — a stuff in which God works to heal us, through which God works out our sanctification in fear and trembling and joy. Our experiences at work shape who we become, are a major medium in which we grow well or off-center.

So we educators ought to help our students get straight the significance of the work they are doing now, in college, and the work they are preparing to do as professionals. They ought neither to bow before it idolatrously nor take it lightly as a mere marking time, messing around. It is deathly, and resurrectingly, serious, yet it is not God, but only one of God's angels. Now, the example that we teachers give as workers bulks as large as the analyses that we offer. Whether our own labors in the classroom and library strike a balance between slovenliness and idolatry is as important as our explaining to our students the golden mean.

For if the majority of our students probably strike us as lazy, a minority probably strike us as driven, excessive. Virtue in the matter of students' work stands in the same middle as virtue in the matter of the work of professors, or farmers, or politicians. In any work, workaholism is destructive, aberrant, sinful — not at all the macho quality that many firms exalt. But laziness, slovenliness, and torpor are equally destructive. Anger and pride are not the only capital sins; sloth and gluttony also make the list. Indeed, the "acedia" (listlessness) so important to the desert sages who make the first lists of the capital sins is a danger, an illness, afflicting both body and spirit. To become a mature, balanced, virtuous worker is therefore no small achievement. To be able to work hard but not compulsively, not always tightened by anxiety, is a sign of considerable development. That is what my theological assessment of the place of work in our human makeup tells me we ought to target. That is the middle way, the golden mean, that would help all whom we influence to move through their time gracefully and courageously.

Love

What we have said about work can save us time concerning love. It, too, is a median concern, inasmuch as by "love" I am meaning here human affections leading to social supports and responsibilities: friendships, collaborations, marriages, ventures in parenting. Certainly, love enters into our worlds of work, and it makes sense that we should try to find works that we can love. When we do, we can work more pleasurably and diligently than when we do not. The doctor who comes to hate her patients because they are eating up her life needs to back away, so that she can get them back in perspective. The teacher or social worker who feels ground down by the low level of her wages or the abusive assumptions of parents and local citizens also needs to back away. When she does, she may decide that what she has loved about her work from the beginning is the chance it offered her to help children or poor people. In that case, if she is to persevere well she has to trim away the worries, insulate herself against the abuse, that outsiders have been shoveling on her from the guff side.

We cannot love rationally work that is making us sick. We have to get our work, no matter how rightly beloved, into perspective. One of the hardest negotiations that many couples have to make nowadays is what their respective works ought to mean, in light of the common life they are trying to fashion. I would hope that a Christian view of human destiny relativizing the importance of work, and also deepening our appreciation of how our works can save us, would facilitate such negotiation, lessening the conflicts between our love for what we do and our love for the other people with whom we are trying to share our lives intimately.

What ought we to tell our students, and bring to our scholarly analyses of human nature, regarding love? It is mysterious, certainly, a more direct entry into the labyrinths of providence than even our work. It is the source of our best energies and our cruelest pains. Without love, infants do not thrive, nor many elders. Without love, even saints suffer more than human wisdom says they should. The little love called appreciation goes a long way toward making offices and rectories run smoothly, be places that those who dwell in them can call happy. The great love called gratitude enfolds an entire theology or spirituality centered on creaturehood. If we look at everything around us as a gift from a great Father or Mother of lights, as an updated reading of the epistle of James could put it, then we can contemplate creation as full of love. God labors for us in creation. The sun and moon, oceans and tides, do what they do for us and our salvation.

Yes, we have to avoid abusing such an anthropomorphism, anthropocentrism, but if you have watched the otters at Monterey without applauding, not thanking them for their show, you had best take your soul to the laundromat, the car wash, the sauna — wherever you go to get back your true colors. The otters do what they do because that is how evolution has shaped them, but this does not mean that you cannot take what they do as a gift made just to you, a marvel the richer for your having been there to perceive it, find in it delight. The tree falling in the forest with no witness from bystanders makes a sound, in the sense that it produces the physical forces that constitute noise. But when someone is there to shout "timber," whether in English or chipmunkese, a new dimension enters, a physiology and psychology that enrich the simple physics.

We love the world best when we appreciate things as coming to us gratuitously. Our responses, our lives, are most eucharistic when we think that most everything around us is grace. God did not need to make us. That we are is a primal datum pointing to a goodness whose importance is hard to overestimate. And that we are with the capacity and chance to multiply our being through love is a further datum — indeed, it is a hint that divinity itself may be a community of friends, a family of lovers. Our students swim, thrash, in the thick of this reality of a creation that makes love capital. Their hormones surge, their fragile egos propel them to search for affirmation, they are as much concerned to find friends, soul-mates, as to find competencies that will put bread on their tables. We owe them wisdom about love, and for Christian educators such wisdom has to derive from the evangelical portrait of Jesus, as the centuries of Christian reflection and commentary have come to appreciate it.

The Johannine Jesus is the strongest champion of love, but the Christ that we find in the synoptics and Paul is no slouch either. God is love, and those who abide in love abide in God. Yes, this love of God is more *agape* than *eros*. It has a stronger component or face of self-spending, even self-emptying, than it does of self-aggrandizement. But nowadays few analysts of the love of Jesus make *eros* unwelcome. Jesus would not have been fully human if he did not take delight in his parents, his friends, even the sick people to whom he ministered. There is no sign among the memories of him that have come down to us that he dragged himself to his preaching or teaching or healing as to works of sheer drudgery. If he suffered much from the dullness of his apostles, and suffered even more from the malice of the Pharisees, such suffering did not take away his tenderness for Martha, Mary, and Lazarus, his humor at seeing Zacchaeus up in the tree. For Jesus God was a father prodigal in his willingness to forgive the wastrel and welcome him home. For Jesus the dutifulness of the elder brother was a mark of religious immaturity, of his not having grasped the full nature of the Reign of God.

The Reign of God is the time when grace rules, love gets in its best innings. The strictures, the constipations, of a rule by law, by justice in the narrow sense of what we can tie down through rules, fall away. God lets the divine heart have its way, and as God does we see why she is as different from us morally as physically. As the heavens are distant from the earth, so is the goodness of God distant from our human goodness.

God loves us purely, without conditions, but also perhaps ardently, mischievously, with great delight. God does not drag the Holy Spirit to the work of moving in our hearts with sighs of love too deep for words. The Spirit moves, broods, willingly, happily, doing what only God can, being as only God is. If Christian theologians find through faith a human participation in the doing and being of God, then that participation, that elevation of human being and destiny into the deathlessness of God, will include our sharing in God's love. We will, or can already, love as God loves. Our love will, or can already, let God love in and through us — our affections can be God's own. Just as our flesh and work are not incidental to salvation, inasmuch as salvation is really human and so historical, so our love and affection are not incidental.

The mother who takes her frightened child to her bosom in the dark of night is letting the child feel the love of God, the care and affection. The father who comes home weary because he has again spent himself to provide his family with milk and meat, rent and furniture, is a figure of the divine Father, the Abba of Jesus, who labors constantly for the well-being of creation. These are interpretations cast by faith, of course, and they do not rule out problems with our moving from the behavior of human parents to what we ought to say about the parental behavior of God. What is most valid in their pertinence to how we ought to think about God, however, is the love that they spotlight. For all its impurity, the love of the comforting mother, the work-weary father, is a sacramental sign of the love of God. People who never were comforted as children, never sensed that their parents spent themselves on their behalf gladly, in delight, know less in their bones, the bottom of their psyches, than they ought to if God is their natural destiny. They have been shortchanged, and a dozen helpers will have to work assiduously to make up for this deficiency.

Who talks about love this way in higher education today? Do even psychologists make plain the crucial significance of human affections, the decisive balance between loving one's neighbor too little and loving him or her too much? Jesus said that we should love our neighbors as we love ourselves, a saying sometimes illuminating but at other times a complication. For some of us do not love ourselves well, with affection but not narcissism, and, moving to another saying of Jesus, few of us love our enemies or do good to those who persecute us, whether inside or out. One might think that even this small slice of the difficulties with which we gain wisdom about human loving would make the argument that love should be a prime matter in our college curricula, but such a thought is more likely to raise a cynical laugh than gain a round of applause.

Just as death, resurrection, God, and creative work all receive much less attention in American higher education than what a Christian theology of education such as mine says that they should, so does love receive much less attention. We can say that Freud was shrewd to have thought that the ability to work and to love constituted an estimable mental health, at least by functional criteria, but little of American higher education is Freudian enough to make our psychological ventures spotlight work and love humanistically, as central or median concerns that bear vitally on our maturation and best ending.

Jesus loved God with his whole mind, heart, soul, and strength, and he loved his neighbors as he loved himself. The gospels take pains to show him not simply repeating this ideal from the Hebrew Scriptures but embodying it. He threw the jacks of his missionary game into the pattern of Isaiah: The blind would see, the deaf hear, lepers be cleansed, the poor have good news preached to them. His first neighborhood, community, was the sinners, the outcastes, who fell outside the social structures of his day. His heart was most tender toward the children, the women, the publicans and whores who got no respect from the establishment. It was not the healthy who had need of a physician but the sick. It was not the righteous who drew his prophetic support but the sinful. Certainly, any preferential option that he made for the poor did not lead him to hate the wealthy, but he apparently thought that it would be easier for a camel to pass through the eye of a needle than for a rich man to enter the Kingdom of God. Underneath the Semitic hyperbole lies a sober perennial judgment. The most lovable among us — those who need our affectionate concern most and tend to draw it in the measure that we are holy — are those least secure, favored, by the bankers and gossip columnists.

Love is dangerous, when we let it go free as Jesus did. Love does not bow to any lesser laws. Thus the Augustine whom I love, not the brooding neurotic and misogynist, said, "Love and do what you will." If we are loving, what we want, the imperatives of our heart, are good. If we are loving, the good of our beloved is at least as important as our own good. Our students need to hear these things, the writs of emancipation enfolded in such traditional dicta. Our gay students and lesbians need to hear them if they are to have any chance of coming to a Christian faith that they can call welcoming, a broad Christian community that they can call home, their family. We need to make our educational ventures challenges to the cynics who scoff at romantic love, and also to the toughs who would trample on artists and welfare mothers in the name of market values. And we need to learn what challenges genuine love sounds in our own souls, how it asks us there to purify our affections and be hard on those springing more from cowardice or self-indulgence than from a true concern for the good of the beloved, whether friend or self. All these suggestive perspectives I would have a Christian theology of education make orientational, thinking such a move an encouraging display of the great gifts that education can offer, when it knows what it ought about human nature and destiny, about the ways and means through which we may, as the patristic sages put it, become what we are — realize our divine potential.

Ritual

We have reflected on what a Christian theology of education may say about the end of human nature, about work, and about love, trying to show through exemplification that such a saying, such an importation or application of Christian theology, can bear to higher education many good gifts. In this section we continue this process of exemplification, focusing now on ritual — the tendency of human beings to conduct much of their business, profane as well as sacred, through patterns grown grooved from custom. There is more ceremony in human affairs than we supposedly democratic Americans tend to think. There is more innate or culturally conditioned scripting of relations between the sexes, between bosses and employees, between the different races, ethnic groups, and churches. True, individuals break out of stereotypical roles frequently, and ours is not a culture so invested in social forms as traditional China or Europe seems to have been. We do not have a caste system approaching that of traditional India. There are now no peasant classes making our societies close approximations of many Latin American ones. And yet — we do have our analogies to all these social stratifications, and we do have our perhaps diluted versions of the ritualistic actions that such stratifications have usually produced. Thus it is useful for us to take to heart works by analysts such as Herbert Fingarette who have found in *li*, the traditional Chinese virtue of etiquette (social propriety, mastery of ritual forms), a powerful stimulus to consider how societies organize themselves best — most peacefully, productively, and gracefully.

There is no society in human history that offers us so clear a story of success that we can say that all groups ought to make it the model for their ritualization of human interactions. Further, few ritual forms arise from completely reflective awareness, as fully rational or intentional creations. Rather, most groups inherit traditions that go back to time out of mind and adapt them slowly, as new needs require. At one time, castes (*jatis*) may have functioned well in India. Indeed, we know that a basically tripartite structure (priests, warriors, and workers: merchants and farmers) obtained in Indo-European societies generally from before their historical periods.

Nowadays we are bound to note that women did not factor into this structure in their own right, in terms of their own works and roles, but rather through their connections to the men who were the priests, warriors, and workers. The "work" of women was to serve men and bring forth children. Sometimes that work gave women high status, but often it did not. Often what we now call "patriarchy" insured that women would be the second sex, possessing less scope for its talents than the first. The fact that the account in Genesis of the creation of our kind, humanity, makes femaleness as aboriginal as male suggests that a Christian theology of education taking aim at providing the ritualization of sexual relationships with the wisest possible orientation may well prove to be anti-patriarchal — opposed to a rule only by "the fathers." As humble as this suggestion may seem to be, it becomes smoking dynamite when one imagines what it could mean for the reform of Roman Catholic Church politics, as well as when one remembers how recently American females did not have the vote and tended to receive a distinctly less academic (rigorous) upper education than males. The great debates in Catholic educational circles about the dangers of co-education have not abated completely, inasmuch as some traditionalists argue that the sexes have innate differences justifying our preparing them for different if often complementary roles. Obviously, though, if we are to see issues such as this clearly, rather than through a glass or smokescreen darkly, we need to look critically at the rituals we use nowadays to ease our way as women and men, blacks and whites, Protestants and Catholics, poor people and rich people, and so forth.

In itself, ritual seems to be both inevitable and oriented toward graciousness. We need some forms, conventions, to get our conversations and collaborations into gear. Shaking hands may not be the only or best way to initiate engagement, but it can do the job. If the alternative is shifting from foot to foot and not knowing how to break the ice, then shaking hands becomes a blessing. More subtly, we need ways of taking into account the full reality of a given interaction, which usually includes both significant differences between the parties and basic similarities. In the setting of a hospital, for instance, the differences between a doctor and a patient can seem enormous. The rituals through which these two parties tend to interact, expect to interact, have to provide for these differences, if they are to ease the interaction along. On the other hand, many such rituals downplay the basic similarities between doctors and patients — their common intelligence, mortality, liability to fatigue, and so forth. An ideal ritual renders full justice to the realities of a given situation. It does not exist only for the benefit of the doctor or the patient. It recognizes the needs and rights of each party and meets them. We might, therefore, amend the present going rituals for the interactions of doctors and patients if we found that they make insufficient provision for the input of the patient. We might give the patient more access to the information that the tests have been piling up, and we might also ease the work load of the doctor, so that there were less excuse for rush, brevity, even impatience.

It is not the place of educators to labor principally at social reform. It is not the function of the theology of education that I am elaborating here to get into the nuts and bolts of ritualistic machinery. What I have proffered so far are simply examples meant to clarify my claim that we human beings create rituals for most of our recurrent meetings, interactions, events, and to lay the basis for an argument that the sacramentality that lies at the heart of the Christian approach to divinity is nothing that we ought to limit to Sunday mornings, churchy surroundings, meetings thought to be religiously significant mainly because they come to us with benefit of clergy. I would instead underscore the humanizing of social interactions when we think about them in light of the Word's having taken flesh, dwelt among us, and shown us what human intercourse can become when it is full of grace and truth. From this underscoring I would then shade higher education as a venture that ought to make those participating in it critical, in a positive sense, of all the rituals that come within their purview, so as to reform such rituals for the better service of all people's growth in gracefulness, helpfulness, effective work, and warm love.

In the gospels we see Jesus both adhering to the ritualistic conventions of his day and breaking them. For example, he expects the Samaritan woman at the well (John 4) to draw water for him, but he treats her seriously when it comes to religious instruction. His disciples are amazed, because the conventions did not allow a rabbi to deal with women as Jesus was dealing with this woman, and because Jews did not interact with Samaritans so freely. Similarly, in his interactions with the Pharisees Jesus both accepted the conventions of debate obtaining in his time and went outside them, speaking with "authority." He was willing to engage in the sometimes nasty intellectual give and take predicated on close knowledge of the letter of the Law, but he was not willing to let such knowledge substitute for just judgments wrought in the soul through adherence to a Lord much greater than the Law. So he would work healings on the Sabbath, if love of his neighbor required that, and if the Pharisees gave him a hard time he would tell them to take a hike (which angered them murderously — see John 7:19 ff.).

Recently there came across my desk the speech of the Father General of the Society of Jesus welcoming Pope John II to the opening of the 34th General Congregation of the Society in Rome in January of 1995. For one interested in ritualism, certain phrases and postures leap off the page. Politic, the Father General bends over backward to assure a pope apparently highly sensitive to the prerogatives of the papacy that the traditional Jesuit fealty to the Holy See remains in force fully. Saint Ignatius Loyola, the founder of the Jesuits, made such fealty a distinctive feature of his group, which grew up in the midst of the turmoils caused by the sixteenth-century Protestant Reformation, some leaders of which stigmatized the pope as the Anti-Christ. The Father General wants to assure John Paul II that today's Jesuits remain authentic sons of Ignatius. That is the end that his ritualistic bowings and scrapings on the page obviously intend.

Well, good, and understandable, but still somewhat sad. The

sources that the Father General must consider constitutive for the juridical status of the Society are, in order, the Holy See, the *Constitutions* that Ignatius wrote, and the decrees of the previous thirty-three general congregations. Among these sources there is nothing directly evangelical. The portrait of Jesus that we find in the gospels must ground the Society bearing his name apart from its juridical status. Now, to put things in a juridical order such as this, think at this distance from the evangelical Christ, is characteristic of "Roman" theology, as people in the trade tend to speak of the mindset at the Vatican, and Roman theology has not changed as much since the sixteenth century as one might expect or wish. For my money it remains all too resistant to the reforms demanded by the sixteenth-century protestors, who based their demands on the New Testament, and so it remains all too legalistic and reminiscent of the Pharisees. The sadness it generates in me comes from my remembering that Jesus was a free spirit willing to face down pharisaism whenever it got in the way of his demonstrating the presence of the Reign of God. The rituals that keep Roman theology going therefore become targets of a critique powered by a desire to keep people free of pharisaism. The better our college students learn how to fashion such critiques, regarding secular matters as well as ecclesiastical ones, the more powerfully we shall equip them to reform the dysfunctional or inhumane conventions they themselves will meet, whether as bishops or U.S. senators, masters of liturgical ceremonies or mistresses of diplomatic protocols. The precisely theological edge to which I want to hone such a critical capacity comes from the Protestant principle that only God is God (and so that bowing to anything less than God is idolatrous) and from the Catholic principle that the full humanity of Christ can make our "imitation" of him sacramental — gracious in virtue of its embodying a love of the free flourishing of our fellow human beings like the love that he himself showed so fearlessly.

Ignorance

Work, love, and ritual are constants — forces or concerns working always in the middle of our lives and shaping significantly where we end, how we finish. In this section and the next we deal with two more constants, both negative. Here the topic is ignorance —

the not-knowing that is as profound in us as our mortality. There the topic will be sin — the inexplicable tendency we have not to do the good that we would do, should do, but rather to do the evil that we would not do, should not do. Together, ignorance and sin summarize the dolors of our condition. Because of them, it is difficult for us to follow the patristic adage and become what we are, actualize our potential divinization. The difference between ourselves and a fully human Jesus, a Logos incarnate like us in all things except sin, turns out to be enormous, because "except sin" points to an enormous variation or distinction. We cannot imitate Christ as Thomas à Kempis and others would have us do, because we cannot get our heads and hearts straight enough, our loves pure enough. Unhappy people, disciples, that we are, who will rescue us from our misery? No one but a God bent on saving us. In the measure that we want to educate our students realistically, we owe them this sober estimate of the human condition that traditional Christian theological reflections on ignorance and sinfulness tend to generate.

But how can I say that human beings are profoundly, indicatively ignorant, when all of higher education is predicated on the student's capacity to learn? What has happened to the Aristotelian notion, capital in Christian scholasticism both old and new, that all people by nature desire to know, and so that the beginning of wisdom is the wonder that swings this desire into action? Do not the natural sciences stand as a wonderful monument to the capacities of human reason, the sweep of the human mind? Though the galaxies extend for billions of light years, we can travel that far mentally. We must, if we can make such calculations. The same with the infinitesimal order of nuclear physics, and with the orders of biology that obtain in our bones and blood. We can engineer towering skyscrapers and bridges that span full bays. We can make and learn languages, turn dreams into celluloid fantasies, imitate Dante unawares in the hellish but immensely profitable shouting of our stock markets and futures exchanges. What then does it mean to say that we are ignorant through and through? How can I make this orientational assessment?

I can make it simply, through questions fit for a child but explicable for philosophers: Where do you come from — whence your genealogical line? Where are you going — what do you know empirically about your end? Why is the world the way that it is —

this evolutionary pattern, this requirement that all human beings die? Why has there never been a society of human beings fully just, a cadre of human beings fully sound psychologically? In the main, educators prescind from basic questions such as these, because they are embarrassing. None of us can tell a ten-year-old child why his parent is an alcoholic and so his home is a hell-hole. None of us knows why mothers of young children are subject to breast cancers that take them away when their children seem to need them most. We can track devastating tornadoes, measure immensely destructive earthquakes on the Richter Scale, but we cannot tell any victim of a natural disaster why the organization of creation is such as to make such a disaster a statistical reality, indeed in some cases a near-certainty over time.

We do not know why we are, and we do not know why we are as we are. Both the that and the what of our human existence, our human condition, stand beyond or below or to the side of our ability to understand. This produces or expresses an ignorance so basic that it shapes our entire human being, individual and social, ecological and theological. None of us can get to the depths of himself or herself — know the "I" through and through. None of us can master the endless variations and changes in our social interactions. Economics is not the "dismal" science only because it must often deal with depressions. More radically, economics and politics and sociology teach honest practitioners that human sociability is too extensive, massive, in its change and reticulation to admit of any characterizations either comprehensive or accurate once and for all. The best social scientists, like the best internists and psychiatrists, are humble because they know that what we human beings do, what we are actively, both together and as individual systems, is far more complex, intricate, fluid than we shall ever understand. This is not to despise any solid knowledge that we gain, nor to devalue the nearly heroic labors through which scientists and therapists gain it. It is simply to remind all involved (in this case, all involved in the higher education purporting to develop good scientists and therapists) that the first and last word is darkness rather than light.

Think of how, in a third realm, that of physical nature, research shows us boxes within boxes, wheels within wheels, living systems within systems. The whole is more than the sum of what we thought were the constituent parts. The laws by which the parts move may be not only more complex than what we can calculate but not amenable to the binary structure of our reason. How can light be both particle and wave? At what point does Heisenberg's principle of indeterminacy require us to become confessed agnostics? The theological grounding for this natural agnosticism, as for its parallels in the social and psychological realms, is the infinity of our Creator. We shall never understand God. In heaven our vision of God will take us on and on, endlessly. There is no end in God, as there is no beginning. God was and is and will be all at once. If we go to the highest heavens, God is there. If we go to the lowest depths, we meet God. We cannot get away from God. Nothing that is is godless. But these are negative routes to theological assertions, not positive. Positively, we do not know, cannot know, what God is. Positively, God is intrinsically mysterious.

And, finally, because the source of creation is a God intrinsically mysterious, we can never grasp the full causality at work in the world. Even if the world is finite, and the architecture thereof, the full reason for the world, the radical reasonableness of creation, is bound to escape us. To this point, the architecture of the world escapes us as well, and every indication is that we shall never master the ecology of the seas or the vagaries of the economies of the large nations comprehensively, in ways that would allow us to control them. But even if we were to verge on such a mastery, we would remain ignorant of God, because we would remain human and so categorically different from God. Kierkegaard's "infinite qualitative distinction" applies through and through. The unknowing preached by the deepest mystics, East and West, boils down to a humble epistemological and ontological realism: That we cannot know is capital, while that we can delude ourselves into thinking that we can know is the source of our worst aberrations and pains.

Take these analyses of our human condition, these deep readings of what we are psychologically, socially, ecologically, and theologically, into the marketplace and you are likely to meet with an incomprehension ironically probative of your thesis. Most of your secular confreres will not even know what you are talking about. Sanskrit or Greek would be less foreign. The ontological realism grounding a traditional Christian agnosticism comes from a different era, a different self-knowledge, than what runs Wall Street or Madison Avenue or the White House. Indeed, it comes from a different knowledge than what runs the Ivy League or the Big Ten. It is nearly as foreign to the *Chronicle of Higher Education* as it is to the *Wall Street Journal*. The lexicon of unknowing, the theology of fundamental agnosticism based on radical human ignorance, that I find necessary for wisdom about higher education would stun most of the people with whom I deal in meeting after meeting, bringing a blessed silence. Those who speak on and on do not know, as Lao Tzu laid down over two thousand years ago. Yes, we have to speak, wheel, deal. But, our speaking, wheeling, and dealing would all be much better if we knew much better than we seem to that we do not know, never will know, simply cannot know what we would have to know in order to become captains of our fate.

When later we deal with the practical implications of orientational angles such as these Christian theological ones that I would foist upon higher education, we can take up the question of how best to bring home to students, make impinge on curricula, the convictions about fundamental human ignorance and sinfulness that I see complementing the ones that I have developed about human finality, work, love, and ritual. We can then move on to theoretical implications — how best to rearrange our senses of what higher education ought to be attempting. Here let me conclude by suggesting briefly the positive benefits in coming to appreciate that our profound ignorance is a negative constant or existential.

What I see as positive in it is more than the realism entailed in confessing that we cannot know. It is well for us to be realistic, at all places and times, and so not to call ice cream what is excrement. We should call a spade a spade. If we are ignorant fundamentally, we can only profit from naming this fact honestly and taking it to heart. But, still more positively, confessing our fundamental ignorance can also be a quick path to freedom — a rapid underground railroad. We are all ignorant radically, constitutionally, so none of us can be much of a pundit. All of us have the right to our own opinion, even though if we are wise we shall also hang loose from that. We can distinguish freely between what may be necessary politically, to keep the traffic flowing, and what is necessary *jure divino* — by divine law. Human laws deserve respect but not servile obedience. We should stop at red lights because it makes sense, helps us avoid crumpling fenders and limbs. We should love the good order that generally justifies our following one ultimately arbitrary way of proceeding in university affairs (quarters rather than semesters) or in church affairs (the given political structure of our denomination), but we should not canonize such a way. Very few things indeed come to us by clear divine decree. Very few things are necessary in either their formulation or their founding. So the maxim that we should maintain unity in necessary things, liberty in doubtful things, and charity in all things is actually a proclamation of our freedom. Because we seldom know beyond doubt, we are seldom constrained as tightly as legalists would like.

This is a burdensome freedom, beyond doubt, but also a yoke that is light. The darkness in which we dwell is terrifying, but also comforting because unavoidable. So we ought not to cede our freedom to those who would lighten our burden, give us artificial light for our journey, by firing up dozens of laws. In fact such laws illumine very little, seldom enlightening our souls. Indeed, for those who have endured the thickest darkness, such as John of the Cross, our ignorance is less a trial than a great blessing. If God did not require us to move by faith, we would move less successfully than we can move, be even more tossed by storm and tide. Now, if this is so (if the saint is right), our higher education ought not to despise mysticism as it tends to do nowadays, and our theologies of higher education ought to make persuasive such logically consequent opinions as that of Karl Rahner that the Christian of the future ought to be — be encouraged to be — a mystic. Thus, our existential ignorance can say capital things about both what we human beings are and for what a realistic education would prepare us. In my view, to ignore such capital things is to condemn one's educational ventures to relatively trivial significance.

Sin

Ignorance places the mind, the intellect, on center stage, and then says that the theater is dark. Sin places the will or heart on center stage, and then mocks us for not knowing why we do not do what is reasonable, loving, good. The darknesses of our minds and hearts flow together, of course, because love both follows knowledge and guides it. We are as integral, as unified psychosomatically, in our sinfulness as in our sanctity, in our sinfulness and sanctity as in our ignorance and sanity. The distinctions that we make between mind and body, ignorance and sin, sanctity and sanity are useful, but they carve up something that itself is whole, and we leave the wrong impression if we do not restore this wholeness. So we should make our distinctions here in order, finally, to return to the basic wholeness of the human being with renewed appreciation.

Our students watch television and read the newspapers, seldom as we theologically minded professors would like. On television they can see in any week enough wrongdoing, apparent sin, to give a theologian employment for a decade. A few years ago the story of the sixty thousand Muslim women whom the Serbs raped systematically in Bosnia captured the spotlight for a while, illustrating human depravity, truly terrible sinfulness, with a force hard to endure. Did the leaders of the Serbian Orthodox Church condemn this heinous criminality with all the moral vigor at their disposal? If they did, it did not make the headlines in the news media that kept me informed in Tulsa.

Moved now to California, I have been subjected to the trials of O. J. Simpson as to a nuisance in my own neighborhood. The deed being judged is terrible, but the effect of how the media have been presenting the judgment may do greater damage in the long run. For the mass media are vulgarizing murder and making it commonplace. They are making so little distinction between the fictional cop shows that they run in prime time and their reporting of a legal proceeding that only people educated critically will be able to keep the two different genres apart. Crime has become titillating, as the mass media have long assumed adultery to be. The way that we treat sin — culpable wrongdoing — is itself wrong more often than not: prurient and so sinful. We members of the audience collude in this wrongdoing of the media by finding virtue less interesting than vice. Why is this our finding? Perhaps because it keeps us safe from the Augustinian wisdom that sin is love of self unto contempt of God, while holiness is love of God unto contempt of self. There is little love of God in the psyches shaping the mass media, the place where the majority of Americans get their sense of reality, and so there are few balanced views of either sin or holiness. Indeed, there is little concern to work out criteria for distinguishing the two, whether extensions of what Augustine intuited or new standards that would call his into question.

Sin, our moral impotence, shows its "original" dimension in the omnipresent stupidity and slantedness that a faithful analysis finds in such pervasive forces as the mass media of communications. Original sin is the sin of the world, the bias on which every infant who is born slides into our midst. It is the irrationality in every large social situation that we meet: education, medical care, business and banking, the church. It is the children's teeth having been set on edge because their parents ate sour grapes, and their parents' parents. Sin shows its individual dimension in our ratifications of such irrationalities person by person. We live in disordered situations and we further their disorder by contributing our own nastiness. We think that we are nice, but if we examine our consciences strictly we find that we resist the demands of holiness — a ruthless honesty and a selfless love — a dozen times every day.

For instance, more often than not we do not want better art, better education, better reporting of the news, if it would cost us more in effort and money. We do not want to pay, in time and interest as much as money, the price for an excellent elementary education for most of our children, or the price for a medical system that would give all our citizens excellent care. In fact we do not want excellence, except occasionally or rhetorically. We prefer hunkering down in our anti-elitisms, intellectual and moral, or in our political correctnesses, more or less nakedly self-serving.

There is an ugliness about all of us — the face that you see in your mirror, and the face that I see in mine. There is cause for shame, and for agreeing with the Westminster Confession that "there is no health in us." If "health" would mean our being the image of God that God deserves, none of us is healthy. Realizing this, the saints hurry to confess themselves to be the worst of sinners. Because they have seen better than the rag-tag rest of us what the holy God deserves, they have appreciated better than the rest of us how sinful we in fact are. For Augustine, the race of us as a whole was a *massa damnata*. This most influential Latin father rendered his interpretation at a time when the Roman Empire was collapsing, but he could have rendered it at a great many other times and places — take the historical epoch and geographical continent of your choice.

Now, there are extenuating and counterbalancing things to be said about human nature, the gist of which is the Pauline "where sin abounded, grace has abounded the more." God has not abandoned us to our worst possibilities, though it remains well for us to realize that only the favor of God keeps us in the running for heaven. Just as human intellectual achievements force us to place qualifications on our sober estimates of human ignorance, so human moral achievements force us to place qualifications on our estimates of human sinfulness. But these qualifications ought not to exempt us professors from the obligation to show our students the full measures of human waywardness that history and theological anthropology say we ought to factor in when we would expose accurately the human condition, the real world, that opens to engulf our students at graduation (but of course has been operating in all our students' lives from their first hours in their hospital cribs.)

Naturally, we have to be as balanced about sin as about anything else, and this means neither averting our gaze from it nor concentrating on it monomaniacally. The right-to-lifers who think that they ought to kill abortionists seem to me monomaniacs and so people who compound the sin of the world more than they lessen it. Abortion is sinful more often than not, I judge, in its social causes if not in the cast of the souls of the individual actors involved. But we become imbalanced when we refuse to admit that many other things are also wrong, sinful, cries to God for redress, and when we refuse to see that our own houses are made of glass and so are always liable to stones.

One can work to limit abortions, as to limit destructive poverty and illiteracy, without narrowing one's focus to such work alone — blocking out the rest of reality, which includes both further wrongs and numerous ameliorating rights. Similarly, it is silly to argue whether American slavery was a worse evil than either the Nazi holocaust that singled out Jews or the modern explosion of abortioneering. Equally, we need not choose between crimes against the environment and crimes against people. We can become sophisticated enough to hold several thoughts, even several assessments and condemnations of evil, in our heads at the same time.

So much popular moral discourse is simpleminded, imbalanced, that I find it hard not to beat to a worn rug the need for balance, for both/and-ism. There is more than enough blame for wrongdoing to go around, more than enough need for repentance and conversion. Indeed, because of this pervasive need I think that we should bring back confession, and not simply because it is good for the soul. We should bring back confession as a kindly, effective sacramental ritual because we are all sinners and need forgiveness every day.

We are sinners in our deeds, our thoughts, the recesses of our souls. We are dark where we would be light, if God were

our surpassing treasure. But we have fouled even so beautiful a
nest of virtue as confession. We have laden it with first foolish
guilt and more recently fatuous narcissism. Sacramental confession
should afflict all of us where we are wrongly comfortable morally,
and it should comfort all of us where we are wrongly afflicted,
discouraged, tempted to despair. The great wellspring of sin is self-
centeredness, and the great effect of proper confession is returning
us to a central God. True, education is not a churchly ministry, in
the sense that professors ought to shrive students in the classroom.
But a proper education, by my theological lights, makes confession eminently human, an amazing cause for gratitude to God. The
more accurately and profoundly our horizon for higher education
surveys the landscape of sin, the more grateful it should make all
involved for the article of Christian faith that God has given us
a humane way to break our vicious cycles, redeem our lives from
the pits.

Practical Implications for Higher Education

I think of my professional self as first a teacher of undergraduates.
What may I do to make ruminations such as those in the first six
sections of this chapter take hold, make a difference, in the lectures
I give, the discussions I run, the readings I assign, the tests that I
create for undergraduates? How can I and colleagues who agree
with a traditional Christian theology such as mine bring about a
better payoff for our students, and how can we get our students
to hear us, cooperate with us, give us the feedback we need if we
are to get our gems into their jewel boxes? These are the sorts of
questions I have in mind trying to answer in this section.

First, we need courses, fewer or more, that would lay out a
basic, mainstream, Christian theological view of human nature.
Call such courses ventures in "theological anthropology," or entitle
them "Human Beings under God," or specify them as dealing with
"sin and grace, death and resurrection" — the requirements of a
given curriculum and catalogue can determine the particulars. The
crucial thing is to have enough such courses to enable students to
see for themselves how the world looks when we espy it through
Christian faith, create enough spots in the curriculum where we

deal with the grounds for our educational venture to let students amble onto where we stand.

Second, we need places in the meetings, the assemblies, that bring together those directing our given educational venture to discuss the assets and liabilities of working from a horizon of a traditional Christian theology. In the church-related schools, it should be axiomatic that faculty members and administrators (and staff members interested and suited) should convene several times a year to refocus themselves on the rationale, the *raison d'être*, of their venture. I assume always that there will be no "orthodoxy," in a pejorative sense, about the formulation of this rationale. I assume that no one will be coerced, and that the rationale will be developed with sufficient sophistication (theological depth) to make it clear than all members of the community have first to honor their own consciences — that our institutional sense of what we are about includes centrally a constant critical assessment of our vision and so is grateful to those who express their reservations frankly.

On the other hand, I also assume that many church-related institutions of higher education are now far less clear, forthright, or courageous about their theological vision than would be ideal. Far too many have lost their nerve, or found themselves so confused that any trumpet they blew would be uncertain. This is an embarrassing situation in which to find oneself, and there are only two ways to deal with it. One is to go to work to remove the confusion or cowardice causing there to be a fog or a void where there ought to be a clear perspective. The other is to refuse to face the disorder or malaise or lack of vision and so keep stumbling blindly. I account as "stumbling blindly" the pathetic efforts of one institution that I once knew intimately to assimilate higher education to a model of management based on corporate business practices. There the jargon brims with "reengineering" and "downsizing" — cruel euphemisms for cutting the jobs of staff and faculty members instead of cutting the jobs of the dumb, visionless administrators who have led the school into disarray.

There comes a point where no amount of slick advertising or massaging of numbers or retreats so talky as to give people with a religious background the teary giggles can do the job. There comes a point (and it is far earlier than many higher administrators seem to realize) where only a vision clear, compelling, and persuasive in its realism, its practicality, is the overwhelming necessity. In scriptural terms, without contemplation the people perish. In Nietzschean terms, people who have a why can put up with almost any how. How is it possible to have three degrees from Harvard and not know these abcs?

To explain why a college or university ought to develop the practice of providing fora for discussing its philosophy or theology of education I have had to venture into theory, the formal subject of the next section. That is well, because a persuasive practice requires a rationale that only a good theory can provide, and a good theory does not zoom along in the clouds but touches down regularly to help people out on the ground, clean up a mess here and give heart to a discouraged bunch there. Returning to practice proper, though, let me add a third and then a fourth suggestion.

In addition to providing courses in Christian theological anthropology — courses in which students could be helped to find, explicitly, the vision directing the education to which they are exposing themselves, in which they are actively involved — and to providing fora where those directing the institution can repristinate the vision on which it depends, colleges and universities ought to (a) help students find in all the courses that they take an at least partial justification in terms of the overall rationale for the curriculum as a whole, and (b) help teachers and researchers do the same.

Students will be the better, in my opinion, for knowing from the outset why their institution sees enough worth in music or chemistry or political science to recommend their studying such a subject, perhaps even to require their studying it. Putting things this way could turn us aside into the great debate about the "classics" that ought to be central, required reading, in today's liberal curricula. I want to avoid that debate at this juncture, thinking it more a detour than a shortcut, but I will say here that I think that my theological anthropology, indeed, any traditional Christian theological understanding of human nature, implies a balance between Western and Eastern classics, foundational texts, as well as between the old assumption that we human beings are all more alike than different and the new assumption that "multiculturalism" ought to be king-and-queen.

The theses that I have laid out about human finality (death and resurrection), work, love, ritual, ignorance, and sin admit of numberless curricular enfleshments. To work out readings, courses, subpoints of view that admit some things old and some things new, some things borrowed and some things blue (red, black, white, yellow, brown), is the task of those in the given place where the curriculum will operate, those aware of the particular ethnic, sexual, religious, and economic makeup of the student body in question. The Roman Catholic political principle of subsidiarity, unfortunately praised better than practiced on my church's home turf, says that we ought to try to solve problems at the lowest level, the most local focus, that we can, because that is the place where we are most apt to find the common sense that such solutions require. The corollary is that we have to give to the people trying to solve such problems locally the power or authority sufficient to accomplish their task.

Back to students in any course contributing to a properly self-consciously visionary educational venture, and then to any teachers and researchers in so visionary an institution. I do not mean that chemistry professors ought to become philosophers, spending large fractions of their time in class demonstrating the place of natural science in a liberal (generalist, undergraduate) education. I just mean that students ought to hear why they, any human beings, ought to study the natural world in the way that course x does.

Most practically, I would suggest that, like the thesis of a good sermon or talk, the thesis or rationale for a good course in chemistry or anthropology or anything solid ought to appear, be made plain, at the beginning, in the middle, and at the end. We should tell the students what we are going to do, remind them of what we are doing, and tell them what we have done. We can be full in the beginning, make our references rather passing in the middle, and be crisp at the end. But students ought to know, ideally in a dawning, growing way, what this given work, this specific study, this intellectual exercise of the moment is contributing to their general education — their intellectual maturation as human beings. They ought to know what we teachers think we are up to.

Thus far I may not have chosen a language adequate for explaining my concerns and practical suggestions to people not accustomed to traditional Christian theological analyses of human nature and higher education, people rather accustomed to take as given, established, the value of their biological study of earthworms or their socio-linguistic study of conversations between women and men at work. So, let me say in quite ordinary language that what have I in mind could be accomplished largely by professors telling their students, simply but clearly, why they themselves are doing the work, studying the data, that they are. Most professors are enthusiastic about their subject matters — think that what they do is valuable, something that students ought to know. A few professors are not enthusiastic, and usually they teach badly, but the majority are enthusiastic. Let the majority merely step back and assess their discipline in terms of what it illumines of the comprehensive reality in which they find themselves living their own lives and they will see the general elements of the orientation that, I think, their students require and deserve. They would move into the best of all my educational worlds if they would also relate what they find in such an assessment to the (presumably well articulated) philosophy or theology of education supposedly shaping their institution, but even if they do not take this further step they will have helped their students crucially.

They will give their students a far better chance to appreciate the contribution of a given course to the human venture as a whole for which the institution ought to be preparing them. Their students will know far more usefully in what coins the lab work and readings and field trips ought to pay off. And finally, as I shall argue in the next section, even so modest a regular self-assessment or orientation as what I have proposed here will go a long way toward solving the problem of integration, of putting Humpty-Dumpty back together again, that bedevils most of our educational institutions nowadays.

Having looked at what students need and teachers can offer, let me conclude this section on practical implications by musing about what a Christian view of human nature has to offer researchers. First, it can help them locate their work on a comprehensive grid of reality. That is, it can help them see better the relation of their research into the debt of third world nations, or the spread of herpes, or the use of the sonnet in recent feminist poetry to the whole fourfold layout (nature, society, self, divinity) that I have presented as requisite for wisdom. Second, our reflections on the end of human beings, and on their work, love, and ritual, apply to what goes on in the life of lab scientist or denizen of the library stacks. The researcher is never not an ordinary human being subject to all the existentials. This implies, third, that reflections such as ours on ignorance can serve researchers as a short course on what we might call metaepistemology or metamethodology, while reflections such as ours on sinfulness can serve a similar function regarding metamorality. Researchers need to know what they can reasonably hope to know. They also need to know how they are liable to distort their work through biases and vices. Last, we need only note in passing that the work of *publishing* the fruits of one's research calls all these existentials into play as much as does the research itself.

Theoretical Implications for Higher Education

Humpty-Dumpty was an oval integrity, a yolk and white that ought not to have been separated. Ideally, a humanistic education is a round integrity, something capable of producing alumni who can echo the poet Terence in saying, "I regard nothing human as alien to me." Tertullian, a rather rigid Latin father, held hands with the pagan Terence enough to say that the soul, the animating principle of our humanity, is naturally Christian. From sources such as these has come the distinctively Catholic and Orthodox confidence that human reason, human eros, is trustworthy, though greatly in need of straightening, healing, and elevation by divine grace. Where Luther called reason a whore and Calvin spoke of it as a factory of idols (both figures had an empirical reasonableness, especially in sixteenth-century Europe), Aquinas had baptized Aristotle, frolicked with reason, and established a lovely, symmetrical Christian intellectualism. Somewhere between these two poles, with their respective dependencies on the Bible and the philosophers, lie the theoretical underpinnings of a properly comprehensive traditional Christian theology.

Therefore, in my reflections on death and resurrection I have drawn on the Bible, while in my reflections on work and love and ritual I have stressed the validity, indeed the sacramentality, of "intermediate" human experience in time, prior to death and resurrection. My section on ignorance has smacked of Catholic mysticism, while my section on sin has owed much to Protestant penetrations of human depravity. What, now, ought I, we, to think about the theory of how we should educate our young people and position our research?

First, we ought to think that there will be no significant integration of our educational ventures until we have comprehensive, whole curricula based on a persuasive vision of human nature. Second, we ought to note that most nonprofessional colleges do in fact acknowledge this fact, inasmuch as they provide for required courses in the three basic areas of the humanities (including the arts), the physical sciences, and the social sciences.

Third, the theological oversight that I applaud most both sends researchers, and teachers, forth into any significant field of inquiry and asks them to report back regularly to mission control, orientation central, so that they not become so arcane, so specialized in a silly sense, as to become idiosyncratic — people who can share what they do only with half a dozen others in the world. A theology to my liking sends researchers and teachers forth to work freely because it blesses all decent (nonprurient) human inquiry as an exercise of the divine image in us. It asks us all to report back regularly because it knows that wisdom never lives in a finger lake, always involves an orderly sense of the whole. A college curriculum that does not love wisdom, pursue wisdom, and so revere the whole, the commons, the uni-verse is a curriculum for students and professors who are dwarfs rather than giants, a course of studies dumbed down for the pusillanimous, those who want to have tiny souls. The educational sin against the Holy Spirit is so to dumb things down, devalue human dignity, that those shaped by one's ministrations come to laugh at the pursuit of wisdom, mock the notion that in loving the world and us so much as to have the Logos take flesh God gave reality an order that we can discover with endless delight.

Fourth, this theological road to a theory of education dominated by wisdom means that the paradigm for undergraduate education ought to be liberal studies: arts and sciences focused on the development of the student's human potential. Any collegiate (undergraduate) education that is professional in the sense of relegating the development of the student's human potential to the margins (or of arguing that marketing can make a woman, that nursing can make a man) is problematic. Perhaps one might argue, in the abstract, that we should take care of liberal education in our high schools. In concrete actuality, it is hard enough to find in twenty-year-olds the experiential basis that liberal education requires, and so it is virtually impossible to find it in fifteen-year-olds. Certainly, one can defend undergraduate students' having "majors" in accounting or botany, as in English or Italian. Certainly professional colleges are much with us and we cannot gas the faculty members and students in them. But I believe that to cede the center of the collegiate educational experience to something specialized, and not to continue to insist that its foremost focus be the whole, the commons, the ways of thought that work in all aspects of human inquiry, is to default on what twenty-five hundred years of Western education have learned about what we human beings need most as individuals and societies. It is, I believe, to reveal oneself to be an educational moron.

We do not live to eat, we eat to live. We do not live to work, we work to live. The life is always greater than the particular preoccupation. Many adolescents find it hard to appreciate this, so their keepers in matters educational have to require that they pursue general studies. In developing an orientation toward such studies, we can learn a great deal from the classical Hindu scheme for the life cycle. In the beginning, one goes to a guru for a thorough grounding in the tradition. Next, one goes into the world, to gain experience. When one's hair turns gray and one's grandchildren beg to be lifted up, it is time to quit the world and go back to studying — to considerable solitary pondering. The last stage is a free wandering throughout the whole of the world, agape in gratitude for its graciousness and giving a model of the wisdom to which our humanity invites us.

Yes, our students need to be able to make a living, to carry out the second Hindu phase. But we can accommodate the humanistic and commercial dimensions of their educations by developing double majors, or by making financial aid more available for both general undergraduate education and graduate professional education. What we cannot accommodate, without turning our backs on our theological heritage, is the desire to turn colleges into training schools, transfer Gothic spires onto quonset huts. For though I think it true that everyone ought to know basic science, mathematics, and principles of technology, I also think it true that everyone ought to know basic language, history, and theology. I think it false that we can produce truly educated people without both teaching them to think critically and exposing them to the full parameters of reality. The pathetic students I have seen whose focus is basketball and whose major is recreation witness to the nadir of many schools' folly. Those schools place in grave doubt their right to be, if a theology such as mine has any wisdom. They give out a message so wrong that it builds up the powers of darkness.

You cannot have an integrated, harmonious life without having an integrated mind and heart. You cannot produce an integrated curriculum or overall education, one properly deep and properly broad, without exposing for students the recurrent dynamics of their intellects and natures. The same person can work problems in differential calculus and play the flute. The same student can excel in history and biology and finance. The problem lies not with the equipment that students bring to us, or with the ecological relations among the disciplines and fields of knowledge. Our students may come with deficient prior educations, but if they are human they can learn to think, study, speak, write, and compute adequately. The smart ones will learn much better than the dumb ones, but anyone who is human has a mind made to know.

Moreover, it is not hard to show that our fields of knowledge overlap intrinsically, because the actual world is as relational, as ecological, as the human mind is generalist, in principle capable of getting the point in any field of inquiry. So the problem of how to effect an adequate undergraduate education does not lie in the ineptness of our students or the highly specialized, separated nature of the world (reality). The problem lies in a great many putative educators' not knowing these elementary truths about the mind that knows and the world that beckons to be known. The problem is therefore the old "Who will care for the caretakers" — give the overseers the requisite oversight? Nowadays in American higher education we have many educators who have themselves been educated badly — with little depth or breadth. Some of them have made their way up the greased pole to positions of administrative power. When that happens, the drone at the top can scramble all the buzz down below.

An honest, perhaps quite effective way to reform Catholic higher education would be to take one's direction from the people who stand out as educational successes — for example, Bernard Lonergan, a man who went as deeply and broadly as any in recent memory. (An honest, perhaps quite effective way to reform the church would be analogous: to use as our directive models people who stand out as religious successes — saints in all walks of life.)

In higher education our sinfulness shows itself most destructively in our refusal to let our betters direct our enterprises — not the nuts and bolts but the overall design. In the church others can deal with how our sinfulness shows itself most destructively, but I suspect that a similar lack of humility (and so a similar Peter principle) obtains.

---------------- *Chapter 2* ----------------

On Physical Nature

☐☐☐☐☐

Creation

Our Christian theological essay on education has targeted four
principal dimensions of reality. In the last chapter we dealt with
human nature. Here we deal with physical nature: the material
world, creation. As in the last chapter our vision in effect was bi-
focal, trying to get faith and reason to work stereoscopically, so
here we attempt to give both theology and natural science their
due. The general principle, clearest in the Catholic theology in-
debted to Thomas Aquinas, that faith and reason are less enemies
than allies, because grace builds on nature more than it replaces
nature, can serve as our justification. From the standpoint of the
theology that I espouse, natural science has full rights to investigate the cosmos freely, beholden only to the canons that articulate
its own sense of integrity.

Nonetheless, theology has much to say about the universe,
about creation, and no higher education wanting to express a
Christian theological vision of reality can neglect such a say for
long without stammering badly. What is the gist, the irreplaceable
core, of what Christian theology has to say about physical nature?
That it comes from God (ultimate reality, the Trinity in whom Jesus
causes Christians to believe) as a free gift. That is the crucial significance of the traditional Christian doctrine that creation is from
nothingness (*creatio ex nihilo*). The only reason that we have a
world — inanimate, animate, and human beings (perhaps angelic
beings as well) — is because God, who alone exists independently,
necessarily, chose to let such nondivine beings be. "Creation," in
theological usage, is a free gift of God, made for no reason or motive ulterior to the divine goodness. God did not need to create

66

a world, make beings "outside" of divine being. The world that God made does not cause there to be more being than what God is alone. The wonder is not how God can be but how the world is — why there is this something rather than the original nothingness that there was "before" (time is not the issue) God made the things that constitute the natural world.

Therefore, when one looks upon the world with the eye of Christian faith, one sees gifts of God. Moreover, these gifts do not exist only singly, as so many angular rocks, sportive rabbits. They exist in orders, systems, evolutionary patterns that suggest a unity in creation. What began with the big bang, if in fact that is how creation occurred, is a single process, now so complex that we human students of it can despair of ever grasping the order that makes it whole. Contrary to what theologians thought as little as five hundred years ago, such order seems to be dynamic, changing, nothing whose subspecies are locked into rigid natures once and for all. The immense spatial and temporal quantities involved in this process make our minds boggle and give our most sophisticated computers full employment. Indeed, if there is a single historical testimony to human beings' having been made in the image of a divine intelligence, it is the achievement of modern science in mapping what it has of creation, discovering what it has of the worlds of the stars and the nuclear particles and the human genes.

A theology confident of the reality and goodness of God, and so of the reasonableness of its faith, ought to be a great cheerleader for natural science. Yes, theology has important things to say about human nature, wisdoms to offer about human virtue and vice, that it knows apply to scientists qua human beings as much as they apply to artists and househusbands. But if theologians should encourage artists to work to the best of their abilities, to the fullest development of their skills, theologians should certainly encourage scientists similarly. The laboratory can be a school of maturation as demanding as the painter's studio or the monk's cell. The work of trying to understand the geology of the San Andreas fault or the hematology of a rare leukemia can ask of a scientist as much as a concerto by Beethoven can ask of a pianist or an interview with the Congregation for the Doctrine of the Faith can ask of a creative theologian. Intelligence is intelligence, wherever it operates. It has to pay attention, hone its ability to get the point, be judicious, act prudently, and love the intellectual life faithfully if it is to come to full maturity anywhere. These imperatives (an adaptation of Bernard Lonergan's "transcendental precepts") are nothing that researchers or creative workers in any field can satisfy extrinsically, heteronomously. Everywhere we can only satisfy them, obey them, from within, with a growing conviction that they spell out our vocation as intellectuals and much of our vocation as plain human beings.

To come to physical nature as an investigator who believes that the world is a free, creative gift of God is not to change any of this intellectual obligation, not to lighten any of this imperative nor add to it any new burdens. What is there in front of us, intriguing and daunting, is the same whether we think of it as a free expression of the divine goodness or we place the question of its ultimate origin in brackets. Similarly, the theological notion that creation has an end, the redemption for which the apostle Paul heard the world groaning, need mean nothing to the practicing scientist, need be no factor in her daily scientific investigations. If it does mean something, as either a conviction she has gained or a question she considers worth contemplating, she has moved from the formality of physical science to the formality of philosophy or theology. That can be a fine move, an admirable exercise of her humanity, but she need not make it. She can be a competent, even exemplary biologist or physicist without becoming a proponent of creation from nothingness or, in contrast, a proponent of an atheistic conviction that the world has always been and in itself has no ultimate significance.

Workers in higher education shaped by a Christian theological vision of their enterprise should not only tolerate natural science, they should encourage it steadfastly. Without reservation they should want ongoing investigations of the material, physical world, and not simply because such investigations may bring a cure for certain kinds of cancer or pave the way to a better disposal of nuclear wastes. No, the first reason for science to be is less practical, more contemplative. All honest, genuine understanding of the natural world is for the Christian theologian understanding of the great gift of God in creation. The being of the physical world testifies to the being of God — the mind and power of the Creator. Certainly, we get no full, comprehensive portrait of God, the Creator, from any of his creatures, nor from the collectivity of them all. But we do get glimpses, appreciations, that can help us to feel about creation as we ought to feel — if in fact we are made to be religious, bound to God for our final significance. The explosions of the stars help us to feel rightly by specifying our sense of the divine might. So do the intricacies of our nerves or the ecologies of the different marine depths, specifying our sense of the divine intelligence. Whatever we learn about creation tells us a little more about our source, the unbounded Other who is always the inmost partner of our journey to understand, be believers, with an appreciation that keeps growing.

Despite their desire to have us develop proper feelings about creation, Christian theologians cannot accept a scientism that propounds dogmas to the effect that the realities with which faith deals have no rational standing. Indeed, a traditional, orthodox Christian theology has to brand such dogmas extrusions from science, excrescences to be judged not by the criteria of science, outside whose pale they fall, but by philosophical and theological criteria, which should find them wanting. For a scientist to say that people can believe in God only for emotional reasons, or, even worse, to say that belief in God is just a refuge for those weak intellectually or morally, is to lay down a proposition having nothing essential to do with the practice, or indeed the theoretical foundations, of physical science itself. What is or is not a rational way for a human being to live depends mainly on the ineluctable, inevitable, unavoidable mysteriousness of human existence. Natural scientists must contend with this mysteriousness as much as poets and bankers must. The children of natural scientists die in automobile accidents or from brain tumors. Natural scientists themselves fall in love, lose their jobs, pass by street people asking for a handout, read the headlines about carnage in Tel Aviv or earthquake in Kobe. There is nothing that scientists can see through their telescopes or their microscopes or in their computer printouts that will dissolve the mysteriousness — intellectual, moral, emotional — of their condition as human beings. Physicists and biologists are human beings before, after, below, and beyond their being scientists, and the mysteriousness of which I speak lodges in their very humanity. They might have been ballplayers or tour guides or movie stars. Their being botanists or theoretical physicists or archeologists is more extrinsic than their being human (and so not knowing, finally, where they came from or where they are going), and it is less crucial.

For a theological outlook such as mine, this means that natural science is a fully human endeavor — an expression of the being that scientists share with writers and accountants and grounds-keepers. Natural science is not an esoteric, arcane kind of work that makes scientists into another species. Students ought to study biology, chemistry, and any other discipline that their college can offer them for the exploration of creation because, in the first place, such a study is a direct way for them to exercise their preem-inently human capacity for understanding the reality in which they find themselves. We educators should set up our students' studies in the physical sciences as we set up their studies in the social sciences or the humanities: as explorations that can turn into wonderful adventures.

Certainly, students will discover that biology or engineering is demanding, at times boring, even discouraging now and then, as they can discover that studying Shakespeare or Dante or Cervantes can be. There are no untroubled romances in the intellectual life, no studies that never leave the rose garden. Moreover, there are no disciplines, no narrowed tracts of studies, that do not require the complement of other disciplines or tracts. Undergraduates need both mathematics and languages, both psychology and political science. If we do not through our tender mercies send them forth appreciating the full range of reality, we have shortchanged them: not given them the truly humanistic education that both their natures and our theological propaganda postulate.

So, not to have undergraduates study physical science is as egre-gious an error as not to have them study theology. In either case the sense of reality that we give our students is dented, thrown out of true by a lamentable, correctable lacuna. But we can fill in the gap. We can give creation its due. In the measure that we regard the natural world precisely as the creation of God, we shall feel a strong obligation to do so.

Last, it bears repeating that it is the task of theologians, not physical scientists, to show students that the natural world is the creation of God. If scientists wish to allude to this conviction, be-cause they are themselves believers, well and good — as long as doing this does not detract from their main work, which is to do science or teach it. "Creationism" is not a matter that scientists ought to have to take up. Until creationism becomes the regnant, going foundation of the principles on which mainstream physicists and biologists and other scientists depend, creationism has no rightful claim to time in the curriculum of natural science. It is rather a matter for theologians, those whose business is the nature of God (one of whose hats carries the logo "Creator").

When "creationism" means the belief that God did in fact make the world from nothingness, that God does in fact conserve the world in being every moment, then a theologian of my liking is a creationist. When "creationism" means a philosophy of science, a metaconception that would force itself into the daily workings of natural scientists, then in my view it is a force that we should brand alien to natural science, a virus that we should consider dangerous to natural science's good health.

The Ecosphere

On scientific grounds, we ought to show students the interconnectedness of the different realms of the natural world. It is not enough for our students to study physics, chemistry, or biology in isolation from the rest of natural science or, indeed, of social science. At some point our curricula have to provide for the ecological character of physical reality, showing that all living things make an impact on other species and receive impacts from other species in return.

Ideally, we will also show students that their human species, *homo sapiens,* is now the decisive force in the natural future of the planet earth. The waste products that human beings generate, and the economic, political, and philosophical forces that shape how countries deal with their wastes, are just one example of how human living is now determining many natural habitats. Decisions about logging in the American Northwest will have as much to say about the future of the old-growth forests as will the quantities of sun and rain that the forests receive, or the physiology of redwood growth. Human activities already determine the number and health of the salmon in the streams of that same American Northwest more than do nonhuman ones. Where even just a century ago the salmon ran in profusion and silvery health, now they are relatively few and stunted. The story is if anything worse in the

American Northeast, where the depletion of fish in the once teeming Georges Bank is a casebook study of ecological stupidity. In the same geographical area, the demise of the forests due to industrial pollution shows all too clearly how right Loren Eiseley was to label human beings "the lethal factor."

The story is the same in many parts of Eastern Europe that used to belong to the Soviet Union, and in many parts of Latin America and Africa. I have sat outside under the stars at a rooftop restaurant in Mexico City and had to wipe grit from my plate before eating. The once prolific numbers of many African or Amazonian species are now so low as to make those species endangered. The poisoning of waters and lands in Japan and China shows that pollution has truly become a worldwide phenomenon. If only because of so many negative, threatening facts of present-day natural life, our college students require a solid instruction in the ecological realities of their environment. Unless they come to their adult works and political activities sensitive to the impact that human industries and recreational activities can have on the natural environment, they will join the legions of their parents and grandparents who in retrospect have lived as assassins.

Beyond the practical problems of pollution, however, ecological or environmental studies beckon as solid ways in which to explore the reticulated character of creation. The niches in which we live are not islands. The plants and animals of our planet are connected along lines that resemble the threads of a spider's web. Where the old images of human nature set our kind outside of material nature, even in opposition to material nature, we now have much evidence that these images are as untrue as they are dangerous. However little most human beings who gaze out at Monterey Bay know about the life moving in the canyons that go as much as two miles deep, the sewage of those human beings makes a crucial impact on the life of the bay, even the life at its depths.

Every creature that takes its food from a given environment and gives back its wastes makes an impact on that environment. We human beings take huge amounts of resources, materials that we convert into energy, from innumerable habitats, and we give back huge amounts of wastes and other forces. Yes, we plant trees, grow crops, reintroduce animal species. We probably do fewer of these at least potentially positive things, however, than we do negative things — take resources away or taint them. Until we realize how widely our intrusions into the lakes and rivers and seas ripple out, we shall not begin to appreciate the way that our natural world actually functions. For the theologian, this represents a new responsibility.

For example, nowadays it is not enough for a theologian to comment well on the biblical verse (Gen. 1:28) that gives human beings dominion over the rest of living creation. It is not enough even to speak of responsible stewardship. As I see the proper upshot for higher education of a dialogue between theologians and ecologists, we should want our students to emerge from their educations convinced that nature does not exist only for their free use. Nature is not simply the maidservant of human beings, standing at the ready to supply whatever human beings desire. Nature has a dignity in its own right, and perhaps a set of further rights in consequence of such dignity. We human beings may have to use other species for our food, housing, clothing, and medicines, but we do not have to abuse other species — hunt them to extinction, pollute them to the point where they gasp and choke. The time has come for theologians to speak up for the sanctity of natural creation, and so for its God-given right not to be defaced, used capriciously, changed or developed with no concern for its future survival and flourishing.

Yes, we developed peoples have made some progress in restoring the lands that we used to strip-mine, replanting the forests that we used to raze. But to date the main reason for such reforms has been anthropocentric: Our excesses have threatened our economic well-being, or the ugliness of our defacements has offended us aesthetically. We have yet to embrace in any truly popular way the notion that it is simply wrong, sinful, to destroy natural habitats, gouge out hillsides, or risk bays through oil slicks. It is simply wrong to put holes in the upper atmosphere or ruin marine beds through the runoff of our chemical factories.

We shall deal later with the issue of what it will require of us educators to equip our students to deal well with the challenge of committing themselves to a sustainable lifestyle. Both there and here, however, we shall have to combat an attitude that Christian religion itself has helped to make ingrained. This is the attitude that, as images of God, vicegerents of God in creation, we human beings have the intelligence and right to command the rest of physical nature for our well-being. We can rip into the bosom of mother earth as we think good, because mother earth is simply our servant, our storehouse. Indeed, we can regard our passage through the byways of mother earth as just a short journey to God's heaven, where we shall live angelically, with no debts to our bodies or the earth. So why not eat, drink, and be merry with the goods of mother earth? Why bother to care for the other species, keep the skies and rivers clean?

These questions suggest how unincarnational our Christian faith has often been, and how self-serving. Because of these deficiencies in our religious outlook, we have been able to give medals of honor to entrepreneurs who destroyed thousands of acres of natural habitat, as we have been able to give them to dictators or oligarchs who made huge profits from the sweat of the peasant masses. The facts of ecological science nowadays brim with moral challenges to the ways that we have treated the earth in the past. Indeed, they brim with moral challenges to the ways that we Christians have understood creation.

It is dubious that we can continue in good conscience to think of ourselves as free to lay waste to the environment as we wish. It is more likely, on both ecological and enlightened religious grounds, that we shall have in good conscience to make ourselves more the servants of mother nature than her masters. Indeed, it is likely that we shall have to consider the earth as a primary object of our remedial ministrations. In the twenty-first century, some of the energies that used to go into feeding the human hungry, educating the human ignorant, and succoring the human sickly will have to go into restoring the rain forests, replenishing the herds now vanishing from the savannahs, making the streams hospitable again to the trout and salmon, the oceans hospitable to the crabs and lobsters. Studies in environmental science, studies of the ecosphere, are so direct a challenge to our prior Christian ways of thinking about creation, so clear a revelation of the dysfunctional character of many of our old assumptions, that they challenge us morally far more powerfully than do most scientific studies.

For there are signs that changes in our human attitudes and practices can make a positive difference — which means that our responsibility to develop such changes is not merely speculative, but rather often is quite practical. For instance, as we reintroduce buffalo to the prairies, where they used to swarm before westward-hoing Americans decimated them, largely for sport, we find that the grasses and flowers that used to flourish there revive. Absent the manuring that the buffalo used to provide, the prairies had changed markedly, in some ways sickening. A new respect for old ecological arrangements shows signs of restoring an important feature of our American Midwest.

Such a new use of old patterns of our lands, such a new attitude toward many natural habitats, will itself require much experimentation and testing. We shall have to learn by doing what are the wisest policies for restoration, what kinds of repristinations make the most sense. There will be no significant efforts along this line, however, no reforms worth bothering about, until a new philosophy (common sense), in fact a new ethics and theology, takes serious hold. We have to think quite differently about the earth, much more ecologically, than we used to think — indeed, than most of us still think at the end of the second Christian millennium — if we are going to give creation its due, either practically or theoretically. We will not be good citizens of the cosmopolis until we embrace the proposition that all living things are our fellow citizens — brother fox and sister marlin, Francis of Assisi might say. As always, it will fall to higher education to be the powerhouse in the shift in consciousness that the twenty-first century will require. Other agents of cultural change will certainly have to pitch in, but our universities are the places where most of the scientific studies that are implied will go on, where we will teach most of the changes in intellectual appreciation of the ecosphere that will be necessary.

Physical Science

I have said that a theological view of higher education such as mine looks at physical science as an eminently human enterprise. In light of the end for which we human beings have been made, toward which we move, physical science stands out as a fine way to increase our appreciation of what sort of world God has made, what is the reality in which we find ourselves immersed through our bodies and minds. The discipline required in the physical sciences, their demand for mathematical rigor and controlled imagination, teaches us that this reality is a tough mistress. She does not give up her secrets easily. She has little indulgence for the sloppy and impatient. Matter is there, over-against us and our minds, seeming not to care what we think of it, whether we make sense of it or give it our applause. The curious thing is that many people find studying matter, its constitution and arrangements, fascinating. Matter presents them problems that soon become absorbing. Physical science is not simply hard work; it is also lively, quickening play.

We assume that matter is intelligible, or at least that it is amenable to rational, mathematical descriptions. We have had enough success applying such descriptions, such hypotheses, in practice to warrant this assumption. At Hiroshima and Nagasaki we confirmed the validity of our leading scientists' views of atomic energy. In hundreds of laboratories every day we confirm the validity of our leading scientists' views of chemical interactions, reading out the state of patients' blood or getting positive results about new synthetic compounds. The method that we credit for the success of the physical sciences boils down to careful, critical thinking. In practice scientific intelligence is far subtler than simply following stodgy recipes, but it still depends on gathering information accurately, assuring that this information is appropriately comprehensive, testing the initial intuition that supplied the formality for gathering this information, working out experiments that can be duplicated and so tested again and again, and finally drawing the conclusions from the data furnished by such experiments — drawing them as cautiously, conservatively, elegantly, and prudently as possible. Physical scientists want results that will stand the test of time. Their confidence rests less on the brilliance of any given scientist or experiment than on the validity of their general method of disciplined investigation — a validity proven again and again.

This paradigm from the physical sciences is precious beyond estimation. We ought to expose all college students to it sufficiently to insure that they get a solid dose of rigorous thinking. We should not transfer the paradigm to the social sciences or the humanities uncritically. When the main agents in experiments are free human beings, rather than molecules or genes, the variables multiply exponentially and our control over them lessens dramatically. But an analogous use of careful research to gather pertinent data and rigorous evaluation of the hypotheses that such data generate and we use to explain them is completely appropriate. Admittedly, sometimes the social sciences seem to strive for an objectivity that their subject matter renders dubious, but any experiment in any field will only profit from the general demand for self-criticism that the physical sciences place at their front and center. In any field, we have to want to learn, to know, what is so, rather than what we might like to be so. Otherwise, we are not honest researchers and our biases will do us in.

I leave it to physical scientists themselves to say whether what they learn about the nature of nature, how they find their years of dealing with matter shaping their sense of human destiny, tends to take them in the direction of philosophy and religion. This drift seems to be a pattern in the lives of many eminent physical scientists (Albert Einstein, for instance), who spend some of their time in their later years thinking about the nature of science itself, even about the nature of the universe. Sometimes their reflections are impressive religiously, often they are not, but what is always impressive is the concern for science and the earth that many mature practitioners exhibit.

The rewards of physical science tend to be quite pure. Occasionally there are prizes or patents or consultantships that are lucrative, but engineers reap more of these than do theoreticians and laboratory scientists. Certainly, there are honors and kudos from one's peers — elections to prestigious academies, recognitions from leading journals, named professorships and chairs. But the material, even the emotional sides of these rewards pale compared to what has to sustain the scientist day after day. Like the painter or writer whose main challenge is the blank canvas or page, the productive, contented scientist has to find the work of trying to understand a given problem, a small piece of the great puzzle of how the stars function or the inert gases work, self-justifying. Physical science is one of the purer forms of the desire to know, the drive to understand, that is a mainspring of human culture.

After one has set aside riches and honors (no small stimuli), the stronger stimulus to higher culture is the simple desire to understand or, in the arts, to make something beautiful. The purveying of the fruits of such understanding is important, but the great thing is the search, the quest, the active exercise of intelligence itself. The real scientist would not trade the work of trying to understand for any of the secondary benefits or satisfactions. The work is the treasure hidden in the field, the pearl of great price, as it is for the real writer or artist or physician.

We mentioned work when we were studying human nature.

There we took note of the high place that work holds in any properly Freudian view of human health. Intellectual work has its frustrations, certainly, but it also has satisfactions with few peers. It is nice when other people give the intellectual worker a pat on the back, but the crucial interaction is less with outsiders than with the materials of the work itself. For the physical scientist, these materials are some portion of material creation. For the theologian thinking carefully about the work of the physical scientist, it makes sense to remember the old description of natural philosophy as "thinking the thoughts of God after him."

The intelligibilities of matter are thoughts of God. That is how the theologian is bound to regard them. Certainly, "thoughts" is a metaphor, a reach for a fragile analogy. But the key intuition seems to hold: The fact that nature is intelligible (despite all the qualifications that chaos theory and the principle of indeterminacy may eventually force us to place) makes nature a medium of divinity, a revelation. The only thing as central to us human beings as our capacity for understanding, our need to understand, and our delight in understanding is our similar relations to love. Both understanding and love work through our bodies, but both also incline us to speak of "spirit." In laboring to understand and love, we go out of ourselves, realize that we are creatures capable of ecstasy. Our minds can travel to the far galaxies. Our hearts can fix our affections on people far away. The imaginations that mediate our thinking and loving operate at the exact border of our matter and spirit, our bodies and souls. In the case of physical science, they give us the figures, the patterns, the formulas that we use to understand what we are dealing with.

Beyond the useful information that students can gain from studying physics and chemistry and geology stands the experience of working to understand. The exercise of intelligence that a good course in physical science can set up can teach students a great deal about their makeup as rational animals. We educators can hope that they will experience the joy of understanding, the pleasure that insight brings. We can also hope that they will experience the amazement that comes when we realize that the natural world has secrets it is willing to disclose. It falls outside physical science as we tend presently to define it to pursue the implications of either the experience of understanding or the willingness of the physical world to disclose its secrets to disciplined inquiry. That is the business of philosophers or theologians of science. But what students learn by studying the material world can inculcate a considerable wonder if the courses that we offer them proceed with a humanistic orientation. We need only position what undergraduates do in courses in physics or geology as explorations of the world given to us human beings as exercises of the intelligence given to us human beings to show the connaturality of physical science with how God has made us and suggest its kinship with all other human studies. Thereby, we may hope to give our curricula the best of integrating perspectives: Education holds together because of the intelligibility of what we encounter in any area of human experience and the capacity we have to understand it.

A Sustainable Lifestyle

The reader will not find in this book extended treatments of the "values" for which those directing higher education ought to plump. That does not mean that I think that education should be "value-free," in the sense of not concerned about practical implications, moral imperatives, ethical entailments. On the one hand, I abhor the tendency of a crude Marxism to subordinate intellectual inquiry to political orthodoxy. The disgrace come to Soviet science from the Lysenko affair can summarize the congruence of my abhorrence with the sentiments of mainstream Western science. On the other hand, it seems to me obvious that both the reality that our academic disciplines explore and the minds with which we explore it are ecological — relational, not sealed hermetically into separated realms. We human beings depend on the health of our biological niches and we make helpful or harmful impacts on those niches. In our own psyches, if we separate crudely what we think from what we do, we make ourselves ill mentally. So, for example, we cannot realize that we are polluting the Chesapeake Bay, ruining that marvelous ecological zone, without moving on to the conviction that we have to change our ways. Not to move on to this practical conclusion would be to give ourselves false consciences, establish ourselves in bad faith.

Thus, there is an ethical component built into all our studies, whatever the area of reality that they explore. Everywhere, we have to ask what difference what we learn ought to make in how we act, live, practice. Sometimes our studies may seem to be so arcane, so basic or specialized, that they carry few implications for changes in our behavior. Other times the implications are so clear that the problem is not seeing them but mustering the courage to change our ways.

For example, the line between the investigations of medical scientists into the dynamics of lung cancer and changes in the lifestyles of smokers could hardly be clearer. In my view, that line continues into the politics of our national support of prices in the tobacco industry, making such support simply immoral. Certainly, little in national politics is simple, as we see in the next chapter. But even the purest, least value-laden research of scientists in fields such as lung cancer can turn out to carry explosive implications for human behavior.

That is the general drift of the heading of this section, "A Sustainable Lifestyle." Many volumes of information, many fields of inquiry, bear on the highly moral consideration of how we human beings ought to deal with the natural world and one another in the next century, but some of the most acutely relevant among them come from physical science. What we are learning about the ecological processes of the skies and the oceans, the forests and the plains, make two things quite clear. First, in few cases do we yet have sufficient evidence to say dogmatically what nature is or is not bound to be like in a given area in the year 2100. Second, in many cases we have sufficient evidence to say that present trends, the apparent results of present human practices, are ominous. For prudent people, such ominousness is enough to warrant a full-scale review, with a firm willingness to change current practices when it becomes morally certain that they are damaging the health of the ecosphere.

"Moral certainty" is not metaphysical certainty. It is the yield of common sense, not an unequivocal revelation from God. If the data on the results of smoking tobacco suggest to a reasonable, prudent person that such behavior is linked significantly to the rise of lung cancer, and perhaps to other cancers as well, then such a person will move to make the appropriate reforms or changes — personal and national alike. She will feel morally certain that she should quit smoking, if she has been on the weed herself, and she will throw her support to those who are trying to remove smoking from the list of national or international human pastimes. Removing smoking need not become her consuming passion. Other responsibilities and causes may continue to take up more of her time. But in the measure that she deems contributing to the demise of smoking important, and to the degree that her financial and temporal resources allow, she will become a solid member of the nonsmoking lobby, movement, or coalition.

Many of the changes in lifestyle that we will probably have to bring about, if we are to keep either the future of our planet or our own human future green in the centuries ahead, come onto our personal and political agendas from research in the physical sciences. Certainly, some changes come from second looks at the demographics of the earth's population, the economics of global poverty, or the statistics on crimes related to drugs. Equally certainly, the information piling up on children born out of wedlock, children living in households without fathers, elderly people warehoused in nursing homes, and so forth suggest large changes in national policies, and so in how we raise monies from taxes and spend them, how we think about citizenship and church membership. Internationally, the problems of poverty, immigration, the despoliation of natural resources, crime, the abuse of children, and so forth suggest similarly large changes. The limits of what goes into our understanding of the word "sustainable" are only the limits of our imaginations, our information, our moral and political fortitude. Still, the most radical considerations come from the ecological sciences, because they report most directly on what our planet seems able to bear, its "carrying capacity."

Consider, for example, the matter of human population the world over. The greatest pressure on the environment comes from the geometrical increase of human beings. The gravest cause for concern about the twenty-first century is the percentage of the global population now under the age of twenty-one. If we say that the vast majority of such people are likely to live to the middle of the next century, then by the middle of the next century we could easily be looking at a planet with over ten billion human beings. We can now only guess, imagine perilously, what the impact of such a population would be. The pressures put on the seas, the arable lands, and the skies are hard to calculate, but even the most conservative estimates will turn the conscientious calculator pale. It seems but the barest of common senses, the most humble of moral responsibilities, to conclude that we have to halt the current rise in the world's population. It seems but the most obvious of instances where moral considerations are built into our computer readouts, our most detached scientific evaluations of the physical data.

A sustainable lifestyle for our species in the year 2050 would probably look considerably different from what we Americans enjoy or indulge right now. Bracketing the crucial political question of how we might move the majority of the world's citizens toward such a sustainable lifestyle, let us confine ourselves to the issue of what rightful impact the problem of our global future ought to make on our assessments of the curricula now requisite in higher education. We can continue this discussion in the next section, where the topic will be the practical implications for education of a theologically astute reading of physical science. Here it will behoove us to line up the most useful theological orientations.

The first such orientation that I would bring to the table is twofold. Taking our human embodiment seriously, and so making us solid citizens of the earth, I would have our Christian theologians use the prestige of the Incarnation to make high priorities love of physical science and care for the earth that physical science investigates. As hallmarks of a realistic higher education, we should want our students to learn about physical reality and embrace the moral implications (for their lifestyles) of what they learn. We should blush to be graduating students illiterate concerning the basic physical and biological laws of their environment, tone-deaf concerning the moral implications of such scientific literacy. Certainly, we shall say the same about social sciences, which in the next chapter we consider under the summary formality of "politics." And, we have been saying throughout, and we shall continue to say, that the reality in which all of us human beings live, move, and have our being is ecological, relational, a matter of both/and rather than either/or. Still, when it comes to the issue of educating students to embrace a sustainable lifestyle, the physical sciences must supply the foundational information.

Beyond this foundational information, theologians ought to develop the obvious observation that we human beings are not either physical or political; we are both. We are not either pure intellectuals or practical citizens; we should be both. To develop the lifestyles that will sustain us in the foreseeable future, we need to become far more sophisticated, far better able to think comprehensively and relationally, than many of us and our students appear to be at present. Relatedly, we need to become far more convinced that all the major areas of human inquiry bear on the survival and prospering of our race — that the arts, the sciences, the humanities, and the social sciences each have an irreplaceable role to play. We have to know the proportions of our problems and also know how to move our fellow citizens to respond appropriately. We have to contend with questions of fact about the current health of nature in a given area and with questions of morale bearing on the possibility that our species will do what is reasonable. Biology is crucial, but so are theology and art. Since none of us can master all the information or insight that is necessary, we have to learn to cooperate, be educated to expect that in the future collaboration will be the order of the day.

A sustainable future will be the fruit of a cooperative venture, a shared comprehensive vision, as much as it will be the fruit of given changes in the ways that we till the land or set up our money and banking. There is no significant zone of human thought or behavior that we can neglect without imperiling our future. Yes, some fraction of our kind may survive even if we do not change, and certainly the earth can survive without our human species. Yes, not even nuclear warfare, bringing nuclear winter, is likely to destroy physical nature completely. But this limit condition or consideration offers most of us only the bleakest of comforts, because most of us want our earth to be fair and all her children wise. Most of us want for creation, the work of God's hands, more than a minimal survival, a minimal victory over our worst human potential.

To this end, it may turn out that we have to challenge, ideally change radically, current Vatican policies about birth control, as it may turn out that we have to change radically current American policies about land development or current Chinese policies about industrial development and the use of coal. Perhaps we need to shift the priorities of the United Nations from managing unmanageable local wars to executing a global war on the use of drugs. Perhaps we need to change the legal codes of many countries so that we execute expeditiously outlaws, those who will not abide by reasonable rules of conduct truly geared to the common good, commending their sorry souls to God. It is hard to know, ahead of a full immersion in the business of working wholeheartedly on developing a sustainable lifestyle, which policies will emerge as necessary, and so eminently realistic, and which will emerge as truly regressive, draconian in the sense of mindlessly brutal. And, of course, we shall not even get into difficult calculations such as these until we become convinced that the situation is indeed critical, that the annual volumes brought out by groups such as the Worldwatch Institute on the state of the earth do indeed create a clear mandate for wholesale changes in our lifestyles (and so in our higher educations).

Practical Implications for Higher Education

These all too amateur reflections on the place of physical science in a higher education oriented by Christian theology suggest that having our students study the material world is absolutely essential. If at the outset we could not give content to the conviction we had that physical science is something to which all educated people ought to have been exposed, at this juncture we ought to be able to fill in many of the blanks. First, it is unlikely that our students will learn to think with the rigor that they ought unless they have been exposed to, indeed exercised in, the foremost modern form of rigorous thinking, scientific investigation. Those teaching physical science will have to say what their disciplines suggest about what competencies in mathematics and computer science we should require of our students. Mathematics is more than the servant of the physical sciences, but its function there as a lingua franca commends it on another score. In addition to the exercise it gives the mind, the humanistic development it offers on its own grounds, competence in mathematics helps students qualify for intermediate and advanced work in the physical sciences. Other things being equal, then, we should encourage our students to become competent at least to the level of calculus.

Second, the relevance of the physical sciences to our grasping the nature of the ecosphere and seeing the consequences for how we human beings ought to live in the next century brings forward another reason for our commending the physical sciences to our students. If they are to understand the debates about the production and use of energy that are likely to heat up again in the next decade, they will have to know the basic facts about matter and energy, heat and light, how an ocean functions or a forest. Too many of our debates about national and international policies about energy or the use of the seas or the repair of the ozone layer skip the level of basic scientific information and plunge directly into economics or politics. Nature is not infinitely malleable. The laws of thermodynamics impose some sobering restraints. The resources of the planet earth are finite. The tolerances within which we must keep the skies and the seas, if we are to have air fit to breathe and we are not to flood most of our coastal areas, are quite narrow. Should we prove that the greenhouse effect is bound soon to melt the icebergs and much of the polar ice, we shall come to a specific crossroads. Either we shall take the path of reducing the forces that are raising the temperature of the planet or we shall walk down the path to flooding many of our coastal cities. Should we come to this juncture, no rhetoric of our politicians will alter the dilemma. The Speaker of the House cannot change the temperature at which ice melts, nor the laws of the elements heating up to produce the greenhouse effect.

A dozen analogies latent in pending crises stemming from the erosion of our croplands, the pollution of our aquifers, the destruction of our rain forests, the overfishing of our prime marine sources of food, and the spread of desertification make the same point. While economic and political (and finally religious) policies and attitudes have much to say about these processes or trends, the base line is physical: the impact working its way out in the material systems under consideration. I would not have all our college courses in the physical sciences take their shape from the environmental crisis that the human species is creating presently, but neither would I let educators, those who plan curricula, avert their faces from this crisis. Ignatius Loyola said that a good is divine in the measure that it is universal. There are few educational goods more universal in their potential impact than our turning out students equipped to deal with the environmental crisis threatening to break forth in the twenty-first century.

Perhaps this crisis would make a fine "problem" around which to organize interdisciplinary studies. I can think of other fine problems (the "feminization of poverty" globally, for example), but the ecological crisis commends itself at this juncture because of its clear rootage in scientific literacy. It would be fascinating, and sobering, to have a competent interdisciplinary team lead students through the physical, biological, economic, political, and philosophical components of this looming global crisis. As well, it would be utterly realistic: All these forces, disciplines, cultural dimensions are de facto at work, in play, right now. We could illustrate cultural differences dramatically by studying how Asians in contrast to Latin Americans or Africans or North Americans tend to construe the environmental crisis. We could show the now inextricable connections of the continents' economies and communications and impacts on such "commons" as the oceans and the skies.

When a group of revolutionaries in Chiapas sneezes, the gnomes of Zurich and London and Wall Street reach for their vitamin C. When a nation cobbled together by force comes apart in the Balkans, centuries of animosity and religious difference come to life again to fan new flames of violence. Consider the ecological dimensions to the war between Iraq and Kuwait, epitomized in Iraq's setting many Kuwaiti oil fields on fire. Consider the dimensions of the nuclear policies responsible for Chernobyl and many other dangerous reactors in the former Eastern Bloc. It is difficult to find a part of the earth where politics and economics, warfare and energy policy, do not carry obvious and frightening ecological implications. It is hard to think about clean water, and so about widespread disease, without getting into matters of tribal hatred, industrial and commercial development, even images of the good life, the righteous way to live.

The point to interdisciplinary studies such as these, whether we promote them directly as straightforward curricular options or indirectly by providing programmatic junctures at which to make links among disciplinary studies pursued less relationally, is that they show students the actual, very complicated operations of the world in which they live. In this world, physical and political and religious forces intersect, color one another, ripple into one another's zones without ceasing to possess their own integrity. People can worship God without knowing what changes such worship may bring to their blood pressure. People can dam streams or blast into rock mountains without pausing to consider what view of nature grants them such license. But if people begin to realize that their prayer and their building roads may be related, influencing one another mutually, they may start to carry out both human activities more responsibly. They may pray as though everything depended on themselves, and so fall on their knees in fear and trembling. They may work as though everything depended on God, and so do what they do peacefully, like developed *karma-yogins,* little concerned for what their more passionate neighbors consider success or failure. All such interesting, potentially life-changing considerations become possible when we let physical science or any other branch of our educational venture display how it can shade other tracts, what pleasure it can give us when we let it show its true ecological colors.

Practically, then, physical science can be a fine prod for us educators to question our traditional conservatism about disciplinary purity and make ourselves face hard issues of interdisciplinary knowing, of the ecological character of the intellectual life itself. If many in the professorate do not want to take the time to deal with the realities pressuring us to rethink our curricula so as to make them more realistic, let the rest of us become astute enough politically to publicize what we take to be the folly of their narrowness or laziness. It is, once again, not a matter of either/or. It is a matter of providing for both the values that a pure, unapplied course in physics or biology can bring to a humanistic education and the values that an "applied" course, in the sense of interdisciplinary and ecological, can bring. Physics or chemistry, like political science or theology, has an integrity in its own right, an order and tradition well worth students' time. But none of our humanistic disciplines actually exists in a vacuum, and none of the zones of reality with which our disciplines deal is an island unto itself, a realm with no ecological connections or entailments.

This relational character of present-day knowledge is as much a fact, a reality begging acknowledgment in any educational venture deserving our full respect and support, as is the need for the disciplines to preserve their integrity and show the value of our pursuing them purely. The argument that there is too little time or space in the curriculum to accommodate this twofold demand I find to be nonsense. We already have several levels at which we require courses. It would be child's play to shift things slightly to provide at the intermediate level for the ecology of disciplines, had we the will. That is the great question: Will we have the will before the crisis engulfs us? The record of human wisdom in matters such as these, including the wisdom of professors in universities, is not encouraging. Still, hope is a theological virtue, so I feel obliged not to despair.

Theoretical Implications for Higher Education

As soon as we begin to appreciate the full range of knowledge, both content and methods, that an educated citizen ought to have in tow to function responsibly in the twenty-first century, we begin to appreciate the centrality of making a college education broad and deep. We ought not to aim at giving students the minutiae of a dozen different fields. We ought rather to aim at teaching students how to educate themselves in any field that commends itself to their study after their graduation. I believe that this imperative or desideratum means that our general effort in college education ought to target two goals.

First, we ought to acquaint students with the major realms of knowledge — the basic tracts of reality. In this work, I would stress a solid exposure to basic information and methodological skills. For example, from their studies in the physical sciences students ought to graduate well informed about the fundamental physical laws running their world, the fundamental biological laws running their bodies, and the mental habits that physical and biological scientists employ. Second, we ought to acquaint students well with how their minds operate transcendentally — always and everywhere. This means a few courses on cognitional theory and many references in many courses to methodology — the practical work of human intelligence in a given area.

So, for example, one might illustrate Lonergan's transcendental precepts — be attentive, be intelligent, be reasonable, be responsible, be loving — in a variety of practical instances. If the same human being might work as a theologian, a lawyer, a physician, and a musician, what are the common denominators of intelligent work, admirable professional practice, that excellence reveals across the board? A good theologian is learned and careful, but so is a good lawyer, physician, or musician. What differences do these two words, "learned" and "careful," pick up when we move them from situation to situation, work to work? Is it true that a good lawyer will recognize her counterpart in theology or medicine? How much does one have to know about the matter of a given field — music rather than law — in order to make such a judgment, or at least feel such an intuition building?

There are encouraging ramifications in this way of looking at collegiate education when it comes to historical studies. One of the challenges that teachers and students always face lies in estimating the differences that temporal era and geographical locale work into a particular problem. For example, between Augustine and Aquinas lie about eight centuries of human experience. What difference did these centuries make in the ways that these two great Christian doctors understood original sin, or grace, or the sacramental function of the church? Moreover, what are we asking about ourselves as knowers, and about the human history that we want to know, by raising a question such as this?

On the one hand, we assume that it is worth our while to study Augustine, or Aquinas, or their likenesses and differences. The experience of our predecessors, and our betters in the matter of intellectual history, suggests that our assumption is not wrong. Moreover, we can verify its rightness for ourselves. On the other hand, however, if we do this conscientiously, we realize the limits of our historical imaginations, coming away humble about our ability to say just what Aquinas felt, just how Augustine construed his problems.

It is not a far step to the issue of cross-cultural studies — how we ought to regard our abilities to appreciate what people different from us not so much in time as in cultural upbringing feel or think. How much can white, middle-class Americans expect to understand of life in South Africa, or Peru, or rural Japan? How much can men expect to understand of what women experience, or women expect to understand of what men experience? And so for the other obvious differences among us — economic, religious, racial.

We learn some of the answers to such questions empirically, by plunging into historical or cross-cultural studies, and so it behooves us educators to afford our students some such opportunities to plunge in. We learn other answers analytically, by examining human knowing itself. The more clearly we understand what understanding entails, the more generic can be our appreciation of the sameness and difference of human living down the ages, across cultural variances. A balanced conclusion, in my opinion, is sober but confident. We may never enter fully into the world of a person or period that stands at some difference from us, but we gain immensely from making the effort to enter as fully, as sympathetically and intelligently, as we can. Through such an effort, we also refine our sense of what kinds of understanding we may expect from other people — what anticipations of awareness and sympathy are realistic. In the past, when a "classical" view of human nature downplayed differences and stressed similarities, people probably tended to be too optimistic about their ability to understand other people. For example, church leaders probably gave too little attention to historical or regional or sexual differences when they went about their tasks of pastoral teaching. Nowadays, many in the university seem so bedazzled by the cultural differences among human beings that they risk balkanizing undergraduate education. By ignoring such common human traits as our mortality, our need to work, our orientation to love, our regular ritualization of social situations, our fundamental ignorance, and our sinfulness, such educators leave their students thinking that diversity is vastly more important than what we human beings hold in common. In doing this, such educators try to render banal or trivial what the theology that I consider capital makes all-important.

As usual, virtue lies in the middle. We need studies that show our students the vast differences among human beings, but also studies that show them the great similarities. For our current topic of the physical sciences, it is germane that people from all continents can learn chemistry or geology and practice it. It is also germane that all people in all continents live in ecological habitats, but also that all such habitats differ, contributing to the different foods, clothings, medicines, and religious rituals that we find among different tribes. Yet, despite such differences, all people share enough biology to enable them to breed across races and cultures. Relatedly, a surgeon in Los Angeles can operate on a patient from Minsk, and vice-versa. This is not to minimize the differences in medical care, medical culture, that one is likely to find by comparing hospitals in Los Angeles with those in Minsk or Peking or Buenos Aires. It is simply to strike a balance in our estimate of the people involved in such hospitals — what we can expect to understand about their medical ways, and what we should plan on not grasping fully.

Stepping back, I find myself noting that people who understand the basic matters of a given problem can move into new situations relatively gracefully and successfully. They can see what is old, common in various situations, and what is new, different. They can even bring their sense of old and new home to their students, helping the next generation to think creatively and effectively about medicine or music or ameliorating pollution in situations initially foreign to them. The theoretical implications that I find leaping off the page from this balanced assessment of likeness and difference amount to a strong pressure to make our college curricula broader and deeper than they now tend to be. I would have theologians and others who study the nature of human beings conspire to help their colleagues in the professorate stress (*a*) fundamental studies in the basic areas of reality (physical nature, politics, psychology, divinity) and (*b*) critical studies of human knowing that apply to all kinds of research and problem solving. What is new in the current educational, collegiate situation is our appreciation of the immense amounts of data that are usually relevant to estimating, let alone solving, any significant problem, and our appreciation of the ecological, relational character of the forces and disciplines that we need to take into account. Our students need a clearer sense of all that is relevant to environmental problems, problems of unemployment, problems of mental health, problems of catechesis, and so on than what we professors can give them on the basis of the range of reality that was laid out for us when we were students a generation ago. They also need a more sophisticated apprenticeship in the working of their own minds — critical thinking, including the moral, aesthetic, and mystical dimensions of human knowing. In my view the representative American college has to redefine its sense of what a humanistic education entails nowadays, paying more attention to fundamental information and intellectual self-knowledge. Relatedly, the university has to do a better job at showing the coherence of its programs of research — at suggesting the unity of the world that we study and the sameness of the mental processes at work in our disparate disciplines.

This means, finally, that we have to pay more attention to the education, the realism and wisdom, of our educators than we have been wont to do. Not all professors are equally competent for the task of devising the undergraduate curricula that we now need to devise. Certainly we ought to provide for all the major disciplines, give the many different specializations their due. But the integration and packaging of how our students ought to move through their studies ought to fall to the educators who see best the proportions of the outlook at which our curricula must aim. This best vision is general and sapiential, rather than specialized and pragmatic. It is well-rounded and critical, rather than narrow and merely informational. We need designers well-informed about what is to be known — a truly contemporary sense of the range of reality. We also need designers well-aware of how knowing itself goes forward — what the transcendental precepts are and how they tend to work out in the major different kinds of knowing. Certainly, such designers ought to be able to work collaboratively. Collaboration, in fact, ought to be one of the abilities they have in mind when they think of what their students ought to graduate able to do — how the products of their educations ought to be able to function. But someone has to guide the collaboration and keep it on course. Someone — ideally many educators well-educated themselves — has to safeguard the integrity of the curriculum, of the education, as a whole. The best candidates for this crucial role will be the scientists who are humanists, the professors in the humanities who think ecologically, the artists who understand top-flight scientists, the historians who love the diversity of human cultures but do not despair of philosophers' or theologians' showing what is common in how all peoples have lived and died. Summarily, in the future collegiate education that I want to help bring into being, the name of the game will be generalism — breadth and depth rather than specialization.

Chapter 3

On Politics

The Common Good

I am proposing a Christian theological view of higher education that is turning out, in my impression, to be both old and new. Among the old components is the effort to provide for the basic, irreducible realms of reality, under the four headings of personal being, the physical world, politics (social being), and divinity. Having considered some of the received wisdom about human nature that a humanistic education ought to take into account, and then having speculated about how we ought to regard studies in the physical sciences, we turn now to the third of our four realms, the political or social worlds that human beings create. As our reflections in chapters 1 and 2 have inevitably been partial, designed to be radical (taking aim at the root issues) and provocative rather than exhaustive, so will our reflections here be.

We begin with the notion that has arguably dominated traditional discussions of how human beings ought to live together, the common good. The common good is a fine antidote to both the individualism that a sociological commentator such as Robert Bellah decries in recent American culture and the totalitarian outlook that has recently fallen apart in the former Soviet Union. For the common good clearly demands that individuals situate their work and play in the context of their being citizens of a socio-political whole, while this same notion shows under analysis that human beings do not thrive when treated like ants or termites — interchangeable members of an impersonal colony.

On the one hand, if we are to live together well, flourish as we ought, we human beings have to look out for one another, cooperate, and on occasion sacrifice our individual pleasures or preferences to meet the needs of our society or group at large. On the other hand, no such society or group at large will flourish as it might if it suppresses the genius of its individuals — if it demands a mindless conformity to general laws and makes no provision for individual differences in talent, need, experience, and so forth. Politics is not only the art of the possible. It is also the art of balancing the individual and the group, the obedience that any society requires of its members and the freedom that any member has the right to expect of his or her society.

At the most fundamental level, the common good is the survival of the species. Unless there is a minimal cooperation among human beings, there is no new generation of *homo sapiens*. Older patterns of marriage, for example, stressed the needs of the tribe for procreation, the needs of the extended family for new blood or better social ties, more than the desires of the individual young man and woman involved. Today we risk making marriage, or less committed sexual interaction, so individualistic a portion of our culture that we neglect the dimensions of procreation and social stability. If the partners to a potentially procreative relationship ought not to be dragooned into their relationship, as they could be in extreme situations in the traditional past, they also ought not to be allowed to think that what they do has no social consequences.

It is a cheap shot to attribute such huge current social problems as teen-age pregnancy, crime, drug use, and poor schooling to the high incidence of divorce and single-parent situations, but it is also foolish to deny the impact of such an incidence. Taken one by one, the stories of people marrying and divorcing and trying to raise children in trying circumstances (economic, emotional, even medical) merit our sympathy. Taken as general trends, as demographic patterns clear on our graphs of the whole, there is much to abhor.

When we orient our political action and thought, our laws and studies, toward the common good, we are likely to find ourselves asking for both more discipline in our citizenry and more freedom in our government — better public service and fewer regulations. In the present context of working out a view of higher education faithful to both Christian convictions and present-day realities, the common good suggests that our students ought to come away from their immersion in social studies — political science, economics, historical studies, sociology, anthropology — more appreciative of the need for both discipline and freedom, both concern for the whole and support for the parts, more aware than they were when they began. The common human good develops in tandem with the establishment of healthy human communities. A healthy community is precisely a whole that is greater than the sum of its parts. Individuals are willing to work for the community, the whole social body, even to sacrifice for it. Yet the community looks out for its individual members, taking pride in nourishing their talents, succoring them in their times of need.

One of the few persuasive rationales for intercollegiate athletics that I have heard stresses the value of the players' experiencing teamwork. The members of a football or basketball team have to play together if they are to achieve more than middling success. They have often to subordinate their individual goals to the smooth functioning of the team as a whole, the optimal overall performance. They have to accept a certain constraint and carry out designated roles, not all of which are starring. One shoots, another passes, a third rebounds. Yes, all have to do all these things, but seldom is the best point guard also the best power forward. Because the goal of an athletic team is so precise and limited — scoring more points than its opponents in the forty minutes of the basketball game — and is such a free zone (play, rather than business or war), the participants can experience their venture in community, their subordination of themselves to the common good, more intensely, perhaps more instructively, than is usually the case "outside," in the wider world where the rules are less tidy, the play is less constrained.

In the next section I shall reflect on the social implications of the Christian theology of the religious community, the church. There our discussion can be more idealistic. Here we may note that politics deserves its reputation for being dirty and illegal, as much concerned to bend the rules or avoid them as to play by them, probably because many of the leading political actors seek not the common good but their own power or status or financial advantage. The current situation in American political life, where lobbyists for large corporations or ideological movements seem to have more influence than ordinary citizens, shows how warped a representative democracy can become. The number of politicians willing and able to dedicate themselves fairly purely to the common good, the welfare of the country as a whole, appears to be depressingly few. The number of statesmen or stateswomen is small enough to give any realistic observer the willies. Once again, the question arises, Who will care for the caretakers? What is a people to think and do when those designated to look out for the common good seem to make that a low priority?

If we take our students through an unsparing look at present-day political realities regarding the physical environment, or health care, or gun control, or support for the education of little children, they may see for themselves that the people in power pay less heed to the common good than to vested interests. They may also see that, in many cases, politicians have to negotiate a difficult line between individual liberties and policies binding on all. This is an ongoing, ineluctable issue in political life. But common sense and traditional Christian ethical conviction can combine to make it plain to our students that the needs of the poor ought to take priority over the wants of the rich, that the good future of all our citizens requires our providing the best education possible for the next generation, that all people ought to have access to basic medical care, to sufficient food, clothing, and shelter. These are the minima necessary for a society to consider itself functional, a group to take any pride in its common life.

Indeed, our students may come to realize from their studies of politics that there is no good reason for any person in the United States to starve or lack shelter, as they may come to see that it is foolish to give education a lower priority than low interests rates or curbing inflation. Yes, one can debate the posing of these issues, and even the estimates of these issues, that I am suggesting here. But in the theology empowering my view of higher education there is no political life, no communal existence, worthy of the name in which all members of the group or nation do not receive certain basic rights in practice (not just rhetoric). Certainly, it is an enormous, in many ways impossible task to try to keep a nation of more than 250 million people functioning well. Certainly, it is a tribute to all involved that we have many excellent schools, hospitals, welfare programs, military units, and businesses. But on Christian theological grounds (apart from the doctrine of original sin) it makes no sense to me that great numbers of our citizens seem unwilling to pay the price for solving such solvable social problems as homelessness and poor education. Again and again I find those directing our politics requiring too little discipline on some crucial matters (for example, taxation) and begrudging the freedom necessary for success in other crucial matters (for example, creative art).

After our students have had an adequate exposure to the history that explains how given political institutions, national or international, have evolved, they need to confront the problems that any people face when intending the common good. For example, how functional or dysfunctional is the legal system that we have developed? Is it now strangling those who would move briskly to reduce crimes, drug problems, abortions, inefficiencies in the workplace, mediocrities in the educational or medical systems? How functional or dysfunctional, by the criterion of its influence on our achieving the common good, is the presently pervasive American understanding of capitalism as justifying our taking financial profits as the bottom line?

Kindly, under control, we have to help our students to ask, Who profits from this obsession with profit — does our economic system in fact serve the common good? What adaptations of this system might make better provision for the poor in our society, the idiosyncratically creative, those drawn to lives of altruistic service? Is the analysis of a more socialistic philosophy of human communal existence that decides that the lack of a sufficiently attractive profit motive dooms such a philosophy to practical failure itself realistic — supported by the empirical facts, warranted by a rigorous analysis of human nature? Our college courses in "politics" of various sorts can offer young people free zones in which they may study and debate these fundamental and fascinating issues apart from the pressures of the marketplace. This possibility makes such studies both liable to a wrongful idealism and beautifully free. It gives us professors the burden of helping our students to become realistic about the problems that politicians face and also helping them to remain rightly impatient with all the feckless excuses. Sometimes there is little that politicians, social activists, can do to improve tangled, troubled situations. Other times there is a great deal that such social activists can do, if they have the will. If we can get our students onto the pathways that eventually lead to discernment and wisdom about these different times, our curricular requirements in the area of socio-economic, political reality will be worth their weight in good citizenship — the gold of any commonweal.

The Church

When Christians think about political life, the social cast of their being human through faith, they have to contend with the church, both its glories and its woes. In both theological analysis and historical fact, the church has been full of grace, holiness beyond ordinary expectation, yet also depressingly sinful. Probably we cannot answer the question of whether the Christian community has created enough goodness in space and time to make it stand out as the people of God in any unique sense. Probably it takes faith to see in the Christian church the city raised up on the hill that shines like a beacon in testimony to the goodness of God. The hermeneutic in matters such as these is circular — faith has to work at the beginning and emerge at the end. The check that we give to God is blank. There is enough goodness on the historical record, a large enough legion of saints, to make the creedal article about the church — "I believe in the holy catholic church" — reasonable, yet there is also enough mediocrity, indeed downright sin, to make reservations about the divineness of the church also reasonable. Nonetheless, when Christians think about what human sociability ought to be, they are bound to bring to mind such New Testament figures as the body of Christ and the vine and the branches.

What stands out in a properly free, uncoopted analysis of the church such as Karl Rahner's is that a tension between the charismatic and the institutional sides is inevitable. In fact, theologians do best when they take both sides as intended by God, part of the divine dispensation. The people who hold office in the church and interpret its laws render an indispensable service. So do the people who respond faithfully to individual charismata — gifts of prophecy, innovation, and wisdom. When officers in the church take to heart such traditional pious self-understandings as the papal "the servant of the servants of God," their work is admirably ministerial. They take a humble view of themselves and their work, delighting in such prosaic analogies as the Rahnerian one of the chess club. As the officers of a chess club exist for the good playing of chess, so the officers of the church exist for the good living of the Christian life. The good living of the Christian life depends on the Spirit of God far more than on any canons (laws) or disciplinary regulations. The officers of the church do best when they serve — second, try to advance — the initiatives of the Holy Spirit.

They do worst when they forget their humble, ministerial role and act as though they were the prime players shaping the history of salvation.

Regarding the charismatic side, a similar humility and ministerial cast of mind is the most fitting. We should be leery of prophets — understood less as those who foresee the future than as those who discern the signs of the current times — who are proud, arrogant, unruly, stubborn, egregiously willful. We should hold suspect nuns such as those of Pascal's Port Royal: "pure as angels and proud as devils." The truly wise are more impressed with the gifts of God, indeed the darknesses of God, than with their own inspirations. The truly zealous exalt no finite, historical cause beyond the providence of God or the discernment of the overall Christian community. Thus the burden of proof lying on those who would murder abortionists, calling such murders necessary to the service of God, is so heavy as to bring their credibility crashing to the ground. Thus the outrage of sisters who insist on forming women-only covens and calling them churches clangs discordantly, because the Spirit who is holy intends our peace and neutralizes our venom.

The danger on the institutional side is usually to become legalistic, occasionally to become too timid to exercise one's rightful authority and require obedience. The danger on the charismatic side is usually to develop an independent, individualistic venture, occasionally to be too timid to speak out the calls for repentance and reform for which the Spirit is asking. On both sides, balance and love are the healthy watchwords. Our courses for students on church history and ecclesiology ought to elucidate this theo-political judgment, showing its relevance to human sociability, human communal life overall. What is plainest in the church, where belief in the movement of the Spirit of God tends to be strongest, obtains actually if more obscurely outside the church, in towns and businesses and universities. Everywhere, those holding lawful responsibility and so power finally come by their stations because of the way that God has created us human beings. We have to live together, cooperatively, and this means that we have to find good ways to organize our interactions, provide for our common ventures, run our shows. We may do this by giving leaders a great deal of power, or by granting rule to a council of elders, or by waiting together for consensus to well up from the whole assembly. The political form (the means) is less important than the political effect (the end): good order, efficient prosecution of what has to be done if all members are to thrive.

My experience is that the best political form, at least for groups of manageable size who share humane goals, who are more than cogs in a machine running to make money or accomplish a very practical ad hoc goal — for instance, raising a barn — is a benign, consultative "monarchy." In such a political arrangement, one person, or a group that in practice is the equivalent — a clear possessor of ultimate responsibility and authority that is inclined to act decisively — holds the power to make decisions binding on the group as a whole. But that person wants to know what all parties whom the decision will affect think and feel, and so that person listens patiently, asks question after question, makes sure that she or he really knows, to the human degree possible then and there, what the members want. Because "what the members want" often is not unanimous, frequently is not even clear, the "monarch" (the one holding ultimate authority) will have sometimes to make decisions, take courses of action, that are interpretative and may be unpopular, at least with some factions. But that is the monarch's responsibility, as it is also her or his responsibility to consult the members assiduously.

We shall have occasion in the next section to ponder governance more fully. Here I raise the matter of political forms because my reflections on the interaction of the institutional and the charismatic aspects of the church have led to it, and because it is another point at which courses grappling with political realities can help our students become realistic about human nature. How has the monarchical model worked out in Roman Catholicism? How have the other salient ecclesiastical models — the collegiality of the Eastern Orthodox bishops, the presbyterian models of many Protestant churches, the congregationalist models of other Protestant churches and, in modified forms, of some monastic groups — worked out?

There is no model so obviously successful that it puts all others in the shade. My preference for a consultative monarchy comes from my desire for action. In my experience this political form offers the best chance for swift, efficient attack on problems, for wholehearted pursuit of common goods. The danger of tyranny and arrogance is high, but no higher than the danger in other models of inefficiency and inaction. The historical record suggests that communities of faith have erred on both sides. The religious ideal in most systems is to give all members a chance to voice what their experience and inspiration suggest while enabling the group as a whole to take action briskly. But most groups in which I have been a member have dillied and dallied until I wanted to scream.

If I am the leader, I want the power to get things done, since getting things done is my (God-given) responsibility. If I am a follower, an ordinary member, a foot-soldier, I want the right (a) to represent to my leaders, those holding wider responsibilities than I, what I think and then (b) to be free to let such leaders do what they think best. They deserve my support, my following of their orders, my generous putting of my shoulder to the wheel. I deserve their really wanting to know what my experience suggests, what I can tell them about the part of their problem that falls into my area of expertise. Granted fair coverage of both sides of this equation, I am willing to live with the errors that human limitations are bound to create.

We Americans tend to canonize representative democracy and the balance of powers established in our Constitution. Among the different models developed for what since modernity we have considered legitimately secular societies, this American one has good credentials. But some of the principles or assumptions underlying it historically are disputable. For example, it may well depend on what a Catholic Christian anthropology is likely to consider a too sour or suspicious view of human nature, leading to an excessive desire to provide checks and balances. And no Christian believer can consider the Constitution to be Holy Writ, which is not to say that it does not deserve great esteem as an amazing human achievement. In other words, it is quite legitimate to push our students to ask whether our American system that divides the legislative, executive, and judicial dimensions of political business is now as functional as what the founding fathers, the Madisons and Jeffersons, would have required to call their brainchild happy, or whether, on the contrary and as a result of historical developments that they could not have foreseen, this tripartite arrangement has lately become dysfunctional.

For instance, does our legislative branch now look out for the common good and move toward it sufficiently expeditiously to earn a passing grade? Is our executive branch free enough of public opinion, of legal and bureaucratic entanglements, to generate crisp, effective common actions? And does our judiciary in fact deliver justice often enough, and expeditiously enough, to deserve our high esteem, or has it rather fallen hostage to legal sharpies, experts at delay and obfuscation, whores selling their talents to the highest bidders? In raising such questions, and suggesting that our students should raise similar ones, I do not mean to besmirch the work of good people in all three branches of government — true public servants. Nor do I wish to imply that there has ever been a political utopia in which no fools or knaves held significant sway. My questions are rather more exemplary and diagnostic, meant to illustrate the critical, activist mind that I think our blocs of undergraduate courses dealing with human beings' political life, with the institutions through which we women and men have arranged our business and governance, ought to develop in our students.

We need citizens well enough informed and secure enough in their faith to keep asking radical, fundamental questions about the arrangements under which they find themselves living, to keep encouraging prophetic and countercultural challenges. At the same time, we college teachers ought to aim at providing our students, our country's next generation of citizens, with sufficient historical and analytical sophistication to make it plain that anarchy (no government) is almost always worse than an imperfect form of government, and that no group profits from changing its arrangements too frequently, that is, that healthy communities are quite conservative. Our theological orientation in this political realm, derived from balanced reflections on the history and revealed constitution of the Christian church, ought to be a prod to a radical political analysis overall. We should not teach students to try to impose ecclesiastical models on other social groups, but we should indeed teach them to import into such other groups the liberty of the children of God. If it is always true in the church that only God is God, and so that no sane, orthodox churchpeople ever confuse the church with God, all the more is it true in secular politics that no form of government has divine sanction — not the American constitution, not the constitution of the People's Republic of China. Certainly, patriotism is a natural virtue and we ought to respect the laws and traditional arrangements under which we live as loyal citizens, but we ought never to worship such arrangements — make them idols. This means that we ought always to be free spirits, and so that we ought always to be suspect in the eyes of all ideologues, whether such ideologues have set up shop in the papal curia or the halls of the United States Congress or Supreme Court.

Governance

From looking at the history and constitution of the Christian church, the political body commanding my fullest loyalty, I have drawn a proclamation of emancipation. In Pauline terms, I have discovered that "for freedom Christ has set us free" (Gal. 5:1). I believe that students ought to discover in the theological courses of their collegiate curricula the grounds for such freedom — the soleness of God, and the singular value of the immortalizing life of God (grace) in our hearts — but not only there. Through a different route, the courses in history, sociology, and anthropology that we offer our students ought to display the considerable variety of the forms through which human beings have organized their communal lives, and so the relatively accidental character of any particular form. People have been human in tribes organized around hunting and gathering. They have been human in larger socio-political units organized around agriculture. The tripartite structure of ancient Indo-European cultures, which distributed the main tasks of social life to priests, warriors, and workers, could function well (or badly). The caste system that apparently grew out of this originally simple tripartite structure has in modern times received much opprobrium, at least from Western observers, but perhaps on its own (karmic) terms it used to function fairly well.

The point is that the appropriate form of governance for a particular people at a particular time is not a matter written in the heavens for all to observe as the manifest will of the deity. It is not a matter cast in stone as the prescription for all time of unchanging mother earth. Governance is a variable human task and creation, an art more than a science. What is clear is the need for people to agree practically to cooperate to create order. What is unclear is how best to do this.

However, observation suggests that a given group of people, working from a given set of historically conditioned traditions, will tend to labor at achieving such agreement in predictable ways. Hindus brought up on the *Dharmashastras* will generally think in terms of castes. Muslims brought up on the *Shariah* will generally think of vesting authority in caliphs and mullahs. Virtually all traditional cultures have been patriarchal, so groups inheriting traditional patterns will usually expect men to hold more official power than women. Modern Western people formed by the American and French Revolutions tend to have little sympathy for more than ceremonial monarchies. Marxists tend to distrust political forms open to the influence of capitalists and the bourgeoisie. Latin Americans tend to take much of their political direction from the recent influence on their continent of juntas and oligarchies. Many black Africans feel the impress of longstanding tribal ways of moving in concert and naming their enemies. Assuredly, nothing in the influence of such traditions determines that a given group of people will act in such and such a way, is bound to choose such and such a political arrangement. The world over, however, more often than not people pass on to their children the political ways that their parents passed on to them, as they pass on the religious ways.

Governance is important but not sacrosanct. I pass over the question of whether the Christian God has given her church certain inalienable political structures, leaving that question to historians and ecclesiologists, and not challenging Roman primacy. For our present concern with social studies in a college curriculum compatible with, indeed directed by, a mainstream Christian theological vision, the pressing point would rather seem to be that monotheism makes all particular political forms provisional. One can see this in the Bible itself. The institution of kingship in Israel, first with Saul and then with David, only came into being with great misgivings. One can still feel in the canonical text the tension between an early charismatic form of government, in the time of the "judges," and the newer form, kingship, that Israel adopted to be more like the surrounding nations. Certainly, the king became a holy personage, anointed for his office. Indeed, this biblical custom and outlook continued into the Christian era, holding through the Middle Ages and beyond. The Holy Roman Emperor had religious grounds for thinking himself the equal, even the superior, of the pope, while the crown that Shakespeare thought made uneasy the head that wore it still conferred a sacral status in Elizabethan England. Analogously, in cultures that Christians used to consider pagan, such as millennial China, the emperor was the holy link between earth and heaven, ruling by a divine mandate (*ming*). Thus while Mencius, the foremost interpreter of Confucius, is at pains to show that a lack of virtue can lead to heaven's withdrawing its mandate, he does not doubt that the emperor is a holy being — a key cog in the way that the sacred cosmos runs.

Nowadays we require a view of our governors that demythologizes their sacrality without ceding the respect that ordinary citizens ought to accord them, in virtue of the governors' being the people most responsible for promoting the common good. Even when the authority of such governors comes from ourselves ("we the people"), the offices that they hold carry by right an aura of pomp, perhaps even of holiness. Holiness derives from the ultimacy of divine being: the way that things are from God is so real that it puts our shabby, halfling human ways in the shade. The way that things are from God for us human beings politically, socially, is that we require order so centrally or crucially that order must be holy — linked with God. For fear of disorder, huge cultures such as the traditional Indian and Chinese ones stratified their populations almost brutally. For the sake of order, many groups have honored a quasi-military model according to which "ours is not to question why."

Now, in democratic cultures "ours" as citizens is indeed to question why, and ours as professors is to prepare our students to do this well. But doing this well means doing it with a keen awareness of the utilitarian limits of questioning. Even when a responsible critique of the American presidency or the Roman Catholic papacy shows much to deplore, such a critique will keep in mind the need for order, and so for respect and obedience. Precisely how one ought to meet this need in a given situation without defaulting on one's prophetic responsibilities to press for reform raises a further set of ad hoc, practical questions. Good people, whether secular citizens or church members, can differ in their answers to such practical questions. What in my opinion they cannot differ about responsibly, however, is the need for both honest critiquing and humble obeying. Somehow, they have to make these usually compatible but occasionally warring postures come together and bow gracefully to the way that God has made us human beings and believers social. Somehow our courses have to prepare our students to find that their yokes as citizens and church members are relatively easy, their burdens relatively light — perhaps in part because their professors have shown them what it means to be, like Jesus, hard on all pharisaism yet meek and humble of heart.

Ministry

We have been zigging and zagging, moving dialectically from secular forms of political issues to ecclesiastical ones to secular ones again. Here we zag for a second time, focusing on the ecclesiastical issue of ministry. As ever in this chapter, the purpose of the dialectic is to illumine the political character of human being, our inalienable and ineluctable sociability. By considering the ministerial posture that power ought to assume in the Christian church, we may hope to see the emperor naked, without the trappings that often obscure the reason for his office to be.

Christian ministry takes its stance, its bearing, from Jesus, who came to minister unto others, not to be himself the object of ministrations. Jesus did not want others to spend themselves on his comfort or self-satisfaction. He did not want his followers to set themselves above the ordinary populace and demand special services. Rather, he saw his followers as servants of the Reign of God, meaning by that term the time when the holy ways of his Father were coming into clear focus and showing their preoccupying power. Practically, serving the Reign of God meant announcing the good news that blind would see, the deaf hear, the lame walk, lepers be cleansed, and the poor have the gospel of liberation preached to them. It meant spending oneself to lift up the downtrodden, make a straight path for justice, hope, the forgiveness of sins, and love. Jesus rejected any notion that his messiahship, the role for which God had anointed him, was political in the sense of oriented toward his seizing secular power or military in the sense of his leading armies against the Romans who were occupying Israel. He thought that his followers ought to render to Caesar the fealty necessary for the good functioning of the state but render to God their ultimate allegiance. Where their treasures were, there would their hearts be. If their treasure hidden in a field, their pearl of great price, were the Reign of God, their service of the gospel would be free and altruistic. They would want to share the joy that the gospel had established in their own hearts. They would consider themselves not the greatest in a given group but the least, the little children.

These are only some of the figures in which the New Testament's remembrance of Jesus' view of power abounds. It is a view opposed emphatically to the way that the Gentiles, the nations, people unreformed by divine grace regard power and might. The riches that the disciples of Jesus are to seek are the virtues that obeying his twofold commandment develops. His disciples are to love the Lord, their God, with their whole minds, hearts, souls, and strengths, and they are to love their neighbors as they love themselves. This twofold commandment of love summarizes the Law and the Prophets — the two oldest and most authoritative portions of Jewish Torah. Let us consider first how this gist of Jesus' ethical teaching orients a faithful disciple's view of political life and then, second, what it implies for college courses in politics compatible with a traditional (and so significantly biblical) Christian theology.

First, the twofold commandment into which Jesus compresses the Law and the Prophets grounds human existence, individual and social alike, in the transcendence of God. It is monotheistic as the Torah is, allowing no idols to compete with God for the believer's allegiance. The classical Israelite prophets denounced idolatry (whoring with fertility deities in the high places) and injustice (neglecting the widow and the orphan). In their interpretation, the experience in the desert that had made Israel God's covenanted people placed human freedom, realism, and social health in a relationship with truly, uniquely, ultimate reality: the Lord who had made the heavens and the earth.

This Lord had led the Israelites out of Egypt with a mighty arm and annealed them at Sinai through Moses. To default on the soleness of this God, the uniqueness of his existence and value, was to strike a mortal blow at what made the people of the biblical God who they were. They could only be what God had invited them to become, and they had pledged themselves to become, by worshiping the Lord alone. The spirit animating the many legal letters compiled as early as Exodus, Leviticus, Numbers, and Deuteronomy shone through this aboriginal monotheism. Only if the Israelites loved the Lord, their God, with all that they had and were could they keep faith with their constitutional reality. Jesus reaffirmed this Jewish monotheism, focusing it on his Father. His disciples could only be who he wanted them to be, could only serve the Reign of God as he wanted them to serve it, if his Father were their only treasure.

The second part of Jesus' summary command to his disciples bid them love their neighbors as they loved themselves. This injunction obviously concerns their basic attitude more than any particular actions. Yet it is sufficiently radical to stand alongside the Confucian golden rule as a touchstone by which we can measure the adequacy of any social philosophy. We should not do unto others what we do not want others to do unto us; we should rather do unto others as we want others to do unto us, because we love other people, our neighbors, as we love ourselves.

Our human existence is as much social as it is individual. Our love of life ought to stem from our love of our neighbors as much as from our love of ourselves. Under the God of Jesus, we are not monads requiring legal bridges to secure our minimally peaceful, benign regard for one another, our cooperative behavior with one another. We are radically social — members of one another through and through, shareholders in the lives of one another, the well-being and the misfortunes, now and always. From the outset — our conception, the way we exist in the world — our being is a being-with other creatures. Stressing the natural cast of this radical sociability, we may speak of the unavoidably, definitionally ecological character of our human being. Stressing the political cast, we may speak of the familial character of human existence, the fundamental brother-and-sisterhood.

Granted this interpretation of the fundamentally social view of Jesus, it is easy to see why he thought of power in his community as ministerial. Those holding office in his circle, bearing signal responsibilities for the common good, ought to regard themselves as the servants of the servants, the people, the church of God. They ought to regard their own welfare as tied inextricably to the welfare, the common good, of this people. And since Jesus put no borders on his sympathy, on the outreach of his own ministerial work, his community was in principle universal. Certainly, he began by attending to his fellow Jews, but he made it clear that Samaritans and Gentiles could also gain his sympathy, move him to heal their wounds and enlighten their minds as his fellow Jews moved him. Indeed, Jesus broke many of the social taboos of his time, establishing table fellowship with sinners and reprobates.

From the earliest decades of the ministerial experience of the disciples of Jesus after his death, as we see most clearly in the New Testament's records of the missionary experience of Paul, the good news applied outside the boundaries of Israel, opening the Christian community to the Gentiles. What Jesus said about loving one's neighbor as oneself and thinking of oneself as the servant of others rather than their lord, therefore came to admit of a universal political interpretation. For the Christians faithful to the original message and example of Jesus himself, political power existed most authentically in the mode of serving other people through a love as intimate and deep as their love of their very own selves.

It is a long way from an evangelical political outlook such as this one of Jesus to most of the political theories that have held sway in the twenty centuries since Jesus' own ministerial work. Lisa Sowle Cahill's recent study of Christian attitudes toward war, *Love Your Enemies,* shows some of the main stops on the journey, in the process reminding us that Jesus extended his disciples' sense of the human community so that it had to include even their enemies, those who had done them bitter injury. How ought we to think about making this striking early Christian view of political reality and power available to our students through their social studies? What are the courses, and the other fora, that we ought to envision when we contemplate the implications of a Christian ministerial view of political leadership for the formation of our students?

We can require courses in biblical and social ethics, of course, and we can encourage students to participate in projects that place them at the service of the poor, or the sickly, or the politically marginalized in their area. But will not these good, necessary maneuvers keep the powder of Jesus' explosive political message unignited unless we find ways of integrating it with the whole range of our offerings in social studies — history, economics, political science, sociology, communications, anthropology, social psychology, law? Each of these disciplines and the other relevant disciplines admits of metaconsiderations, of course (philosophy of history, jurisprudence), and organized together as the "social science" component of the curriculum and professorate the courses and teachers concerned with the political dimension of reality might easily sponsor times when such metaconsiderations come out on the table at panels, on the floor at debates, into the space of the circle of armchairs at friendly discussions to show their great significance. In the context of the Christian education that I am imagining in this book, representations of, developed forms of, the evangelical social vision of Jesus would be altogether fitting; theologians and other believers would be altogether welcome to pitch in their contributions.

Furthermore, pointed curricular discussions among the faculty members bearing the primary responsibility for designing, modifying, and executing the core curriculum could show how such metaquestions might function at the outset, in the middle, and at the conclusion of regular courses in the area of the social sciences. This is not to demand that sociologists or anthropologists become philosophers or theologians. It is only to try to make concrete, practicable, one way that a Christian undergraduate education could work out its proper distinctiveness. No professor ought to be pressured by any orthodoxy. Any fears of any professors about risking the integrity of their courses would deserve a fair and full hearing. But in fact courses in the social sciences already brim with metadisciplinary issues. In fact the people whom sociologists and anthropologists study, whether they are Africans or Latin Americans or antebellum American Southerners, all carry in their heads images of how their leaders ought to exercise political power. The founding or leading figures in most social sciences — the Webers and Durkheims, the Geertzes and Turners and Douglases — are acutely aware of the dynamics of power and the problems of studying those dynamics well. So the kinds of discussions that I envision, both outside the classroom in special events and inside the classroom in the ordinary unfolding of established courses, need not be extrinsic or artificial. They need only take seriously the responsibility of undergraduate teachers to expose their students to the most basic information and issues in their fields, and not to back away from the existential implications of social theory, the distribution of wealth, and the forms that political power takes when one studies them humanistically, as vital portions of a young person's education in the ways the world actually runs, the unsuccessful and successful ways that people actually work out their social orderings.

Law

The great Christian biblical instance of reflection on law is the polemic of Paul in the letters that he himself apparently wrote (in contrast to the deutero-Pauline letters such as Colossians and Ephesians). There Paul's wrestling with the role of the Torah in the process of justification provides a classical instance of the ambiguities that Christians ought to feel about legal efforts to channel right action. Few Jews are happy with Paul's interpretation of the Torah, but most Christians should agree with Martin Luther that justification has to come through faith rather than works sanctioned by the law. Whatever the problems with pitting the gospel against the law, it is clear from the experience of the Christian saints that the letter can kill while only the Spirit quickens divine life in us. Perhaps this is equally clear from the experience of Jewish saints such as the Baal Shem Tov, for whom the Torah was a lovely path to freedom.

The point for our broader consideration of the place of law in human communal life and undergraduate social studies is that Christians ought to find it hard to justify law as an end in itself. Just as the officers in the church exist only for the good living of the Christian life, so the canon law of the church exists only for the good living of the Christian life. Analogously, the Constitution and the other codes of federal law exist only for the good living of American life — the common good of the citizens to whom these codes apply. It is surprisingly difficult for people to keep this simple, axiomatic view of law in focus. It is surprisingly common to find churchpeople ensnared in canon law or other church decrees, to find ordinary American citizens afraid of the codes governing how they are taxed or how they ought to register their cars. In both cases, the small-mindedness of many bureaucrats administering the laws contributes greatly to the problem. Too often such bureaucrats are pesky little tails wagging the dog, puny establishmentarians trying to elevate toward scriptural status what ought to be mere rules for keeping the traffic flowing. Our studies in politics will not be realistic unless they help our students estimate rightly this all too common reception and administration of the law.

Prescinding from the problems in character (guilt, pride, self-importance, concern about status) that abet such disorders regarding canon or civil law, we still have to wonder about how to care for our great caretaker, brother law. On the one hand (how often

I find myself getting into this grammatical construction, because how often the reality that I am trying to describe is complex and demands a nuanced, balanced treatment!), we have to respect the law, even revere it, because historical studies can show us easily that lawlessness has done many peoples in. On the other hand, our monotheistic commitments as Christians or Jews or Muslims, epitomized in Tillich's Protestant Principle, force us to relativize all laws — make them servants rather than lords. God does not need any laws, including the religious ones (talmudic, koranic, canonical) that many believers tend to associate with God intimately. The intuition of an early Taoist such as Lao Tzu that before laws proliferated people lived better lives, lives both more vigorous and more moral, merits patient contemplation and rewards it. Making laws can encourage criminal behavior. The legal mind can incline people to think in terms of what they can get away with, instead of what is simply right. The 613 laws of Torah can be a blessing, concretizing the *mitzvoth,* the good deeds, that please the Lord, but, as Jesus found with the Pharisees, such laws can also deaden the spirit, blinding people to the real import of the Sabbath or the real point of a kosher diet. The Sabbath was made for human beings, not human beings for the Sabbath. All foods are clean. It is the intention that is crucial in observing the Sabbath or taking food and drink. It is the faith and love with which we use the goods of creation that determine the health of our religiosity.

Take this free attitude into public affairs, indeed into church affairs, and you may well seem dangerous to the establishment. Take to heart the response of Peter to the Jewish leaders who forbade him to preach about the death and resurrection of Jesus ("We must obey God rather than men") and you will seldom feel enslaved to human overlords. We are required, by Scripture as well as enlightened common sense, to revere those who hold authority in human affairs, but we are bound to keep them from bullying our consciences.

Indeed, any wise, truly holy authority wants us, its subjects, to have mature, free consciences. It does not want us to remain children or to obey it mainly from fear. Yes, there is a place for discussing the sobering light that the Christian teachings about the sinfulness of human beings casts on political questions, including questions of obedience and compulsion, but this place is not, in my opinion, at the beginning or the center of a proper analysis of law. The law that Christians ought to obey most urgently is the inner direction of the Holy Spirit. The good sense that secular citizens most need to possess is a balanced view of the necessity of legal constraints for both good order and the common good. Education comes into its own as a mode of public service, a benefaction to the people at large, when it builds up the credibility of these inner sources of good church membership and secular citizenship. The courses in politics that will outfit our students best are those that show them the reasonableness and graciousness of being law-abiding.

We cannot live mature human lives heteronomously. Neither can we be fully human, I believe that Christians must believe, if our dominant model is that of the autonomy canonized by Kant and some other leading figures of the European Enlightenment. We human beings are too intrinsically creatures of God and social animals to make such an autonomy realistic. The model that we ought rather to develop is a persuasive theonomy — an exposition of our rule by the Spirit of God that would make it experiential and beautifully compelling. To this end the theologoumenon that I find capital is the thesis that we increase in our humanness by drawing closer to God. Conversely, God is not the enemy of our freedom and flourishing but the best enabler and guarantor. We shall deal with issues such as these more leisurely in the next chapter, where the topic is divinity, but they are so crucial to a proper understanding of law that I feel obliged to anticipate them here.

For the Christian orientation to higher education that I am trying to develop, the liberty of the children of God is surpassingly important. Just as we educators ought to want to develop students who are equipped to take over their own continuing education, and therefore are also equipped to challenge what we have taught them, so we ought to want to develop students who are free spirits, more beholden to the grace of God than to any extrinsic, purely human authorities. Any experienced professors know that sometimes they have to want this against what their students themselves seem to want. Only the inexperienced think that being a free spirit is easy, or that surrendering one's mind like a dummy does not exact the lesser toll, at least in the beginning.

Law is precious in the measure that it helps people order their lives, both the private and the public dimensions. Law applies most obviously to public processes but, if only as a cast of mind, a disci-

pline of spirit, it carries ascetical overtones for the private zones of
work, prayer, study, and love as well. Natural law — the order built
by the rationales of the creation — is a participation in the eternal
law that we imagine to be the expression of the divine mind that is
light in which here is no darkness at all, that is, in fact, the divine
Logos, the eternal "person" who took flesh from Mary. That is a
good Thomistic view of how the world gains its rationality.

Human law ought to be a similar participation in the eternal law
of God, peculiar because human nature is most characteristically
rational and so able to generate laws on its own. The interesting moral and ontological overtones to the task of harmonizing
human laws with the eternal law of God used to be mediated by
Scripture, inasmuch as precritical times and theologies considered
Scripture to be revealed law — an authoritative manifestation of
the divine will in human beings' regard. Nowadays all questions
about the revealed character of Scripture beg considerable sophistication, and prudent interpreters are slow to claim that a given
stipulation represents the eternal legal mind or will of God. Even
the Decalogue seems to be more hortative than prescriptive, which
is a secondary reason why I limited myself to the twofold commandment of love that the evangelists present as a summary of the
law of their master Jesus. It would be enough for me if the theological understanding of law that we gave our students worked itself
out as a commentary on this twofold commandment.

In the next-to-last section of this chapter we deal with the practical implications of these theological reflections on political studies.
Here let me say that, regarding the curricular implications of my
views of law, I think that law is an obvious candidate for the role
of "pegging" that good courses for undergraduates often spotlight.
Since most undergraduate courses ought to be basic, concentrating
on the main patterns overall and the fundamental methodological principles (the highlights of what is to be known, the range
of the reality in question, and the highlights of how educated
people best apply their minds in this given area), it can work
well to offer students four or five pegs on which to hang their
thinking caps. These may be interesting, apposite texts (readings).
They may be central or challenging notions (problems, issues). Law
beckons to my teacher's mind as a good peg on which to hang several matters of behavior, custom, and social intelligence that recur
in representative tracts of history, economics, sociology, anthro-

pology, and other disciplines bearing on human social behavior. How did Colin Turnbull's pygmies of the Congo keep their villages in order? What laws did they develop, honor, interpret — with what flexibility and according to what criteria? In contrast, what had law to do with the breakdown of order among Turnbull's Ik of Uganda? What does such a breakdown suggest about the connections among ways of interacting with the natural environment (outside politicians took away the Ik's traditional areas for herding their cattle), longstanding customs, and international laws (regulations from supervening powers)? These are examples of the "thought questions" that duller students hate, because which answers are "right" or "wrong" is less clear than which arguments or interpretations show the best study and intelligence. They are also examples of the kinds of questions that have become habitual and congenial for students educated well and humanistically in the social sciences. I believe that our goal in Christian collegiate education ought to be to produce precisely such students, because they hold the most promise for developing for their contemporaries and children the intelligent responses to political problems, both perennial and new, on which depend the common good and the gracious credibility of the gospel.

Persuasion

Law is one necessary, good, but limited means of moving people toward the common good — life civil in the sense of making the local community a place where people can flourish in relative peace and prosperity. Persuasion is another means, one more fragile, subtle, and ultimately decisive. We cannot make people good through laws, even when our laws are eminently fair and wise. "We," outsiders, cannot make people good by any means. People have to take their own lives in hand, their own souls and destinies, choosing to cooperate with God, to say yes to grace.

Perhaps the key to the warfare that goes on during many an adolescence is the dawning realization of this necessity on all parties' parts. Parents have to let go, but also stay in touch. Children can puff themselves up to strike out for independence but also feel their courage shrink and run back to hide under the bed. They have seen the dark and been scared by it. So have their parents, forced to visit again the bogs of hormonal muck, the confusions that social life presents when first we have to take responsibility for our forays through it. Thus whereas the ride across the mountains, or high hills, to Santa Cruz is for the adult merely a bit harrowing, for the teenager it can be a killing adventure, literally. And so for the parent the teenager's trip can produce a wait all too imaginative and harrowing, much worse by far than when the parent must negotiate it herself. The parent can only try to persuade the teenager that prudence is much better than valor, let alone than taking risks. But at some point the teenager has to learn this for herself, himself, perhaps best after having run through the twists of it with Dad or Mom along riding shotgun, taciturn and stoic.

On the larger social scene, I find that good politicians are those who can persuade the populace to vote for, support, pay for, endure what is right — the best courses of action that present insight, wisdom, can come up with. Ten years from now such courses of action may show themselves in retrospect to have carried serious flaws, heavy oversights, or economic liabilities. But we cannot refuse to take necessary actions today because ten years from now history may show that we made serious miscalculations. We cannot let the press and other egregious second-guessers push us into abulia — the paralysis that freezes would-be deciders into inaction. The theological imperative relevant at this point is Luther's wonderful *pecca fortiter*. We have to "sin" — risk mistakes, moral as well as operational and political — because that is our human burden.

More injustices and sufferings have come from human beings having done nothing than from their having done their best and plunged ahead. Honest mistakes we can usually clean up, beg forgiveness for and receive it. Cowardly inaction takes us out of the picture, the flow of the history of salvation. It saps the will of good people and often it wastes much hard work that they have put in. It causes far more cynicism than unsuccessful action, many more dispirited comments about the proclivity of "great men" to care first for covering their own asses. Just as lying is the cancer surest to ruin intimate friendship, so waffling, being "political" in the pejorative sense (gutless), is the disease surest to render public service ineffective, toothless. The gods whose mills grind too slowly ought to lose our respect and burnt offerings. The Rome that builds nothing in a day, a week, a year, a decade rightly becomes a figure of fun.

I do not mean, of course, that precipitousness is long persuasive. I do not mean that thorough preparation is not essential if our projects are to move ahead smoothly and succeed. I simply mean that, when I survey the political scene from my admittedly protected corner of the world, I wish that more leaders would get on with it: Clarify what ought to be done — or what period of doing nothing, simply watching carefully, is appropriate, not because they are afraid to act, but because the situation is truly neither so clear nor so bad as to force some action, any action — and start doing it. Having started, they, we, need to persevere. We cannot keep pulling up our plantings every other day, stop and go with new ventures every other week.

So discretion, prudence, a keen sense of the signs of the times — these become precious political virtues. Pacing, timing, the ability to marry boldness to restraint all pitch in. To be effective, politicians have to be enough in touch with their constituency to know that the folks back home will support what they have in view. On the other hand, effective leaders do not rest content with what the lowest common denominator makes certain will be popular. The art of leadership is, consequently, very demanding. The potholes in the road are many, that there will be some bumps is virtually certain. Being in favor, being loved politically, is a fragile commodity indeed. Persuasion is a carroty stick, a sticky carrot. So having a sense of humor, and a genuine willingness to step aside when the fickle electorate has turned thumbs down, are political qualities that grow in importance. Thus I enjoyed the response of Dan Glickman, our congressman in our Wichita days, when the massacre of '94 turned him out of office: "The people have spoken, the bastards!" Fortunately, he got to take his powers of persuasion to the office of the Secretary of Agriculture. Fortunately, the eye of newt he had to swallow did not prove a lethal potion.

What I find most persuasive, and would hope to make persuasive to my students as the crucial requirements for good politics, is an ordinary combination of brains and goodness — a combination that, sadly, can seem to be an extraordinary thing in politics run as "business as usual." The problem is the prevalence of fools and knaves. The great political cause for fear is that so many caretakers are dumb or venal or both. So the solution is to secure caretakers bright and pure of heart — find them, and then keep them as they were when found. In this process, we common citizens have to want leaders who are bright and good. We common citizens bear most of the responsibility when politics stinks. Our is the right and power to throw the rascals out. So the bad conduct of public affairs lies on our own heads. If the climate of political service becomes such that few good people are willing to endure its surfeit of guff, we ordinary citizens are the final causes. We could have changed the climate. The politicians who get elected by pandering to our baser instincts — the greed that keeps us unwilling to pay necessary taxes, the fear and resentment that make us love to hate aliens — have only been shrewd at reading the state of our souls.

In a democracy, the great problem is always the state of the people's souls. The people get what they want, what they are willing to pay, vote, work for. The people are often too lazy or narrow or self-centered to demand good leadership. They, we, choose to become sheep bleating before those who slaughter us: the lobbyists employed by big business, the reporters and editors who care most for selling papers, selling advertising time, boosting ratings. The dumbing of America has also been the vulgarizing of America. We could turn off Oprah and Donahue and Geraldo with the flick of a wrist. But, en masse, we love the sleaze that vulgarians such as they shovel at us. We conspire with Rupert Murdoch, take pleasure in yellow journalism, a press tabloid, prurient, and pornographic. God have mercy on all us unholy co-conspirators. God help the educators among us who do not fight the debasement of public opinion with might and main.

It would take me afield to make all the distinctions necessary to get in focus the hard sell that a proper persuasion, a fitting adaptation of the Platonic *peitho,* would require in the church, especially in my Roman Catholic portion of it, where the polity *ex professo* is not democratic. Suffice it to say here that I hope to help produce students who are as critical of the ugly power-plays that go on in the church — leading recently, for example, to the demise of ecumenism and a waffling on sexism, if not in fact an inciting of it — as they are of the ugly secular political climate in many countries. The nadir for me recently in ecclesiastical politics was the papal ban on discussion, debate, concerning the ordination of women. I do not know what to make of a veto on free speech — on honest exchanges of heartfelt conviction. I do not know how to respect a community whose leaders try to ride roughshod over people's consciences (perhaps the most godly part in any of us), a community whose leaders do not want its members to tell the truth under God, expose the current needs and hopes of their faith. This state of church politics leads me to think of Dostoevski, the Grand Inquisitor versus Christ. It reminds me of Pilate on truth, of the Pharisees judging the evangelical, especially the Johannine Jesus. And so it leads me to the juncture that many of my students will reach if I help to teach them to love the church fiercely, with a will never to leave it, yet to judge the church unblinkingly, with a mind that will not be bribed. It leads me to the place where I must choose whether to laugh or to cry.

The gospel is a divine comedy, so I feel bound to laugh. Most persuasive to me is the interpretation of Julian of Norwich: All manner of things will be well. Until that parousiac day, I have to guard my soul against corrosion, including the corrosion of bile. I owe too much to the persuasive beauty of the gospel to let a few leaders pissantly poor turn it sour for me. I owe my students the laughter that John Climacus found deep in the soul of those who try to mount the ladder of virtue by prayer. Indeed, one sure end of my political reflections is realizing the need to hie myself off to the chapel. There from time to time I recall Aquinas's remedy for depression: Contemplate the figure of Christ crucified, and go home to take a warm bath. There I recall the words of Jesus on exorcism. This kind of devil, little students, is cast out only by prayer, fasting, and gentleness toward your whole self, body and soul.

Practical Implications for Education

We have now taken serious looks at three of the four major portions of reality that my theological approach to higher education requires humanistic educators to honor. Perhaps it is time to muse about the best ways to structure the curricular walk-through that we ought to structure for our students and require them to complete. In following my muse, you may be relieved to hear me say once and for all that I realize full well how unlikely I am to receive from the rest of the professorate anything like unanimous support for my curricular stipulations, but that this does not really matter, since my purpose here is more to lay out what I think should be than what I think is likely to come to be. A solid fraction, perhaps a majority, of the professors at even Catholic colleges appear not to share the theological imperatives that burden or enlighten me. It is too easy to say that this is the reason for the crisis of identity now afflicting Catholic, or simply Christian, higher education, but in my view it is also obtuse not to realize that this lack of Christian theological conviction plays a major role in the crisis.

Indeed, I think it naive religiously and politically not to realize that this lack of theological conviction makes the program stipulated in Pope John Paul II's document for the reform of Catholic higher education, *Ex Corde Ecclesiae,* attractive on many scores. The argument on behalf of American instincts, in fact on behalf of an American Catholic educational wisdom gained through thorough experience of working in a pluralistic culture, has to be made in good part on theological grounds better than those of Roman theology. The fact that to date American Catholic institutions of higher learning have seldom developed a crisp theological rationale and shown it to be operating obviously in all aspects of their campus life, but most saliently in their curricula, has left them vulnerable to a dangerous Roman woodenness, anti-intellectualism, and apparent lack of awareness or even sincerity about the rights of individuals' consciences.

Enough orientational ferverino. Let us get down to cases and sketch what a curriculum faithful to a humanistic and theologically astute desire to expose students to the full range of reality and the best critical thinking might look like. Our context is the traditional four-year college. It does not matter what age our students are, only that they accept the premise of the college that its first charge is to excite, shape, guide, and challenge their human potential. After we have laid out the main lines of the curriculum as it could take shape in a representative Christian college of arts and sciences, we can attend to the tailorings that would be appropriate in professional colleges — undergraduate educations in business or engineering that were serious about their desire to be as humanistic as possible.

Take the temporal framework in question here to be four years, eight semesters. Take the work load of the full-time student to be five three-credit courses each semester — a heavy work load, but not an impossible one. This would mean a total four-year accumulation of 40 courses, 120 credits. Were I dictating the distribution of these courses and credits, they would fall into three categories. Students would take 30 percent of their work (12 courses, 36 credits) as specific required courses, three in each of the four areas of reality: personal nature, physical nature, politics, and divinity. Specialists in each of the four areas would determine which three courses all students would have to take. For example, in divinity I would require of all Christian students courses in Scripture, Doctrine, and Ethics/Spirituality. Of all non-Christian students I would require courses in Christian Scripture (the Bible), The World Religions, and Contemplation and Action (worship and ethical practice). Professors in the natural sciences might agree that all students had to take Physics, Chemistry, and Biology, or Physics, Biology, and Mathematics — whatever they thought was the triad best able to (*a*) show students the range of material nature and (*b*) exercise students in the basic methodologies that organize scientific thinking nowadays.

Concerning personal nature (the humanities), again it would be the province of professors in this area to work out the sequence of three specific required courses (9 credit hours). They might stipulate English, Philosophy, and History, or Shakespeare, Plato, and Toynbee's world history — whatever they thought would best (*a*) show students the full range of personal nature and (*b*) exercise students in the methodologies of the humanities. Concerning the dimension of politics or human sociability, the relevant professors would be free and responsible to work out what triad of courses they thought could best (*a*) show students the range of political reality and (*b*) exercise students in the critical thinking that dominates the best work in the social sciences. They might decide for courses in Political Science, Economics, and Sociology. They might think Anthropology or Social Psychology or Law more important. The triad would be their responsibility, their choice.

Let me add at this juncture that I would require students to show sufficient competence in a foreign language, in handling a computer, and perhaps in quantitative skills (mathematics or statistics) to assure their being able to carry out both what their professors could rightly require of them in standard course work and what their meeting the demands of responsible citizenship in the global cultural world of the first decades of the twenty-first century portended. They could show this competence by passing competency exams, and the college would have remedial or preparatory courses available (at no credit and for a minimal charge). Moreover, students could "test out" of basic courses if their high school transcripts suggested and their own confidence warranted the assumption that the given required course in Physics or Scripture would be redundant. They would still be obligated to three courses in each of the four zones of reality, but with the advice of a panel of advisors that met regularly they could choose another course to meet their requirement in divinity or physical science.

So, the first set of courses in my ideal collegiate curriculum would be twelve that guaranteed a minimal coverage of the range of reality that my theological vision discloses and of the ways of thinking that in this vision we come to consider expectable in people well educated nowadays. The second set of courses would be another twelve (another 36 credit hours, another 30 percent of the overall total required for graduation) that would ensure a further but freer coverage of the four major zones of reality and the ways of critical thinking that now set shop there. In other words, students would, with faculty guidance, select three more courses in the humanities, the social sciences, the natural sciences, and theology or religious studies. Each curricular branch of the faculty would be offering a full menu. Depending on what each department thought best and could staff, say, on a regular teaching load of five semester courses per year, duly adapted when the same professor carried both collegiate and university (graduate) responsibilities, there would be conversational courses in Spanish and Japanese, literary courses in Chaucer and Dante and Molière, history courses in Chinese, British, American, and European history, courses in various aspects of mathematics, chemistry, economics, and so forth. Professors would encourage students to make this second triad of courses in their quarter of the pie representing the full range of reality and critical methods complementary to what the students had taken in the first triad (specified more exactly and described above).

I would expect the result of imposing both triads on all students to be their emerging as well-rounded and well exercised critically as possible, because 60 percent of their undergraduate education had pounded out the crucial foundations. Each student would have spent eighteen curricular hours, six courses, on each of the four constitutive zones of reality and ways of scholarly thinking. No amount of hours can guarantee an adequate formation, but eighteen in each area would offer the best chance for achieving this that

I can imagine realistically (without changing radically the overall current format of the American college).

The final component, the third triad and remaining 40 percent of the curricular courses and hours, would go for electives: filling out the requirements of a major concentration, responding to the student's personal needs, interests, ambitions. There would be sixteen courses available for this third triad, forty-eight hours. Majors (which I do not consider pressingly important) could be a combination of new courses and courses already taken in the first two triads. A rough rule of thumb might be to set a maximum of eight courses for the major (twenty-four hours of "advanced" work) and a minimum of eight courses that students had to take fully freely, at the dictate of their own interests — music, dance, computer programming, Italian, economics, whatever. The limits of the offerings would be only the limits of the competencies and imaginations of the faculty and students working in concert. Each professor would ideally be able to offer one such free course each year. Each student could in effect take one such free course each semester (though prudence would suggest accommodations in scheduling based on the prerequisites that made sense).

In the next section I shall deal with the theoretical implications of giving "politics" the due that I have given it here and asking all parties to American collegiate education to work from a theologico-humanistic model such as this. I shall only nod now toward the justification for making "divinity" an equal quarter, expecting that choice to become clearer in the next chapter. Here let me simply repeat that the theology at the wellsprings of my view of higher, especially collegiate education makes each of the four zones of reality for which I am providing irreducible to any of the others and a necessary part of any education able to give all of reality its due. I care less about how colleges might arrange their coverage of each of the four zones than that they make their best effort to do that well. If a given group of faculty members and administrators wanted to make more of psychology or music or art or computer science than I have, fine and dandy. I have no conscious prejudice against any discipline, no desire to depreciate the potential of any discipline for contributing to the overall humanistic education that I find fitting best the job of turning freshmen into seniors reasonably well-rounded intellectually and sufficiently developed critically to let us hope that they will be good, effective, citizens in the communities that they come to live in as adults.

Theoretical Implications for Higher Education

The first theoretical implication that I find in this layout of both politics and a curriculum that would give each of the four primal zones of reality its due is that the human mind, indeed the human personality, is in principle equally well equipped to study the self, the material world, and the social world. Individuals differ understandably in their interests and talents, but human intelligence itself seems equally apt for studying poems, rocks, and congresses. The theological foundation for this view of human nature takes shape from such planks as the fact that the image of God in us human beings emerges in part in our capacity to deal with a wide range of creation — in our having minds ordered to grasp the intelligibility of whatever exists. Second, my theology says that the effects of human mortality and sinfulness, though sobering, are not so debilitating as to cast crippling doubt on the worth of what we can learn by studying in different fields.

Third, I also count as a theological contribution to the theoretical foundations of a humanistic education, or as an implication of the curriculum that I have proposed, what I think of as the priority of contemplation in a college education. For while I consider it a good thing for students to become involved in projects of worship and social action, as well as in organizations that help them make friends and mature socially, and even for them to become involved in athletics of some measured sort, I do not think that these concerns are central to the nature or mission of a college. Central is the intellectual development of the student, and so the studies that students must do to fulfill the requirements of their courses.

One can get a good academic education, experience and fulfill the main reasons why we have colleges, without spending much time in the chapel, or helping out in a soup kitchen, or socializing in a sorority or a fraternity, or playing varsity tennis. This is not to say that these activities are not good, nor that they are not "educational" in a wide sense of the term, nor that life is not broader than study, nor that religion is not finally more important than academics. It is simply to say that one cannot get a good collegiate education without taking solid courses, moving through a curriculum that is wide, deep, and demanding, and studying hard. It is simply to say that a college is not a church or a welfare agency or part of a farm system for professional athletes. The measure of the quality of one's undergraduate education is the change in the range of one's vision and the power of one's thinking that occur in one's running through its curriculum.

We should regard college students first under the formality of "student" — one who is eager to learn what precisely the college has to offer. We should make aptitude for academic work the principal, though not the only, criterion when we make our decisions about recruiting, admission, financial aid, and so forth. We should not be Marxists, more concerned to change reality than to understand it. We should be intellectuals fully engaged with reality, and so well aware that we ought not to separate our contemplations from our actions. But as professors and students and administrators in a college we ought first to focus on specifically intellectual maturation.

This said, let me agree with what I think of as intellectual ecologists that we should certainly try to make our students aware that what we do, the "praxis" in which we engage, has an impact on what we see, how we feel, when we contemplate the different zones of reality. To say that the rightly ordered college is primarily contemplative is not to say that it is blind to the influence of practice or willing to disregard the niche in socio-economic reality from which a person contemplates the entire human ecosphere. It is simply to insist, with Eric Voegelin, that the old meaning of "ideology," where the word named something pejorative, a prejudicial outlook often formed by a political agenda, remains firmly in force, even when newer ideologues try to coopt the word and relativize it, so as to suggest that everyone has a prejudicial slant and none of us can be objective or truthful. That sort of misunderstanding of the workings of the human spirit — which is peaceful and joyous only when moving, or being led, out to deal with what is simply so, with whatever reality or truth seems to be revealing itself to be — leads to the dementias of political correctness and dogmatizing — in the pejorative sense; "dogma" also has a perfectly good old meaning: teaching that is authoritative.

So I think that students should not study politics in college primarily in order to press forward an ideological agenda but rather because "politics," in the broad sense that I am giving the term here, is an irreducible part of human experience and objective reality — a zone different from the self considered alone and different as well from what the physical sciences and the "divine" disciplines study. In studying politics well, students will discover a great deal about human nature, about history, even about the material world and religion. The four zones that I have sketched do not stand off from one another refusing to touch, any more than one can collapse one into another without great loss. The theoretical implication of studying politics, of being required to take at least six courses (15 percent of one's total) in the area of social studies, is the proposition that to be educated well any human being has to be familiar with both the main contours of this area of reality and the best ways of understanding it. The further implication or assumption is that all human beings are social, just as all human beings are animals making their way through the material world, and all human beings are individual personalities, persons, who stand apart to some important extent from both the natural world and any group in which they are members.

Finally, though people who do not believe in God, and so do not accredit the zone of reality that I am calling "divinity," will not accredit this further theoretical implication, all Christians have to hold that human destiny stems directly from God's being the Creator of the universe and so that nothing purely material or social or psychological, nor even the combination of these three concerns, can be the measure of the reality that we human beings must deal with. The measure of the reality that we human beings must deal with is the full range of creation and its Creator. If politics deserves six courses, at least 15 percent of the curriculum, so do the humanities, the physical sciences, and the disciplines that deal with divinity.

In other words, I believe that the full reality that we human beings must deal with establishes the range of what a solid undergraduate curriculum ought to take aim at. Relatedly, I believe that the ways that we human beings best study the main contours of this range of reality suggest the methodologies that we should want our students to master. Politics has so much to say about the quality of the lives that human beings experience, both as citizens in secular communities and in the church, that it would be reprehensible for educators not to offer college students a solid instruction in the ways and means of politics. The same for the humanities (the studies bearing on the self), for the physical sciences, and for theological studies.

Moreover, a college is itself a communal and so a political venture. A college is itself a place where the citizens have to develop law and persuasion into a machinery for achieving a common good — here, a good education. One interesting way of focusing the political side of an undergraduate education would be to make some aspect of collegiate business the basis for a case study. Students could analyze the anthropology of dorm life, or the economics of varsity sports, or the politics of the faculty or student senate, or the history of their given college. This could help them realize quite concretely that they live in the midst of political animals, that they themselves are political animals subject to laws and persuasive or not so persuasive politicians. They could study the significance of patterns of interaction among the generations, as this worked out in their relations with faculty members. They could do papers on the function of tradition or apprenticeship, or on the group dynamics of teaching, as one of these worked out in their major field of study. The significance of race, sex, ethnic background, religious upbringing, and economic class could all gain specificity by students' applying the theories to which their classes exposed them to what they experienced in their own dorms or eating clubs or work on the student newspaper or interactions with the secretaries or groundskeepers. The limits of the practical applications of the theoretical commitment to social studies that I envision are only the limits of our imaginations (how often that is the case!). Leadership and good citizenship hang out on every lamppost as semaphores. We only need professors and students with eyes to see them.

_____ *Chapter 4* _____

On Divinity

Transcendence

We begin our study of the fourth dimension that I would have undergraduate education explore by reflecting on transcendence — the "beyondness" of God. In the next section we shall deal with the immanence of God — the "hereness" that balances the divine beyondness. For the moment, though, let us content ourselves with thinking about how God is beyond everything limited, created, and mortal. Another way of putting this would be to say, Let us deal with what justifies our considering "God" to name reality of an order for which we cannot account by humanistic studies, social studies, or the natural sciences.

Our minds go beyond the realms that we can study in those three ways, and so do our hearts. From the human side of theological studies, we find lines, energies, reaching out toward something, someone, who is always greater. From the divine side of theological studies, inasmuch as these studies take shape from "revelation" (texts or traditions thought to be given or inspired by God and so more than human), there seems to be a voice, a realm, that presents itself as beyond the human, more than what space and time contain. Certainly, one may say that it takes faith to accredit this divine side of theological studies so as to make it a pressing factor in one's own life. However, to accredit divinity so as to give it its due in "religious studies," the humanistic enterprise that limits the degree to which the personal implications of revelation enter its scholarly probings or professorial voice, one has only to let Christians, Jews, Muslims, and others be themselves — the believers, the patients and agents of faith, good or bad, that they actually are or have been. Simply by doing this, scholars in

128

religious studies have to admit the transcendence of God almost as much as theologians do. There is no "religion" without a binding to divinity or ultimate reality, to use a rough equivalent more befitting aspects of some Asian religions. One cannot make honest sense of the myths, rituals, ascetical exercises, and ethical codes of traditional peoples without accepting their view that they have long dealt with a God or ultimacy not reducible to the psyche, or the group, or the natural world.

Augustine is famous for describing the human heart as restless for God — finding no lasting fulfillment in creatures. A Christian can interpret Mahayana Buddhist teachings about the "emptiness" of all *dharmas* (individual realities) as implying largely the same thing, at least psychologically. Thomas Aquinas said that even in heaven God will remain a mystery. The beatific vision of God in which Thomas placed human fulfillment would be an endless moving into the inexhaustible light of God. Gregory of Nyssa spoke in a similar vein, giving Eastern Christian mysticism a way to speak of endless growth or development in "theology" (the zealous search for God that engaged the whole mind and heart, and that would not cease in heaven). These authors, and dozens more — female as well as male, non-Christian as well as Christian — offer evidences that when we human beings exploit or enjoy the full range of our capacities, the boundaries of our ordinary reality dissolve.

In their different ways, mystics and yogins, as well as shamans and transcendental philosophers, all tell us that we contend with more than space and time, matter and politics. They all say that there is more to reality than the sum of the different zones of our synthetic (physical-biological-psychological-religious) selves. Always we have an objective intentionality that presses beyond our limitations. Always the unbounded into which we head and about which we can only stammer gives us our boundaries. In crucial exegeses of experience that Eric Voegelin credits to the classical Greek philosophers and the Israelite prophets, including Jesus and Paul, humanity realized in two distinct yet complementary ways that transcendence, the divine mystery, is the definer, the most ultimate maker, of what we human beings are distinctively.

The noetic experience that Voegelin finds coming to clarity with Plato and Aristotle heads for a beyond, an unmoved mover, who under later refinement comes to be seen as the constitutor of our world and selves. We seek this beyond of creation, this ultimacy (which, in the next section, we shall consider under the formality of its immanence to creation), but it also draws us. We have the sorts of drives that impressed Augustine, the kinds of hungers that begot the Hindu Upanishads, but as we actually experience them these drives are more than just our own products or strivings. As we actually experience them in study or prayer or love, they are responses to solicitations of reality, of drawings by reality. Reality has "words" for us, "revelations" with a small "r."

Martin Heidegger spent a long philosophical career brooding over this originally Greek ontological problem. Voegelin is clearer about the transcendence of the solicitor, the drawer, than Heidegger was, and Rahner and Lonergan are clearer still. The drawer, the solicitor, the lurer is divinity. Indeed, the mystics are "patient" of divinity dramatically. They have no doubt that God has acted on them, come and gone unexpectedly, freely yet indelibly. They cannot describe their experiences adequately. In their own eyes, something ineffable — the simplicity and infinity of the divine — always renders their speech more false than true. Yet what or who they have experienced, have felt at the fine point of their souls, is the realest thing, or no-thing, that they know, or do not know. They want to affirm and deny at the same time, so as to point to the "eminent" (unique, *tertium quid*) character of God. Yet some of them, for instance, al-Hallaj, have died for their conviction that God is the realest reality of all there is, including their selves.

The noetic mystics have stressed the intellectual, lightsome side of God or nirvana. Platonists, pagan or Christian (one could include Augustine and, with qualifications, Aquinas among the Christian Platonists), and Indian mystics, both Hindu and Buddhists, have often exhibited this intellectualist, ontological movement into divinity, this sense of being drawn forward by divinity or ultimate reality. The pneumatic prophets, theologians, and mystics have stressed love, the heart, the entire soul. In Jewish and Christian biblical revelation, this is the voice that has predominated. Until Christian theology became fully Hellenized, it was far more pneumatic than noetic. Prior to the second and third centuries, it took Paul, the Johannine Jesus, and the great writing prophets (Isaiah, Jeremiah, and Ezekiel), as its great instructors in the dynamics of the spiritual (pneumatic) life, which it considered to be the life of our deepest engagement with God. In the pneumatic life, the Spirit of God is more significant than are our human spirits, but the special "sensorium," as Voegelin calls it, of the Spirit of God is our spirit, our soul.

The pneumatic life may be prophetic, formed in the cauldron of a divine call for political action — protest against injustice or false cult. If we move outside the biblical sphere of influence, we find that it may also be yogic, inasmuch as yogis such as Patanjali move below the mind to deal with ultimate reality, with the Atman, at the base or core of the self. As well, the pneumatic life may be ecstatic, giving the experience a modality of erotic going out, after or in response to the beauty of God. Such exstasis likens it to shamanism, whereas yoga tends to shape it to "enstasis" — trying to find its fulfillment (the transcendent God) in its own being, for instance, as a limitless ocean on which it floats. A Christian mystical classic such as *The Cloud of Unknowing* is enstatic in a loose sense: The cloud as which divinity appears overshadows the mind, but this overshadowing helps contemplatives to realize that divinity is the being of their being, and that letting one's heart pulse with love for divinity is the best way to be in the cloud. Whatever the adjectives that one wants to use, the point for our purposes is that divinity becomes the destiny of the person's mind and soul. The covenant becomes internal and personal as well as external and political (a compact forming a people). The imagery of the Song of Songs comes to the minds of many Jewish and Christian mystics, making the spiritual life a romance. We shall see later how the specifically Christian images of crucifixion and resurrection suggest further tonalities in this experience of the transcendent divinity. For the moment let it be enough to have indicated the noetic and pneumatic sides and to have suggested that they are possibilities, in some ways even hard facts, in the consciousness of all human beings, and so in all our cultural worlds.

Perhaps the main reason that I labor year in and year out teaching in the area of divinity is because I think that we Christian educators have nothing more precious to offer the younger generation than these noetic and pneumatic treasures from the students' global cultural inheritance. The beyondness of God is the greatest source of liberation that I know. The loveliest gift of monotheism is the freedom it can establish in our souls. There is only one Lord to whom the monotheist bows. All human authorities are limited. Moreover, this one Lord or Mother or divine Mystery is what we know intuitively is our only adequate fulfillment. If there is no God, no beyond that is holy and pure, just and loving, then Camus and the other phenomenologists of the absurd are correct. For then we have been made as existential contradictions, intrinsic frustrations, Sartre's "useless passions." But there are phenomenologists more persuasive than Camus and Sartre, at least to Christian minds. There are reporters such as John of the Cross who speak of things that Sartre at least seems too small-souled to know (ditto for Marx and perhaps Freud). There are experiences of being drawn out to the divine beyond, which can also be experiences of having the divine beyond show itself to be one's own inmost within, that reshuffle all the pieces in the kaleidoscope. In this new design or pattern, our movement toward God, our drawing by God, is the center of the puzzle. God is the known unknown to which we have to attend, if we are to come to the only answer that makes full sense. Granted, this full sense is mysterious, but in the process of coming into it we realize that to be God God has to be other, more, ever-beyond. Nothing set to our limited, creaturely scale can do the job that our minds and hearts, our souls and strengths, demand be done. So we realize that in the transcendence of God lies our fulfillment, and our delight is to pass this good news on.

Immanence

If transcendence suggests how God is beyond us, immanence suggests God is within us, present to us, available everywhere we go. The extreme of the intuition that divinity must be immanent comes in pantheism. There everything is God. There the intuition that all things derive their being from God goes to what Christian orthodoxy considers excess and becomes the proposition that all things are divine. What this intuition misses in becoming excessive is the lack, the limitation, that marks us creatures off from God. We are finite, mortal, ignorant. God is the opposite: infinite, immortal, omniscient. Indeed, we work out our human inklings of God by denying the limits in ourselves and other creatures — by making God transcendent.

Yet, we also want to say wholeheartedly that God is with us, in us, making us be, because otherwise there is no explanation for our being. Without God, we cannot explain why the whole system of us limited beings came into being, nor why any one of us obviously perishable parts of this system continues to be while it does. There is a nothingness in us, a gravity toward death and dissolution, that makes it mysterious that we do not fall apart or evanesce. Why *is* there something rather than nothing? This question of Leibnitz strikes Christian philosophers as a direct avenue to God.

Present to us outside, in the milieu that other creatures compose, and present to us inside, at the center of our being, God could not be more immanent or intimate. We might reach conclusions, appreciations, such as this by reasoning in the wake of ontological thinkers, but for Christians the more secure route moves out from the God with whom Jesus was involved. As the gospels portray the religion of Jesus, he was at one with his Father. John is the gospel that makes the most of this unity, but the synoptics present Jesus as a man led by the Spirit and committed completely to the cause of his Father, which was the coming of the Reign, the Kingdom, of the Father. Jesus strikes us as a man grounded in God, a man whose relationship to God gave him his inmost identity. The miracles that he works seem like an overflow from this relationship. The graciousness of his words appears as another overflow. So, contemplating Jesus, Christian theologians are primed to think of God as with his people, close to her family.

The immanence of God gives the field of studies that I am calling "divinity" a unique relationship to the three other curricular areas that I would have students study. Certainly, the humanities, the social sciences, and the natural sciences overlap among themselves. Clearly, the human being is simultaneously individual, social, and biological. Yet the human being does not relate to the natural world as he or she relates to God, nor does the natural world relate to the human social world as it relates to divinity. God is the creator of all beings, human and natural. God is the Lord of all individuals, groups, and gophers. Nothing that is exists apart from God — that is a staple teaching of traditional Christian theology, both doctrinal and mystical.

Indeed, that is a defensible, perhaps even probable entailment of the biblical theology of Genesis, the prophets, and Jesus. If so, then God is present everywhere and none of our studies can prescind from the omnipresence, the constant influence of God except for the sake of convenience. There is no self to study, unless God gives it being, living within it as its inmost reality. There are no groups composed of people, apart from the influence of God. And, finally, there are no mountains and stars, no oceans and trees, that do not get their being from God. God is present in, is immanent to, all of them as the final reason that they are.

When theologians set their thinking caps at an angle that orients them toward ecology, they can find the immanence of God a good starting place for a Christian spirituality of the land. The land is promised to Israel, as the Torah tells the story, and Israel comes to think of itself as a people covenanted in this promise. The land is not so central in the Christian covenant. The Lord is present in all places, including all hearts that have said yes to his command to love purely. The being of God is the final reason for all beings, whatever their form or place.

Thus the ascending Christ commissions the apostles to preach to all nations. Thus neither Rome nor Constantinople nor Moscow could ever exalt itself convincingly. If there was a holy place that could not be replaced, it was Jerusalem. However much the later Christian capitals proposed themselves as the omphalos of salvation, *the* holy land remained the place where Jesus had walked — more specifically, it remained the places around or in Jerusalem where Jesus was born, died, and rose. Jesus himself, the Logos incarnate, was God at his most immanent, so the places where Jesus was were the most sacred sites in the world. In time, they came to include the chapels where Jesus was present eucharistically and the assemblies where two or three gathered in his name.

So it is the incarnational character of Christian faith that comes to dominate a course of divine studies such as mine, when the topic is immanence. However much the ontological reflections of the late medieval mystics capture the pure presence of God in all beings, both the historical spur to these reflections and the antidote to the impersonalism that they can create is the specific figure of the Logos incarnate, of Jesus the Christ. Jesus has a presence in individuals, in groups, and, as the Logos, in nature that humanizes the divine immanence and makes it material. The creative being of God can become something familiar from the disciple's contemplations of Jesus. In Christian conviction, this incarnation or materialization of divinity can make any place of the psyche, or the social world, or of nature less foreign than otherwise it could seem.

Concerning individual human being, the saints are the most human of personalities, because in them the light and warmth of the biblical God are strongest. Concerning social human being, the best communities are those that sponsor a creativity, a justice, a worship, a love worthy of a God as good as the Father of Jesus, the nursing Mother of Isaiah. And even as nature keeps us mindful of the impersonal character of God (the ways that the divine transcendence takes "God" beyond anything that we can coopt), it is still amenable to images of maternal bounty and paternal fertilizing that suggest a personal creator. This does not mean that I wish natural scientists to anthropomorphize nature. It does mean that the rationality of nature, and also what we may find to be nature's chaos, admit of theological interpretations that keep them the products of a divine artisan. The beings of nature are always beings come from, and dependent on, a Being that is, by analogy to us rational, human beings, "personal." In other words, God's presence in rocks and streams and even earthquakes is a power that we may ultimately predicate of a who as much as a what.

Wherever we go, God is there, having preceded us. Whatever period of history we study, Christian faith forces us to assume God's care. We shall deal in later sections with how this care works out, what students need to take away from what Christian studies of divinity say about suffering. Here the main point is that divinity is not remote from us, sequestered in high heaven. It is not limited to sacred places such as churches. It is all around us, and it is in each of us. Old people show forth the image of God, but so do infants. The energy of young people speaks of God, as does the stillness of the very sick. God inspires good priests and nuns, but also good mothers and fathers. A priori, as a general orientation, Christian faith bids us to be on the lookout for God everywhere.

Moreover, the speech that we summon to talk about God can be innovative as well as traditional. We may use impersonal speech, perhaps most appropriately when discoursing on the presence of God in nature or the experience of many East Asian contemplatives. We may also use personal speech: friend, parent, lover, lord. Elizabeth Johnson's fine work of feminist theology, *She Who Is,* deals with theological language with a special awareness of the needs and insights of women. Catherine Mowry Lacugna's good book on the Trinity, *God for Us,* shows what the old and the new can mean for our thinking about the economy, the interactive ways and means, of God's dealing with us most personally, as an eternal community of knowing and loving.

These are just a few of the many examples that any current student of divinity might pursue, to the end of realizing that God is with us all days, all good ways, unto the consummation of the world. We cannot be without God. Our humanity depends on our relationship to our Creator and Savior. Secular humanists deny this proposition. Thus, this proposition puts a sharp edge on what can make Christian college curricula distinctive. Where secular humanists limit the range of reality to the first three areas for which we have provided, Christian humanists have to add divinity. Doing that, we change the entire constellation, the whole gestalt, of the curriculum that we ought to consider stipulated by reality. If divinity is as real and irreducible a dimension of what our students encounter as are the other three, then divinity deserves equal attention in the curriculum.

Specifically, in terms of the assignment of courses and credits that I sketched in the previous chapter, the reality of divinity requires of all undergraduates in my proposed college of arts and sciences three specified courses and three freer ones — six courses, eighteen hours, 25 percent of the required portion of the curriculum, at least 15 percent of the whole undergraduate education. I find it hard to respect as Christian a school that would find this allotment uncongenial, or undesirable, or even impractical in principle. I would suspect the wisdom and guts of the administrators, the faculty members, and the students who could not move from the adjective "Christian" and the noun "college" to support the claim of divinity to a minimal 15 percent of the courses that students take. Naturally, the immanence of God in our Christian institutions of higher learning is not limited to the courses that we offer, but when we are so ashamed of our Christian identity, so disabled by crises of nerve, that we will not make God as important a subject of study as the personal, social, and natural worlds, we have blocked the obvious avenues by which God can enter the critical minds of our students, the cultural endowments. How is that not a large academic sin?

Healing

Both transcendent and immanent, God works for our healing. Put perhaps more exactly, the being of God, which is both far and near, gives our human being the order it needs for health. When we relate ourselves, our communities, and our natural world to a divinity always greater than they, we clear the space that these lesser zones, lesser beings, need if they are to appear in our minds rightly. Professors presumably want realities to appear in the minds of their students rightly. Professors open to Christian theology therefore ought to encourage the study of divinity, seeing in divinity the context that all studies need if they are to make maximal sense.

Recently I saw an article complaining that many of the statistics that the press offers us are virtually meaningless, because the reporters do not give us the context necessary for the figures to disclose their significance. For example, if we read that last month 250,000 new jobs appeared in the U.S. economy (a whopping figure), we have only a fraction of an insight. We need several more figures before we can estimate the significance of this figure 250,000. For instance, we need to know how many jobs there are in the U.S. economy overall. How many new jobs appeared during the same month last year? How many old jobs were lost in the period when the 250,000 new ones appeared? If there are 25 million jobs in toto, then the gain was 1 percent — one new job for every hundred current ones. If there are 50 million jobs in toto, then the gain was only .5 percent. If last year the figure for new jobs was 125,000, then although the gain this year was double that of last year, if the overall, base number of jobs remained 25 million, then the gain was only .5 percent — one new job for every 200 old ones. If while gaining 250,000 new jobs the U.S. economy lost 150,000 old jobs, then the real gain was only 100,000 new jobs or .25 percent — one new job for every 400 in the base. So, what "The U.S. economy gained 250,000 new jobs last month" really means depends on further data and a broader context.

The same for what even so already broad a statement as "man is a rational animal" really means. First, we have to know that there are animals who are not rational. Second, we have to know that there are creatures who are not animals. Third, we have to know that human rationality is the most important source of culture. Fourth, we have to know that human rationality is the distinctive resource that our species has for making its way in the material world, most impressively through the natural sciences and the technologies allied with them. Fifth, we have to know that human rationality allows us to deal with the total context of our lives, which is, first, creation (the universe) and, second, God. Last, we have to know that animality and createdness limit human rationality, while sin beclouds it and throws it off course. It is also well for us to know that, nowadays, "man" will clang on some of our readers' ears as sexist or insensitive language, and it is desirable for us to know that God is the immanent and constant designer of human rationality, structuring it intrinsically by being the most constitutive and crucial "other" over and against which it defines itself.

When J. H. Newman made his famous argument for the place of theology in a university, he worked along the lines that I am pursuing now. His argument was that without theology you could not have a "university," because without theology you would lop off a crucial zone or area or foundation of what is so, of the range of reality. When Clark Kerr described modern institutional ventures in higher education such as the University of California at Berkeley as "multiversities," he did not focus on a lack of theology so much as on a lack of coherence. In my view, joining Newman to Kerr allows us to diagnose the genetic flaws of the modern institutional ventures as syndromes of a mental disease. Inasmuch as a diagnosis is the first step toward healing, let us consider a few paragraphs elaborating this diagnosis and clarifying it space well spent.

There can be no coherence in the intellectual life as long as we do not have a rational, healthy hold on what is to be known and what capacities we human beings have for knowing it. We do not have to know what is to be known in all its details. In fact, obviously we cannot know what the next round of developments in microscopes, or telescopes, or genetic theory, or mathematical theory will stimulate. But we can know, heuristically, enough about the major zones of reality, and about the major ways that the human mind can work well, to make our progress in any field, and our progress overall, sufficiently coherent to keep our world a universe and our comprehensive institutions of higher learning universities. The zones of reality that I have laid out, and the undergraduate curriculum that I have derived from that laying out, are one way of conceiving of the universe and the realistic college. To conceive of the consonant university, one need only open the four major branches of study to advanced, more specialized work (nuclear physics, the religious philosophy of Nagarjuna, marriage practices in the Indian *jati* of rice farmers, the Icelandic saga).

Many "applied" studies (business, law, social work) would

fall into the general area of what I have called "politics." Some (medicine, engineering) would fall to the natural sciences. A few (psychotherapy, perhaps the performing arts) would fall to the humanities, inasmuch as the humanities focus most directly on personal (individual human) being. And divinity? The practical studies falling to "divinity," taken as a collection of disciplines designed to explore the individual and social implications of what we learn about the fourth dimension of reality from detached theological or religious studies, are in sum pastoral studies — effective preaching, performance of liturgies, effecting reconciliation, and so forth.

The theoretical healing that divinity implies for the aberrant modern mind comes first from the crucial role that divinity plays in ensuring that the range of reality covered by our intellectual work be adequate. Immediately, establishing divinity as an irreducible fourth realm of reality takes away much of the wobble, indeed fracture, of modern intellectual life. Mediately, in a further move, this medication begins to disclose much of what is wrong, unrealistic, in our approaches to other zones of reality: for example, our flight in many humanistic studies from the overwhelming significance of human mortality; the baleful effects in the political realm of our neglecting the workings of sin and grace; and the metascientific and so orientational import that a theology of creation carries for the natural sciences.

Third, beyond these immediate and mediate benefactions, the introduction of divinity adds to our studies of how we study, to our knowing of how we know, the new factor of mystical understanding. This factor bears similarities to aesthetic knowing in the arts, to intuitive intelligence in politics and the natural sciences, but we are wrong to reduce it to those. For when not falsified by the assumption that mysticism must be mainly the product of sensory deprivation or cultural conditioning, mystical knowing shows itself to depend on direct encounters with ultimate, unlimited reality. East and West, it shows itself to be both the defeat of ordinary knowing and the foundation of ordinary knowing.

Paradoxically (the adverb most important for describing mystical knowing well), those who deal with divinity most directly, with the least constraints from their acculturation, experience an unknowing. It may take the form of Lao Tzu's worry that while all others are sunny, he alone is clouded. It may break out in exclamations like that of Parmenides: "Is!" In many other mystics it expresses itself in images of darkness, in predilections for silence, even in instincts that gesture or dance is the closest rendition that one can get. The point is that, taken seriously, through a study of its foremost practitioners or experients, divinity enlarges our sense of the human mind. Thereby, it puts into our overall sense of how we can know a complement parallel to the complement that it puts into our overall sense of what there is to be known. And, in both cases, divinity gives us our most important "limit factor," or, in better English, "limiting condition."

The incomprehensibility of God is the medicine that we need most if we are to restore our stereotypically modern intelligence to health. Stereotypically, that intelligence is razor sharp but also razor thin. Thin, narrowed, it does not deal well, if at all, with the limitlessness, the infinity, of divinity — with the expansive Being of all beings, the rich isness that we cannot understand. Aquinas put this as well as it can be put: We cannot know what God is — because what God is is that God is; in God essence and existence coincide, and both are simply unlimited. The divine aseity ("from-itself-ness") of God assures that we cannot deal with God as we deal with any creature, for any creature is dependent and derivative — carries in its being and bones an intrinsic "from-another-ness." So the divine and the created are incommensurable, which means that we human creatures, however rational, cannot comprehend God. God is intrinsically, ineluctably, inalienably mysterious. God cannot not be mysterious, and in this mysteriousness lies our peace. One way of looking at the therapies that Newman sought in arguing for the inclusion of theology in the university is to see that he wanted to bring the troubled modern mind to a great source of peace.

The biblical equivalent of Kerr's multiversity is the Tower of Babel described in Genesis 11 and painted effectively by Pieter Bruegel the Elder. In Bruegel's painting, Nimrod, the king who has commissioned the tower, is more interested in the obeisance of a few peasants than in the obvious problems that his construction is having. The moral for the multiversity is several-fold. First, there can be no mastering of total reality, because there can be no language or notation covering God, let alone all of human diversity. But, second, the reason that even our best stereotypically modern educators fail to build as well as they might is that they do not take care of the whole. They are so seduced by the adulation of the little parts that they let the grand building fall into tatters. Instead of going deeply, broadly, and ecologically, they construct more and more eccentric corridors, suites unto themselves, useless fire walls.

In educational constructs, both theoretical and practical, virtue lies in the middle suggested by divinity. No human intellectual work will ever remove the mystery of creation, but only when the mysteriousness of creation, its divinity, stays in focus will such progress as our intellectual works can make stay in balance. To return to the therapeutic image at the head of this section: Divinity is essential for the healing of our current mental disease. If we are to get back our healthy minds, we have to make the mysteriousness of God, and the mystical knowing of those who deal with God best, capital in our calculations of what we are about in higher education.

I am not asking for a return to the medieval days when theology was the queen of the sciences. I reaffirm now all that I said previously about the autonomy of the disciplines — those of the natural sciences, the social sciences, and the humanities. I simply make the observation that seems to be inevitable if one is a Christian believer: Without God one has a false image of reality, and without knowledge of God one has mental aberration — the foolishness of which the Psalmist speaks, the simpleness that Lady Wisdom decries, the twistedness that the Johannine Jesus hates in his unbelieving enemies, weeps over in his beloved Jerusalem.

Grace

Christian theology speaks of grace as both healing and elevating. Indeed, it thinks that healing (radically: salvation) only comes through grace, since only God can make us divided creatures whole. It also thinks that God is so good that the divine gifts not only heal us but move us into God's own life. This is the feature of divine grace dearest to many Eastern Orthodox Christian theologians: divinization (*theosis*). In this section I want to reflect on the implications for higher education of both of these senses of "grace," adding the incarnational condiment that the grace of God often shows itself in the gracefulness of those who live close to God, who are in love with God.

First, let us think about the healing of grace, the graciousness of our coming back from illness to well-being. We once were lost, but now we feel found. Like the wonderfully ironic and highly instructive man in John 9, we once were blind, but now we see. Coming home, finding the place where we ought to be, gaining the sight that we ought to have, enjoying the being that we were made to be — these are implications, overtones, grace notes to the firm, plain chant of God's daily dealings with us. Whatever removes our amnesia about our actual nature and position in the world — the brevity of our time, the smallness of our knowledge and power, the record of our sins — comes from God. Whatever softens our hearts toward those against whom we have hardened them, which may include God herself, comes from God. Whatever stirs up our faith that honesty is worth serving, stirs up our hope that where sin has abounded grace has abounded the more, and stirs up our unreserved love of God, our desire at least to love our neighbors as ourselves — all this comes from God as well. This is the sense of grace that we find Paul commending to the Philippians in chapter 4 of his letter: Whatever is true, noble, just, pure, lovable, gracious, excellent, or admirable (the list of adjectives in the NEB translation) is good for our souls, heals us, comes from God and bears God to us. To have right order, good health, in our souls, and so in our work, our family lives, our citizenship, our prayer — anywhere — we need a presence of God, an action of God on us, that we cannot compel or assume or claim as our just desert. We need the gift of God to be ourselves — right, healed, forgiven.

But the gift of God exceeds our healing, however radical and wonderful that healing is. *Gratia elevans* is more than *gratia sanans*. Elevating us, God makes us partakers of the divine nature, 2 Peter 1:4 says. This is the end, the goal, of the Incarnation, Athanasius says. God (the Logos) became human so that we might become divine. For classical Greek thought, mortality was the key mark of humanity. The key mark of divinity was just the opposite: immortality. The gods did not die. In having the Logos take flesh from Mary, and then raising the resultant Jesus from death to life, the Christian divinity transformed human nature. What is mortal has become also immortal. Joined to God personally in bonds of faith, hope, and love, the believer moves into the common life of the Father, the Son, and the Spirit, which is deathless and eternal.

This is a perspective that takes us far beyond healing. This is a response to the deepest stirrings of our spirits, which are for a light and a love that never end. Such a prospect would be merely ideal, pleasant dreaming, apart from the Incarnation and the Resurrection. Only the historical experience of Jesus, as Christian faith accepts it from the New Testament, anchors our hopes for conquering death in the real world. Because God has raised Jesus, Paul tells the Corinthians (1 Cor. 15), Christian faith in the resurrection is not in vain. Immortality and resurrection, the Greek and the Israelite symbolic strands, come together in the actual person of Jesus, the Word become flesh. Apart from Jesus, there is no sufficient warrant for the articles in the Christian creed that assure the believer of "the resurrection of the body" and "the life of the world to come."

Thus far, we have reminded ourselves of the two primary connotations of grace, healing and elevation. When asked what we Christian educators want our students to take away from their studies of divinity — more specifically, from their studies of how divinity comports itself toward us human beings — healing and elevation should dominate our intellectual agenda. Moreover, our ambition should be more than catechetical. We should want our students to ponder the huge consequences of thinking that divinity offers human beings radical healing and eternal life. For example, if one accepts this part of the Christian creed, any pessimism about human nature has to be qualified. The great sinfulness of human beings certainly should make us sober, but the healing grace of God should stir us toward a peaceful, patient, prudent hopefulness. We cannot write human beings off, either as a collective entity or as the specific individuals Samantha and Mike, because God is able, indeed apparently is eager, to heal them of their narcissism, their sensuality, their pride — of any and all the debilitating, deranging effects of their capital sins. What may seem impossible to them clearly is never impossible to God. If we believe that God is working in all people's lives (a conditional statement far from rhetorical), then we have always to keep open the possibility that the Bosnian Serbs as a group, or the specific yuppies Connie and Regis, will, like the prodigal son of Luke 15, "come to" themselves and get back some sense.

It would take me afield to discuss the sacramental aspects of healing grace, which in any educational case would fall practically to campus ministers more than professors. However, I should note that the gracious actions of God, for signs of which Christian faith bids us to scan the horizon like Ezekiel's watchman, though in a more hopeful mood, can use the sacraments of penance and the Eucharist as a matter of course. Both sacraments can be regular ways of focusing on God's work to heal us of our sins, restore us to our better minds and hearts. Indeed, let either ritual be simple, spare, free of psychologizing fussiness, and the desert will often bloom, rocks will often break open with water.

In liturgies rightly ordered, God is the agent placed front and center. Christ is the obvious healer. The Mass is not the priest's show. The confessional is not the place for stroking. The encouragements of God are the only ones that do not fail us. Human applause is terribly suspect. And the greatest encouragements of God let us hope not only that the Spirit of God has washed the selves that we had dirtied, has watered what we had let run dry, but also that she has insinuated into our souls divine life — light and love stronger than death.

When we discourse on divinity, trying to describe for undergraduates how it moves toward us, how what it is in itself becomes our human own, we ought, finally, to try to suggest the graciousness of God's effects. Without God, we limp and stagger, stammer and cock our ears. So Jesus drew on the messianic expectations of his people to describe the graciousness of the presence of God (of the Kingdom) as a time when the lame would walk, the blind would see, lepers would be cleansed, the poor would have good news preached to them. Every valley would be exalted. All the rough ways would become smooth. It would be good palpably for sisters and brothers to live together — like oil running down the beard of Aaron. The messianic banquet (a figure for heaven that our puritanism has led us to overlook) would not be riotous revelry, freshmen out on Friday night. It would be free, lovely, laughing — good food, good drink, creative twinkles in every eye.

When we speak of "Christian humanism," we ought to imply this gracious, graceful, good partying. Indeed, we ought to imply the best of music, dance, poetry, friendship, and warm feelings, without any of the hauteur that high art or cuisine can connote. The grace of God sings simply, close to silence and the music of the spheres. To my mind, it comes more in Gregorian chant than in acid rock, in Sung Dynasty landscape paintings than in twisted modern portraits. But tastes, aesthetic minds, vary legitimately, so no one has a lock or preemptive option on what is humanity so gracious as to evidence the workings of God. Let me only note, therefore, that in the traditional rules for the discernment of spirits, as they come down to us, for example, in *The Spiritual Exercises* of Ignatius Loyola, the good spirit works on the good soul gently, quietly, entering and leaving without clamor. The bad spirit, in contrast, is violent and noisy. Let those who have ears to hear use them for Bach and Mozart. Let all the parties to Christian higher education make it a central part of their ambition to show students winning models of human graciousness and give them cogent theological analyses of what makes such models winning.

Crucifixion

Granted the graciousness of divinity, how ought our studies of it to stake out a Christian tract on suffering, pain, defeat, apparent uselessness — on the crucifixion of our hopes, our flesh, our spirits? What does the painful dying of Jesus say about theodicy — our efforts to justify God's ways, the ways of God's world? Moving into these questions, professors ought to tone down their volume, notch up their receptors. If ever there were a place in the curriculum for going gently, treading lightly, it is here. Our students often carry burdens that are shocking. Our Christian God comes to us despised, rejected, a man of sorrows acquainted with grief. Like a lamb he was led to the slaughter. At his end, there was nothing comely in him, little joy or grace. Only a small band of disciples stayed faithful to the end, waiting and watching under his cross. Most of even his inner circle were like those whom he met later on the road to Emmaus, unable to comprehend a messiah who was a suffering servant.

If you limit your sense of how we human beings die to Sherwin Nuland's prize-winning *How We Die*, the best you will come up with is a stark stoicism. As this surgeon sees it, death is usually brutal and ugly. Certainly the death of Jesus portrayed in the gospels is both brutal and ugly. Certainly what AIDS or cancer does to many people is difficult to bear, observe, contemplate. Yet no symbol of Christian faith is more central than the crucifix. No identification of God with human beings, across the entire repertoire of what the world religions have to offer, is closer or fuller. In virtue of what theologians call "the communication of idioms," it is fully orthodox to say, "God died on the cross." The man Jesus drew his deepest existence and definition from the Logos to whom belonged his flesh. Though fully human, "like us in all things save sin," Jesus was yet also fully divine. Dying, he took divinity through what we must all go through. The way that God chose to make us immortal was a way that made divinity itself mortal.

We see this paradox everywhere in Christian worship and art. For example, there is the liturgical response, "Dying he destroyed our death." In patristic thought there is the near-commonplace that, strung up as a criminal, Jesus became Christus Victor. In fact, for the gospel of John, Jesus' mounting the cross is a glorious moment. For the liturgy of Easter, the death of Jesus is the crux of the process through which the fault of Adam, the sin and seismic cleavage afflicting us all, becomes a happy fault.

Christian faith, speaking of the communion of saints, the forgiveness of sins, the resurrection of the body, and the life of the world to come, demands that we look at death differently than Sherwin Nuland does. These articles of the Creed, which look back to prior ones about the suffering of Jesus under Pontius Pilate, his crucifixion, his death, his burial, and his resurrection on the third day, demand that we limit the authority of our senses and deal with death as believers, children of God. The demand seems easy when we come to it in youth, before our own oxen have been gored. But after we have gained some experience of pain and death, and so can appreciate the books of Job and Qoheleth, we find it hard to look on death as Francis of Assisi did, hard to call her our sister.

Suffering and death are our natural enemies. The cries of the wretched of the earth rise up to heaven, asking God, "Why?" Does God ever answer? Can we ever be sure that Golgotha holds the key to Auschwitz? These are not questions that one of us can answer for another. Professors cannot can adequate responses to them into lectures. Students cannot find notes from which to crib passing grades. At the end of the day, picking through the bones of the meal, we find ourselves alone. Only God can be our comforter. Only God can see us through and pass us over.

Our students need to know how Jesus is the Christian response to the horrible question seared into human flesh by death, as they need to know how Jesus is the Christian response to the wonderful question grinning from a healthy infant's face. How did Jesus die? Why did Jesus die this way? What does his dying in this way, and then his rising to the "right hand" of his Father, imply is the best way for other men and women to go to their deaths, go through their deaths?

The simplest sign that healing grace is at work in these matters is the relief that comes with the thought that they may not be settled, shut down, a dead issue. It is hard to have this thought when one is wracked by terrible pain, but even then the memory of once having had it can become a preserver to which to cling. In less troubled times, the thought tends to work as do many of God's other graces. It tends to open further possibilities, ways around what had been dead ends. Thereby, it lets us hope. A great cloud of witnesses have gone through their deaths hoping that the Christian symbols tell the truth. A great many brothers and sisters have died with such an anointing. Ashes to ashes, yes, and dust to dust. But, there is more to faith than Lent. There is Holy Week. There is Easter. There is Pentecost. Ecce homo — behold, good people, the full sweep of what being human can mean. See how the life of all born of woman can end and then rebegin.

Not with a bang or a whimper. Not as just another turn of the karmic screw. Rather, with a silence that can become congenial. With an invitation to contemplate the mortality of all flesh. With a cry of abandonment to God that tears away all lesser props. At death, we finally have to let God be God. There, if not before, we can run to no other option, can buy comfort from no alternative god. One of the main blessings in a Christian view of death is that it makes life properly serious. If now, in the wood made green by the symbolism of Christian faith, we remain so superficial, what would we be in the dry wood of unbelief? How easy it would be for us first to blanche like skeletal bones and then flee into complete distraction. How rare it would be for any of us to read Thomas à Kempis with understanding and pleasure. But now, with faith, theologian and peasant can huddle together on the same mourner's bench and accept the same call to imitate Christ. They can recall that Christ whom they have to call master and lord set his face for Jerusalem, knowing that it would be the city of his death. He wanted to embrace its people as a hen gathers her chicks, but Jerusalem would not accept his things for its peace. A good question that Jesus continues to ask from the cross is whether we will accept these things. Will we take his dying and rising as our own paradigm, the template to which we ourselves have been formed?

Or will we agree with the pagans, many of them no doubt wishing they could feel differently, that death is only dark and empty, and so that contemplating death is a sure recipe for sadness, even depression?

If you contemplate the death of someone you love, certainly you are bound to feel sad. However, if you contemplate it with a restrained, judicious Christian faith, you are also likely to feel your spirits rise. Whatever their literal references, the figures of Paul and John about resurrection and living forever can become stations at which Christians may find peace, perhaps even find eager expectation. The Johannine Jesus says that the disciples who eat his flesh (eucharistically) will live forever. Paul says that the resurrection of Jesus warrants our own hoping that in the twinkling of an eye all will be changed. We cannot see these transformations, cannot feel these happening, but we can believe in them, can hope for them, and can love the comfort that they bring us. We can find our own version of the conviction, crucial for our remaining in the church with good faith, that it is enough that the word of God's good news be preached, the sacrament of God's immoralizing grace be celebrated. We can find one day that these are enough to found and feed a community of Christian faith, and so that all the ecclesiastical rest is only commentary.

We professors do not have to point out to any student that life is often painful. Those who do not know this already will learn it all too soon. The one surety, stronger than taxes, is death. The one common denominator is suffering. Even the fortunate few, the gilded rich and intelligent, come to know pain in their bodies, frustration in their families, winter chills in their spirits. Few places on the globe have Mediterranean climates, and most that do are liable to earthquakes or monsoons. Thus Karl Rahner, and Martin Marty after him, has written of a wintry faith. Thus the compassion of the Buddha sprang from his realizing that all *dharmas* are painful, fleeting, and soulless.

The Christian interpretation of crucifixion makes the way of Jesus humanistic in a sober sense. Because its God has died, Christianity can say to the world that it knows human suffering to the depths and beyond. Yes, there certainly is a distinction between Christianity and Christ, between the church and God. Nonetheless, in my studies of the world religions I have found nothing so humanistic as the Christian interpretation of death that takes the experience of Jesus as linking death with descending into hell and then ascending in resurrection to the right hand of the father. It is certainly true that many putative Christians do not know what they are talking about when they recite their creedal prayers or babble at the bedside of the ill. But it is not true that Christian faith, or the Christian church, does not know what it is talking about, because it never forgets the way of its Lord completely.

Christian faith, and the Christian community formed from it, knows about God from within, through the testimony of God's Spirit, and from without, through the testimony of its Scriptures and sacraments. What it knows is in many ways blank, far richer than propositions. But the gamble and conviction bred into its sinews is that God has said that he will see us through. When Jesus cried out to God in abandonment, God led him to surrender his spirit, and God kept his spirit well. In restoring the spirit of Jesus to his crucified body, God made Jesus whole and glorified. We can gaze on this restored, glorified Jesus in biblical imagination, standing with Thomas to put our fingers in the hole in his side and becoming not unbelieving but believing. We can tell our students that many Christians have made this contemplation down the ages and, if in fact it is so, that we ourselves make it profitably again and again. We can also remind them that what has been done, and is still done now, probably can be done in the future. What actually occurs is always possible. Some people actually do believe, beyond all their doubt and fear and trembling, that their redeemer lives. Therefore, such belief is possible. Therefore, crucifixion can take us to terms beyond its bare initial own.

Resurrection

On the cross, as the main feature of a single picture rather than the center of a triptych, Jesus is a tragic figure. Flanked by his ministerial life on the left, and his resurrected life on the right, he becomes the hero of a solemn comedy. The resurrection does not take away the pounding, reeking evil of the crucifixion. But it does set this evil in a wider context, one relieved by aloes. The Jesus of the ministerial life clearly has resources greater than those of his enemies. The Jesus of the resurrected life has been vindicated by God, his Father. How ought our studies of divinity to extrapolate consequences from this Christian triptych, so as to appreciate "resurrection" as an existential force applicable to all people's lives?

A gentle approach beckons in some naturalist poetry, which reads the death of nature in winter and its requickening in spring as a universal rhythm. Traditional Indian thought developed a cosmological mythology out of similar intuitions: Dying and rising is the way of all the earth. Indeed, for human beings karma produces a cycle of death and rebirth, but the best comfort that this analysis offers us is the consolation of patience. If we detach ourselves from the desire that keeps us chained to the cycle, we may escape to moksha — freedom from karmic conditioning. This escape is not the same as resurrection, but it is a foundation for hope.

The Jewish developments that led to the apocalyptic literature, as well as to hopes for both resurrection and the life of the world to come, could claim a grounding in prior figures such as Ezekiel's vision of dry bones taking on flesh again, through the breath of the living God, but resurrection and the life of the world to come have not dominated Jewish faith as they have dominated Christian faith. The weal in this situation has been that Jews could be this-worldly, concerned about beauty and justice, with a passion that Christians often did not show. The woe has been that without the world to come this world could easily become either overly depressing or overly important.

In the last section we considered crucifixion in predominantly personal terms, because it comes to each individual as the perceptible climax of a unique story. Perhaps resurrection comes to each individual equally uniquely, but since we do not perceive resurrection it is difficult to say how it occurs. Let us therefore consider resurrection in more social terms, stressing the cultural impact that taking it as an article of our creed can make. Doing this, we may say first that resurrection is more than extending the tribe for another generation. Procreation does create a kind of immortality, but what the Christian creedal symbol means by "resurrection" is more than procreation. For the creedal symbol means that all of our current human existence, our entire "human condition," will be transformed — indeed, is already in a process of transformation.

Teilhard de Chardin is the recent Christian thinker who has pondered the cosmic implications of the Incarnation and the resurrection most persuasively, and for him the Christ is at the center of a universal process of evolution. The emergence of thought has led in Christ to the emergence of divinization, thereby showing to matter its final destiny. What will be at the Pauline "all in all" is a Christ who has led the whole universe "upward" to his Father. In constructing this sense of the cosmic future, Teilhard is extrapolating from his faith-filled analyses of the prior stages of evolution, where he finds that the "within" of matter has become ever more intense. It is hard to call the Teilhardian extrapolation "science," yet it is easy to love the materialism, the radical incarnationalism, of this scientist's religious vision. Here is a sense of creation and resurrection that does not leave the world behind — that never succumbs to the temptation (both Greek and Indian) to become acosmic. Here is a reading of the resurrection of Christ that clarifies Paul's intuition that all of creation, laboring now for its redemption, will find itself reborn one day.

I find these Teilhardian ruminations, imaginations, more interesting than apocalyptic scenarios filled with angels and vindictive visitations. I also find them far different from the gnostic readings of cosmic history that became the arch-foe of the early Christians. It is pertinent that Eric Voegelin found himself describing modernity as a new gnosticism, precisely because it has denied the openness of the classical Western view (both Greek and Christian) of the soul. Rendered wholly immanent, never allowed an exit to a beyond that measures the world, the stereotypically modern intellect thinks that it harbors a wicked secret: we make all the sense there is. Voegelin's study of sorcery in Hegel reads out this gnostic ambition. His charge that Marx was a swindler, forbidding further, transcendental questions because, though no Hegel, he was a sufficiently competent philosopher to realize that transcendence would push his materialistic scheme into tatters, remains in my view an accusation as trenchant as it was courageous.

Gnosticism, both ancient and modern, misses the balance established for Christianity by the twofoldness of Christ. Gnosticism does not want us to dig our toes into the sand of mother earth and accept our bodiliness gratefully. It also does not want us to travel beyond the cosmos ecstatically, to a God we cannot imagine, an infinity that dwarfs our psychic inflations. For Voegelin, Heidegger was a modern gnostic, not reaching the Platonic beyond. For me, Jung was another gnostic, thinking that he knew God because he had surveyed the human psyche.

The resurrection of Christ takes the balance of the Incarnation to another level, without destroying the twofoldness of Jesus and ourselves. Jesus resurrected remains one divine person with two natures, divine and human. We hoping for resurrection remain creatures who will come into our own, find the fulfillment that God has whispered into our marrow and soul, only when our bodies are glorified and our spirits can contemplate our Source face to face. The images of the resurrected Jesus, quite restrained and dominating only a few of the many chapters of the four gospels (even when one interprets such events as the Transfiguration in light of Easter), are enough to let us think that a glorified body is still a body: It eats and drinks, it enjoys table fellowship and walks to towns outside cities. The restraint, though, is important, reminding us that if our Christian faith in the resurrection is to be canonical, it ought to chasten any tendency to rattle on about what it cannot know. The puzzles about what will happen at the resurrection to the body of the man thrown overboard and eaten by a school of sharks miss the point. Similarly, in his debates with the Sadducees, who denied the resurrection, Jesus refused to get into equivalent puzzles, such as who would be the husband of the woman married seven times, contenting himself with saying that in heaven there would be no such marrying.

"Heaven," complete fulfillment, lies at a level that we cannot comprehend with earthly minds (a recurrent Johannine theme). Thus when Karl Rahner took up the heavy-sounding topic of "the hermeneutics of eschatological assertions," his conclusion was light and brief: Seldom can we say what the last things (death, judgment, resurrection, hell, heaven) will entail. Usually the best course is to content ourselves with minimal affirmations: I believe, with the creed, in the communion of saints, the forgiveness of sins, the resurrection of the body, and the life of the world to come.

What I would have the resurrection of Jesus, and "resurrection" as an existential attribute now applicable to the human condition overall in virtue of the resurrection of Jesus, imply for our work in the undergraduate academic area of "divinity" is that the God coming to us on the wings of Christian faith is a God full of life. We have already stressed light and love, the other two leading Johannine attributes for God. Equally important is life. Because God is living (deathless), we have vital creation — life expressing the divine vitality. Because God is living, death will be no more, and God will wipe every tear from our eyes. Jesus comes to us as the human filiation of divine life — the Son of the Father in human flesh. Jesus fights with Satan, the personification of evil, death, and darkness, proving to be stronger, indeed tossing Satan out of the house to which faithlessness has given him access. After being defeated in the temptations in the desert that followed on the baptism of Jesus by John, Satan withdraws to await a more propitious hour. That comes when Jesus is arrested, beaten, mocked, and crucified.

But the paradox so central to evangelical theology extends even to this hour of darkness, when evil reaches its nadir. Jesus dying on the cross is a victor. He has kept faith with his God, guarding the holy of holies at the fine point of his soul, and the Father shows a complete satisfaction with Jesus by raising him in triumph — displaying him to the world as a cosmic victor. For Paul this makes Christ a new Adam, the first-born from the dead and lord of all. For the first chapters of the book of Revelation, the life blazing from the risen Christ is coruscant — whiter than what any fuller can bring about. The risen one holds the keys to death and Hades because he has gone to those zones and conquered them. Dying he destroyed our death. Rising he restored our life. If the flaw in us, the fall of Adam and Eve, was a cog for the wheel that turned history into such a triumph, it was indeed felicitous — a very happy fault.

Why, in Lukan perspective, it "had" to be that the Christ should suffer to enter into his glory will always escape us human beings, hiding out in the inscrutable counsels of God. That it had to be, we can say after the fact, is another suggestion that the divine wisdom is both harsher than we might assume and more radically glorious. God has redone the human condition. Elevating Jesus, God has elevated healing grace into divinization. Because of the resurrection of Jesus, we can say that the end of human beings is nothing less than the community of God — light, life, love. Take that to your stereotypically modern mind and, as you hear it scoffing, watch it shrink.

Practical Implications for Higher Education

We have scratched the surface of the implications that a Christian concentration on divinity might carry for a collegiate education, but here we may take up the practical matters of what teaching theology, or religious studies, should entail and how it may best take shape in our curricula. The assumption that I am making throughout is that divinity is to receive by right its 25 percent of the required portion of the curriculum and its minimal 15 percent of the overall number of courses that students must take, since I am assuming that I have established that "divinity" is as irreducible a domain of reality and preoccupation of the human mind as are "the humanities," "politics," and "the natural sciences."

For Christian students, as I have indicated, I would require a sequence of three stipulated or specified courses: Scripture, Doctrine, and Ethics/Spirituality. For non-Christian students, I would require a sequence of Bible, World Religions, and Contemplation/Action (Worship/Social Impact). Let me first deal with these two stipulated triads and then move to the second triad of courses that I would foresee as required in divinity, the three that students would have to take but could do so more freely.

Depending on their prior education, Christian students could take the three specified required courses at introductory or advanced levels. The point at either level would be to cover both the essentials of the Christian sense of divinity and the critical or hermeneutical tools of Christian intellectual work. The course in Scripture would show students the basic literature of the Christian Bible: Law, Prophets, Writings (to keep the divisions of the Jewish *Tanak,* which I find neater than those of the Christian Old Testament); Pauline, synoptic, and Johannine materials. Simply getting a clear sense and deep grasp of the main images and theologies of these six basic subliteratures in the Christian Scriptures would be a considerable accomplishment.

While one can argue on purely cultural grounds for the value of attempting to achieve such a mastery of the biblical literature — an argument that becomes stronger when we consider why it makes sense to require a course in Bible for non-Christian students as well as Christian — in a theological approach such as mine the cultural value is secondary to the precisely intellectual one. These biblical images and appreciations of God have formed the soul of Christianity, of Christian faith, of the Christian community. Christianity, Christian faith, and the Christian community are the sponsors of the collegiate education being offered in the institution of higher learning that has been our presumed focus in this book. (I worked for many years in state institutions, where there was no theology, only religious studies, and where the curricular assumptions and arrangements therefore had to be considerably different.) If we are to show students the contours that the fourth irreducible zone of reality, the divinity that both transcends the other three zones and is immanent to everything in them, has assumed in Christian history to form the basic Christian worldview, we have to pay close attention to the Christian Scriptures, which have been the primary book that the community of Christ's disciples has fashioned and read as God's word.

Second, the course in Christian doctrine that I foresee as a stipulated requirement for all Christian students would make clear what the document of the Second Vatican Council on ecumenism calls the "hierarchy" of truths in Christian revelation. Some teachings are more central or primary than others. It is imperative that educated Christians know what is primary and what is secondary, so that they can develop the perspective on divinity that qualifies as wisdom: a sense of its natural order. I have found useful Karl Rahner's conviction that the three cardinal mysteries of Christian faith are the Trinity, the Incarnation, and Grace, so I would have the basic course in doctrine pay most attention to these three. The Trinity is the essential symbol for the precisely Christian understanding of God, an understanding developed by sustained reflection on the religion of Jesus himself, as the New Testament remembers and develops it. God is a community of "persons" (unlimited centers of consciousness) traditionally called Father, Son, and Holy Spirit. We have some freedom to add other names for God (Mother, Lover, Friend), but we also have a large obligation to probe how Christian theology has in fact worked over the traditional three.

The Incarnation is the precisely Christian view of how God has chosen to be with us, of the covenantal form that the trinitarian God has assigned to us. The Logos, the second person of the Trinity, took flesh from and in the Virgin Mary, becoming fully human while remaining fully divine. The twofoldness of Jesus, the balance that I see as the best source of all the other balances that we should want to develop in our approaches to the personal, political, and natural worlds, makes Christianity a religion whose usual speech is not univocal but analogous (the Catholic trend), dialectical (the Protestant trend), and mystical (the Orthodox trend). Because Jesus holds together in his own being time and eternity, human flesh and divine spirit, mortality and immortality, crucifixion and resurrection, and so forth, he is the microcosmic balance, equilibrium, measure by which we can keep all the other lines of our wisdom, our sense of the order of creation and reality, aligned and true.

Grace, the third cardinal mystery, the third of our principal doctrines giving order to the hierarchy of Christian truths, is the actions of God, the bearing of God toward us, that we have already described under the formalities of healing and elevating. As well, it is a constant reminder that God is the source of any gracefulness there is in us — mental, cultural, or religious.

My course in doctrine would also deal with the church, Scripture, and the Sacraments, as a second tier or rim of Christian doctrines (perhaps in a bow to feminist insight, the "hierarchy" of truths can also be something concentric). This placement is not an effort to deprecate the importance of the church, or Scripture, or the Sacraments. It is simply to suggest that, in analytical perspective (Aquinas's "order of teaching"), they come after the three primary or cardinal mysteries. Further subdivisions, such as the history of the church and the forms of governance that it has developed, or the history of scriptural interpretation, or the liturgical rituals developed for the sacraments, ought to get the nods that they deserve, but the heart of my course on doctrine would be the three principal mysteries — an elaboration of the core of what "divinity" means in Christian understanding.

The required course on ethics/spirituality that I foresee would take up the main themes that Christian faith has developed through thinking about fitting action and prayer. Ethics deals with the main personal, political, and scientific or technological problems that we have to negotiate: truthfulness, love, sexuality, medicine; economic, legal, and social justice; ecological responsibility. Spirituality deals with personal, social, and natural religious living. Students ought to learn the basic Christian theory of prayer, both meditative and contemplative. They ought to learn the main rationale for Christian worship and love of neighbor. And they ought to get help in thinking about the material world as a creation of God that they ought never to deface, that they ought always to regard as a family of fellow expressions of the divine generosity.

The three courses that I would stipulate for non-Christians, elaborated under the rubric of religious studies and so not animated by the prior convictions of faith that shape a properly theological study, run parallel to the three courses that I have stipulated for Christians. The Christian Bible has been so prominent a cultural factor in the West that one cannot be considered literate, educated well, without a good knowledge of it. (Do professors in English still feel the same way about Shakespeare?) The world religions offer the basic data that any student needs to survey in order to estimate what humanity's main responses (shamanic, prophetic, sapiential) to divinity have been through the ages and around the globe. The course dealing with worship and action would pursue in the mode of religious studies a generic form of the course in Christian theology on ethics and spirituality, showing students selected examples of how the various world religions have regularly developed for their people a twofold regime of worship and practical action.

The other courses that I would have all students take as "free" (nonstipulated or specified) requirements in the area of divinity would ideally enable all graduates to exit reasonably well educated about both the objective contours of this fourth zone and the main ways that specialists study it. I would urge Christian students strongly to study the world religions. I would try to get advisors to tailor sequences that fit students' individual needs: more on ethics for lawyers, more on sexuality for prospective doctors, more on ecological spirituality for prospective natural scientists, solid courses on marriage for those in serious romantic relationships, and so forth.

As always, the actual constitution of the given faculty in divinity and the given student body would have much to say in determining what free required courses, and also what still freer electives (courses beyond the six that all students would have to take), would enter the curriculum. If many of the students came from third world backgrounds or ethnic minorities, then courses in liberation theology and the spiritual traditions of the given ethnic groups would be fitting. The same considerations, along with the competencies of the faculty members, would color whether the religious studies courses in divinity ought to stress East Asian, or Indian, or African, or indigenous Latin American traditions. It would be highly desirable to have advanced courses in Scripture, so that Genesis or Luke-Acts could receive a more extensive treatment than that possible in the required courses. The same for courses on individual theologians, for example, Rahner or Barth or Schillebeeckx, and on methodology, especially in biblical and ethical studies.

The assumption throughout would be that students would work hard, reading demanding but rewarding original sources and contemporary analyses. The aim would be an exposure to the fourth realm of reality as adult and rigorous as any exposure developed for the other three realms. In their six courses in divinity, students would be expected to grapple long and hard (and deeply) with the significance of God. They should come to see why agnosticism and atheism can be responsible options, and also why Christian faith, and the faiths of the other world religions, can be at least equally responsible ones. Finally, I would expect our theologians to sear into their students' souls the challenge of Christian faith, indeed of all the religious experience of humankind: the proposition that none of us can become fully mature, a human being of truly estimable stature, without striving for a wisdom that it is hard to separate from holiness. Relatedly, I would expect our teachers to show, as a matter of intellectual analysis (not homiletics), that religious contemplation and responsible political action are the twin engines of any such full human maturity.

Conversely, I want my students to leave our college with at least the germs of an understanding of why a secular education and worldview, limited to the first three zones of reality, is terribly truncated; with a fierce intellectual love of God and theological studies; and with a gentle compassion for all the people pained by the malformation that comes when they do not know God, have not been educated in the beauties of divinity.

Theoretical Implications for Education

Taking divinity seriously as a full partner in one's humanistic collegiate education is one more vote for viewing that education as liberal rather than applied. The first intent of the sort of education that Christian institutions of higher learning ought to promote is to free the mind to know all that is to be known — to remove the blinders that make for partiality. For Christian faith, it is more important to know God than anything else, in part because until one knows God one cannot know oneself. Divinity therefore puts Christian higher education in touch with the Greek tradition of self-knowledge and also with the modern (Enlightenment) tradition of liberal education. Indeed, Christian educators should share many of the high ambitions of their Ivy League counterparts, though Christians must change the generally secular assumptions that dominate the Ivy League.

Second, I think that a representative offering of solid courses in divinity implies that a good education helps us to overcome what Robert McAfee Brown has called "the great fallacy" of opposing spirituality to political action — of making them out to be antagonists. Having in mind such friends and fellow-travelers as Gustavo Gutiérrez and Elie Wiesel, Brown contests the simple-mindedness of either denouncing liberation theology as though it had to be averse to prayer and transcendence, or denouncing liturgical worship as though it had to be apolitical. In the background of this analysis might stand Karl Barth with the Bible in one hand and the newspaper in the other. In the foreground might stand the many critics of liberation theology who seem unwilling to see how the poor actually live, to hear how the cries of the suffering sound when we listen to them in concert with the biblical text. For my purposes here, the graduate who does not see why liberation theology is today an imperative form of Christian faith, and who does not also see why the Christian tradition of contemplative prayer is a resource for holiness with few peers, ought to strike his or her professors as a failure — a student to whom they did not get through.

There will be occasion to speak of wisdom in the last section of this book. Here, though, it seems fitting to suggest that making divinity a partner equal to humanistic studies, social studies, and the natural sciences offers Christian educators a fine chance to form their students toward wisdom. Teachers cannot make students wise. For wisdom, experience and the Spirit of God are the key factors. But professors can orient their students so that by graduation their students long for wisdom, sensing that only it can cap the education to which they have been exposed. Clearly, a good education keeps on ticking long after graduation. Students get used to studying, and so in later life they continue to read good books, to exercise their analytical skills. Ideally, they agree with the Roman poet Terence that nothing human should be foreign to them. Ideally, they enjoy dipping into Lewis Thomas on medicine, Stephen Jay Gould on paleontology, Oliver Sacks on neurology, Barry Lopez on naturalist biology, Lawrence Sullivan on South American religions. Enjoying good books, good plays, good theater, good dance, good music is not pretentious to them, nor is reading about Zen gardens or Chinese philosophy or Koranic jurisprudence. These are all estimable products of the human mind, of human biology and politics. So are studies of the Chesapeake Bay, or the history of warfare, or the shifts in women's fashions. Divinity simply adds an overall context — nothing human should be foreign to us because the image of God shines in our universal humanity. Through reason all peoples are akin — medieval Christian pilgrims, Chinese emperors visited by Matteo Ricci, Indian holy men visited by Roberto de Nobili, painters such as Cassatt and Goya, and ourselves.

The term, the goal, and the lure (the final mover) of a truly humanistic, catholic mind is God, Voegelin's "Beginning and Beyond," the more explicitly Christian Creator and Savior. We do not see our human situation correctly, we do not appreciate the dynamics of our own spirits aright, until we recognize the constitutive force of divinity. God makes us human. God gives us our world. And God does not do this simply extrinsically. Rather, the mental horizon that allows us to scan the world, and the sense of self that allows us to wonder at the ineffable aspects of human creativity, come from the presence of God in our awareness — from the company of God as the tacit "other" and partner in all that we do.

This liberation of the mind, of the human spirit, to explore far and wide suggests that studying divinity is not the sole prerogative of ecclesiastical theologians. Rather, it is the birthright of all human beings. There is nothing more congenial to the deeper human mind (*intellectus* rather than *ratio*) than contemplating the mystery of Being, the actuality of divinity. We live and move and have our spiritual being in the divine mystery. Whether we find ourselves on Easter Island or Manhattan, the light in our minds comes from God. Equally, the proper end of the education that we receive, traditional or modern, is the divine mystery. Wisdom, negatively, is knowing that we shall never know. Wisdom, educationally, is coming to what Lonergan calls an inverse insight: We cannot know God conceptually with the tools that we apply to knowing finite things. We cannot know what God is; we have to sacrifice our natural tendency to keep pursuing the essence of something initially unknown, the characteristics and relationships that make it distinctive.

God is distinctive in having no essence apart from the unlimitedness of the divine act of existence. God is distinctive in having no part, nothing that we can take apart by analysis. The mechanic in us therefore turns away from "God" in frustration. The ratiocinist has to give way to the mystic. But none of this phenomenology of how the mind works in the trans-academic portions of divine studies is peculiar to any particular religious tradition. Neither Muslim mullahs nor Jewish rabbis nor Christian magistrates nor Indian gurus nor Japanese roshis can tell us once and for all what God is. No group of religious teachers, divines, has a monopoly on God. None has been the council that God consulted when fashioning the world. Each is a very human body, conditioned thoroughly by its given space and time. The greatest wisdom that any has to offer comes from the particular exercise of its own people in the abcs of divinity: Divinity is always prior, we are always running after. Divinity is always greater, we can never grasp this majority. Always our good relations with divinity depend on its grace. Never are we profitable servants, people with the right to sue. A good sequence of courses in divinity leaves our students well schooled in this fundamental reality, this bedrock fact about their own minds.

Properly mystical, the divine portion of an undergraduate education tends to turn out students who are countercultural. On the one hand, they have their feet on the ground, loving the earth and working hard to make it a place of justice and beauty. On the other hand, they have "here," on earth, no lasting city. Indeed, they follow Augustine in knowing about two realms, the city of the holy God and the city of sinful human beings. The city of sinful human beings is potentially lovely — sacramental, eucharistic. The city of the holy God, the heavenly Jerusalem, is mysterious — eye has not seen, ear has not heard, what God has conceived for it. The tension that comes from holding citizenship in both cities ought to be creative. The incarnate divinity that comes to us in Christ requires that we love God with our whole minds, hearts, souls, and strengths, *and* that we love our neighbors as ourselves.

Remarkably, many of our students do get this message. Even now, with all the imperfections in our curricula, we Christian educators turn out many students who know full well that they are bound to two allegiances. They must render to Caesar and time what these masters have the right to require. But they must also render to God and eternity a further, in many ways deeper, fealty. In fact, I wonder whether the 1995 flap among the alumni of Boston College (in whose company I stand) over the proposal to award a Saint Ignatius medal to Margaret Thatcher could have been as intense at a secular college. For I doubt that the alumni could have turned on the (to my mind foolish) Jesuit administrators who allowed this award to become a possibility had those alumni not been formed to think that Ignatius would want no honoring of politicians who dismissed the poor programmatically and were quick to recur to violence. Yes, it was a special insult that the Irish-Americans whose grandparents' dimes built the original Boston College had relatives in the old country to whom Thatcher had been particularly nasty. But the heart of the matter, as it came to me in the press (always a ground for caution), was the incompatibility between the political outlooks of Christians schooled in a preferential option for the poor and Thatcher, and so the shameful incongruity of the award. The further shame was that the alumni of Boston College on Wall Street who proposed the award should have, could have, thought that Margaret Thatcher represented admirable political policies. Something in their undergraduate educations had misfired badly. Those with Ignatian sensibilities about the poverty in which consecrated religious ought to live, or with any memory of the directives of the Thirty-Second General Jesuit Congregation on the essential place of social justice in the ministries of the Society, had to witness all this sadly, the educators among them hearing a painfully cautionary tale: what they had delivered, practically, and perhaps also what they had conceived theoretically, had aborted painfully.

_____ Chapter 5 _____

Education Revisited

Students

We began, in our Introduction, with teaching — trying to turn freshmen into students. We ended, in the previous chapter, with alumni — former students giving cause for grief. In this chapter we return from our introductory orientations, and then our four-chapter-long reflection on the realms of reality that a humanistic Christian undergraduate education ought to survey, to the matter of education itself, searching again for what theology ought to say about this fascinating and utterly central human concern called teaching.

"Students," etymologically, are those who are eager — who want passionately to learn. That definition can separate the audience in any undergraduate classroom into sheep and goats. As well, it can remind us of the limits constraining what teachers can accomplish, and also of the motivational portions of the teacher's task. We cannot educate those who are not eager to learn. Students have to give us a minimal docility and cooperation. Any course in higher education entails an implicit contract between the professor and the students. The professor is bound to providing the leadership and direction that the course requires, on the assumption that the professor is the professor in virtue of possessing greater knowledge than the students. The student is bound to offering a proper acceptance of this leadership and direction, most importantly by doing the work that the professor requires.

Both partners to this educational contract must make an act of faith. The professor must believe that enough students will do their work to give the course a chance of succeeding. The students must believe that the professor stands at the podium because he or she can provide the leadership and direction that the course requires if it is to succeed. "Success," both parties have to agree, is a matter of the students' knowing more at the end of the course than they did at the beginning — of their having grown, matured, ideally in both breadth and depth. Professors so jaded or cynical that they have no faith that students will do their part ought to retire, or to withdraw into pure research. Students so callow that they do not hold themselves co-responsible for the success of their courses ought to leave until they acquire enough maturity to make this responsibility plain to them.

A good teacher loves her or his students. This love is nothing syrupy, nothing that detracts from a proper rigor and a prudent skepticism. But it is also nothing that vetoes affection. Unless you like the kids, love what they could become and in their best moments want to become, you are in the wrong profession. Teaching is not a substitute for parenting, but it does carry some of the potential of a good parent-child relationship, of a good, mutually beneficial exchange between the generations. It is a cliché that students teach their teachers nearly as much as they learn from them, but it can be quite true. It seems to me obvious that the responsible teacher does not let classes degenerate into bull sessions where students simply pool their ignorance, but the balancing obviosity is that until the teacher engages the students, so that they make the course their own — make it an intellectual property in which they have invested substantially — her success will remain limited.

The connection between teacher and student is one of Martin Buber's primary instances of the I-Thou relationship. It is not completely convertible. Students and teachers are not intellectual peers, however much they both remain simply human beings whose lives are short, who have never seen God. They can be friends, but for the academic exchanges that constitute proper teaching to occur the two cannot be equals. Naturally, this does not mean that teachers ought to think of themselves as dictators or omniscient judges. Naturally, it does not mean that students have no knowledge or wisdom and ought to be craven. It just means that students have to respect the credentials that make the teacher the teacher, and so they have to offer the teacher a proper docility, while teachers have to use such docility well, earning the students' respect through displaying a manifest competence. In a word, teachers have to know what they are talking about, and students have to be open to, eager for, the knowledge that competent teachers are offering them.

In fact, much more often than not this happens. The number of truly incompetent professors in Christian colleges such as mine is small, as is the number of students closed to the possibility that their teachers have good things to offer them.

Loving my students, I want their good. Love is precisely wanting the good of the other, the beloved. Specifically, as their teacher I want the intellectual growth of my students. That is my formal goal. I may also want my students to do well in the band, in their social lives, in the chapel. But, specifically as their teacher, I ought to stick to my intellectual last. In my course, the goal is that students understand, get the point, grow intellectually. I want them to see more of what "divinity" connotes, since that is my area, and to appreciate better how critical, educated intelligence works in theology or religious studies. (One of the blessings of religious studies is that perforce it uses many methods: historical, sociological, literary, and philosophical.) If students do not leave my courses with such an improvement, such a growth, I ought to be dissatisfied with our performance, theirs and mine conjoined.

Recent Catholic ecclesiastical documents that refer murkily to the impact that campus ministry ought to have on the intellectual life of college students therefore set off alarms in my system. I want no bending of the intellectual effort that students ought to be expending in divine studies so as to make the results serve piety. Certainly, I think that excellent theological understanding is a major support for excellent, truly adult piety. But in the classroom the dog is intellectual understanding. Ministerial applications or influences are at best the tail. Neither prayer nor social action ought to preempt the study that is the proper focus in a college course. Neither practica nor oranda are the first order of business. If this implies that a college is neither a parish nor the whole of life, fine. I think that is indeed the case. I also think that students as students are embodied intelligences, and so that teachers as teachers ought to be paid first to exercise those intelligences, make them more robust and refined.

There is a largely discouraging literature about how to test the success of a given college course, even a given college education. Perhaps the best overall index is what the student thinks ten years later, but even that index labors under the assumption that the student has in fact matured into a responsible, incipiently wise adult. I believe that good courses show students things they had not seen before. These things may be completely new, or they may be things that students thought they knew, and so considered old hat, but then had their teachers redo to disabuse them of their ignorance. Many of the things that professors working in courses in Christian theology try to teach fall into this second category. Most students in such courses have been through the catechism, so they assume that they know the Christian tradition. Therefore, the first step toward succeeding with them is often to disabuse them of their assumption.

Always this necessity reminds me of Kierkegaard's analysis of his situation in nineteenth-century Copenhagen, a city that considered itself "Christian." The indirect discourse that he felt he had to employ to speak of Christian faith effectively was a tribute to the deadening effect of "Christendom." Before he could get his readers to hear his message, he had to make it seem foreign to them, ironic and pseudonymous. Often the situation in our classrooms is not so severe, because the paganism of our students is more blatant than that of the burghers of Kierkegaard's Copenhagen, but it is still hard to overestimate the resistance that comes because students think that God is a settled issue.

I would like God, divinity, to be a quite unsettling issue. I would like the sequence of stipulated required courses for Christian students to shake up their bourgeois, prematurely sclerotic minds. The biblical theologies are a fine means to this end. It is hard to read the books of Ruth and Jonah consecutively without starting to realize that the Hebrew Bible delights in challenging the Israelite faith from which it springs. Ruth is a pagan Moabite, yet she becomes the ancestor of King David. Jonah is an Israelite prophet, yet his God finds the pagan Ninevites more religious than he. The situation does not change in the New Testament, when Jesus comes on stage. The Pharisees are nothing if not correct, in terms of the religious law, yet Jesus lashes them again and again. The story about the two men who go up to the Temple to pray, one a Pharisee and the other a publican, shows the gist of what Jesus thought about religion (Luke 18). The continuance of pharisaism in the church of Jesus is ironic as well as scandalous.

In the gospel of John, the authorial voice is ironic consistently. Again and again his hearers do not understand the Johannine Jesus, cannot grasp what he is telling them. He is from above, they are from below. Until the Spirit of God begins to elevate them, they haven't got a clue. The professor of biblical studies is not above his students the way that Jesus is above his unperceiving hearers, but the message of Jesus that the professor tries to elucidate may indeed continue to be. Perhaps the major benefit of biblical studies is how frequently they bring any honest student, professorial or undergraduate, up short. As the heavens are distant from the earth, so are the ways of God from our human ways. That is the biblical perspective, and much of the best biblical literature delights in driving home the wisdom consequent upon it: Let God be God.

Professors of divinity have to let God be God with their students. They have to try to make their own the Ignatian dictum that they should work as though everything depended on God and pray as though everything depended on themselves. In their precisely intellectual work at guiding students so that the students come away with a better understanding of Scripture than that with which the students began, and so of making students more able to take the Bible on its own terms than they were at the outset, professors ought to proceed freely, peacefully, joyously. Equally, professors should think of their charges, and their failures with their charges, when examining their consciences each night. We are responsible for the charges given to us. It is a limited responsibility that we professors bear, certainly, yet a serious one. If our students are not learning, we ought to be sad — on the verge of doing penance. If we have piped them a good, happy song, and they have not danced, have sung them a poignant, affecting dirge, and they have not mourned, we ought to speak to our God pleadingly, lamenting the youthful heart of darkness. In other words, to be an estimable Christian vocation, teaching has to touch the roots of our being, set up shop deep in our hearts, so that we pray for our charges, wanting their intellectual maturation more than we ever suspected we would when we began.

Community Service

The litigiousness of present-day American society has forced most colleges to make explicit the criteria on which they base decisions about tenure and promotion. As a result, most professors find themselves working in a judgmental framework that attempts to parcel out their profession in terms of three primary responsibilities. These three are teaching, research/publication, and "service." A representative weighting of them is 40 percent for teaching, 40 percent for research/publication, and 20 percent for service. Though service comes in for only one of five shares, while both teaching and publication come in for two, it nonetheless remains a vague player in the games of current higher education. Indeed, when combined with the equally vague "collegiality," it can become a player of considerable moment.

For students, something similar has come into play. As the preferential option for the poor and the essential quality of working for social justice have made a substantial impact on the Christian sense of ministry, some educators have thought that public service ought to become a requisite for collegiate graduation. Let us therefore muse about what an ideal Christian view of the place of service in higher education would entail for both students and professors.

I am all for public service, as I am all for contemplative prayer. But I have serious doubts about giving service any privileged status at a Christian college. It delights me to find students deciding to spend their first year after graduation participating in programs of service such as the Jesuit Volunteers, because I think that the students usually benefit greatly from the dose of reality that such a program can provide and that usually they do considerable good. But I consider the Jesuit Volunteers, and parallel programs in which students may engage while undergraduates, peripheral to the main task of a Jesuit or other Christian college, which to my mind is engaging students full-time in the exploration of the humanistic, social scientific, natural scientific, and divine realms of reality.

I expect my students to work hard. I assume that their studies are their first order of business. And so I resent strongly anti-intellectual comments from the margins of a college to the effect that the real business is engaging students with the poor, let alone comments that stress giving students the circumstances for interesting friendships. If is fine for students to engage with the poor. It is dandy for students to enjoy interesting friendships that perdure long after they have graduated. But all this is secondary. Primary for students is learning, by doing well the work required by their courses. Primary for teachers is teaching and, to a lesser extent (as I see a properly ordered college), publishing. For both students and teachers, service of the community is markedly secondary — something for their spare hours.

To be candid, I do not think that diligent students have many spare hours. If students are taking fifteen hours per semester, and if they are putting in two hours of study for every hour in class, then already their studies are claiming forty-five hours per week. Certainly, this leaves them some time for good works, as for exercise and socializing, but not luxurious amounts. Relatedly, 90 percent of the time, in my experience of more than twenty-five years of college teaching, students who complain of overwork are lazy or disorganized. They have not put in two hours of study for every hour of class. They have not pursued further readings beyond the few required in the syllabus. Now and then I meet a student who is a workaholic and needs to be shown why workaholism is sinful. For every one such student, however, I meet nine who work too little, for whom the precisely intellectual focus of their collegiate years has yet to become compelling.

When we get into the intellectual life, we realize that there is no end to the books we ought to read, the studies that are pertinent. Learning is an ecological enterprise: No study is an island unto itself; every study touches a dozen others. That is the splendor of the intellectual life: It has no perceptible end. In heaven there will still be things to learn, things justifying an eternal exploration of God. On earth, we do indeed have to reach a balance about our intellectualism, taking its endlessness as a call to go peacefully, not burn ourselves out. But when an education is catching fire, getting itself on track, there are not enough hours in the day to read all the books that one would like to read, do all the assimilating and connecting that one's engaged mind desires to do.

I do not say that this potentially devouring aspect of the intellectual life ought to produce a veto on community service. I simply say that, for the four years of an undergraduate education, educators, parents, and students themselves ought to have enough faith in what a college is about to let study be the predominant passion. Applicants who show little likelihood of making study their predominant passion ought to be advised to seek other employment after high school, regardless of their ability to pay or their skill at bouncing a basketball. A college is for study, learning, intellectual growth. When this primary focus comes under assault, those in charge of a college ought to react ruthlessly. It is their job, their duty, their moral obligation under God to keep their enterprise faithful to its charter. In my view a college that makes more of practice than of contemplative study is in the process of losing its soul.

Let me be clear that what I am saying about the focus of a Christian college is not what I would say were the question, What should be the focus of a Christian life? To answer that question, I would refer to the twofold commandment of Jesus, and I would agree that one valid interpretation of the law of Christian discipleship would make community service extremely important. But I have already stated or argued that a college is not a church and that the collegiate experience is not the whole of life. I have already agreed that there is more to life than study, as I would be happy to agree, in the proper circumstances, that love is more important than knowledge. Still, here our topic is a theology of education, especially the education befitting an American Christian college. In this context, I feel obliged to defend with might and main the precisely intellectual character of the enterprise, largely because so many people, inside our colleges as well as outside them, seem not to understand it or believe in it wholeheartedly.

For example, at a putatively Christian college where I once taught, the Dean of Students told a 4.0, Phi Beta Kappa graduating senior that she was exactly the sort of student the college ought not to want. It ought to want the solid B and C students who manned the fraternities, womanned the sororities, and gave the college "spirit." Ay chihuahua! For such a statement alone, the man should have been thrown out on his ear. But his uneducated boss at the top of the pyramid needed mediocre subordinates, so philistinism such as this received a tacit sanction. Students got from the dean in charge of their living arrangements and social lives the clear message that college was a time for drinking beer, acquiring buddies, and participating now and then in a car wash to raise $100 for unfortunates. Any good professors ground their teeth and found their dreams turning grim. Their worst enemy was in their midst, seated on a throne of honor. A man of power had not the slightest idea what his business ought to have been. He should have been released to sell Rice Krispies.

The entire dynamism of the undergraduate education that I have designed moves students toward graduating equipped and motivated to work hard in the world, for the good of all creation. There is nothing ivory-towerish in what I foresee, because everything in it strives to engage students with reality — with what is so in their own personhood, in the political realms in which they participate, in the natural world, and in the realm of ultimacy. Moreover, I have proposed that ethics/spirituality or worship/action be stipulated required courses in divinity. I want students to graduate fully inclined to try to make a difference in the world. However, I observe that many good intentions go awry because the people who have them don't know what they are doing. Some of what they need to know can come from experience, but if they have not gotten the habit of studying, of doing research well and contemplating the implications of what their research uncovers, they will never become activists with a vision, agents of change who respect what history has to teach them, what philosophy and theology say about the human nature that they are trying to transform.

When you look at the U.S. House of Representatives or Senate from a perspective such as mine, the most pathetic aspect is the lack of depth and vision. We have plenty of technocrats, or at least of people able to boss technocratic staffs. We have few people who are wise because they have followed the example of a Lewis Thomas and spent their late nights listening to symphonies such as the late ones of Mahler. What has Mahler, or any contemplation suitable for midnight, to do with improving the world? If that question wells up in you despite yourself, you are further evidence for my argument. With all the good will in the world, what you have to offer any community that you want to serve (including that of your own family) will be strikingly limited. You can't get blood out of a stone. A person deaf to great music will not generate public policy concordant with the music of the spheres.

Academic Freedom

College professors, who are the force most crucial in effecting a good undergraduate education, need to be free to do their job. Sometimes the connotation of "academic freedom" that rules in the popular mind has it that professors need protection against being abused because they hold unpopular views. That is an important issue, but the more fundamental one, as I see it, is the freedom of professors to do what they ought: Lead their students through demanding courses. Professors cannot do this if the local culture is anti-intellectual. Strange to say, we do have campuses where many people are anti-intellectual. Seldom would they confess this boldly, but each day many students, administrators, and even teachers shy away from talk about excellence, from ambition to hone their minds sharper for better work.

Indeed, a significant thesis in many platforms of political correctness lays it down that "elitism" is a great evil. Is that supposed to mean that mediocrity should be king? The only elites in athletics or business are those people whose performances are excellent. So ought it to be in our colleges. In our colleges, intellectual excellence ought to be the great badge of merit. Intellectual excellence need not be snooty, let alone mottled by racism or sexism. In fact, when it matures intellectual excellence will tend to become humble, because it will tend to become aware of the mysteriousness of reality — of all that it can never know. But whether full of prideful beans needing further baking, or already properly modest, intellectual excellence is the pearl of great price that we have to leave our professors free to nurture in our students. Otherwise, we cut the hamstrings of our teachers and force both them and their students to limp along.

A liberal education is one that frees the mind from the shackles of ignorance. Ignorance subsumes many kinds of not-knowing, but some are quite obvious. Students who do not know the facts about global population, global use of natural resources, global warming, and the like are ignorant of some of the things they must know if they are to make good estimates of the future of their planet. Students who do not know the facts about sexual prophylaxis in a time of AIDS are ignorant perilously. The facts, the basic information, is always relevant. We can never dispense with knowledge of what we are contending with, what is in fact shaping our situations.

Beyond the facts, however, we have to know how to interpret them. Recalling T. S. Eliot, I think at this point of having the experience but missing the meaning. It is not enough to go to the site and record the facts. One has to offer the facts a patient, sensitive mind, so that they can present their significance. In other words, teachers have to help their students appreciate the canons of good learning. Whether or not they want to cite Descartes on how to direct the intelligence or refer to Bacon's new organon, teachers ought to give their students a good sense of how those who have thought best about the workings of the human mind tend to advise the rest of us.

I have already cited Bernard Lonergan's five transcendental precepts. We have to pay attention, be intelligent (work our brains), be reasonable (root out our prejudices, provide for what we do not know), be responsible (decisive), and be loving. The fourth and fifth of these precepts step off toward a full religious living, but the first three apply to any form of study. Certainly, quick people of common sense exhibit these three traits: attentiveness, sharpness, judiciousness. To be sure, we need to distinguish between knowing such precepts instinctively or operationally and knowing them with reflective clarity. A Dick Francis, possessed of little formal education but gifted with a good brain, can educate himself so as to become not just a successful writer of mystery stories but also an interesting purveyor of information about horse-racing, flying, the liquor industry, the remodeling of houses — whatever he wants his characters to get into. But the best policy for training writers is not to leave their education to pick-up-sticks. For every Doris Lessing, quitting school at fourteen, we have a lot of adult dropouts who neither write nor read nor think well. Just as prehistoric tribes found it useful to train their hunters and medical people through an apprenticeship, so does our modern American tribe find it useful, when it reflects sensibly, to train its future leaders broadly, deeply, and critically. The freedom that college teachers most need is the "space," temporal and cultural, to do this well.

On the one hand, it would be naive to expect that the processes of formulating curricula and making academic appointments could ever become unpolitical. On the other hand, those who want to keep these processes properly pure need to fight to protect them from ideologues and pressure groups. The controversies that we have seen recently about what ought to be considered the classics, and so the backbone, of a solid collegiate education, have been salutary, inasmuch as they have forced all involved to reconsider critically the criteria for deciding the first order of collegiate business. However, when a writer of the stature of Saul Bellow suffers insults from punks because he presumes to speak up for Tolstoy, our culture is in serious trouble. The same when innovators try to reduce Madison and Jefferson to a par with Abigail Adams.

In theological studies, one of the reasons why we have no obvious successors to giants such as Karl Rahner and Bernard Lonergan, Karl Barth and Reinhold Niebuhr, is that an anti-elitism has kept chipping away at the supposed "difficulty" or "obscurity" of their work. Certainly, one has to slug away, at least in the beginning, if one is to raise the level of one's game sufficiently to start to get their point. Lonergan himself found in his doctoral studies of *gratia operans* in Aquinas that he had to abandon the Suarezian framework in which he had been schooled. But such slugging away is the most precious part of a collegiate or university education. We do not grow by continuing to move around the same little counters. We grow by realizing that the game can rise to a new level, or a new depth, or a much broader context. In the best of collegiate experiences, what changes most significantly is the temper of our own minds. It is less the facts that we come away with than the new, more developed and powerful capacities we gain for dealing with any set of facts that measures the success of our four years.

If professors are to be free to concentrate on nurturing this sort of transformation, the educational context in which they work has to be protected from the slings and arrows of pragmatism, pressure politics, the major disturbances of what Lonergan called "the pure desire to know." The glory of the natural sciences, which even the occasional story about the fudging of data does not really tarnish, is that they live by a method, an intellectual protocol, that renders bias and prejudice as insignificant as possible. Yes, scientists wage fierce battles at the moments when history requires them to consider changing their paradigms. Certainly, Thomas Kuhn's work on the structure of scientific revolutions, and the refinements of this theory proposed by such fellow scholars as Stephen Toulmin, provide due cautions against disembodying natural science. But I think it remains true that the natural sciences inculcate a respect for what simply is so, or what now seems most likely to be so, from which all other bodies of knowing ought to take a lesson.

Perhaps nowhere is this lesson needed more than in the social studies that I have labeled "political." The debates about testing for intelligence are a case in point. It is well for us to question thoroughly the assumptions behind any experiments designed to explore this issue, but in itself the issue admits of rather simple study. It is imperative that philosophers and theologians point out that human rights depend on something more basic than an intelligence measured on a fallible current scale for predicting academic success, but tests that reflect fairly the kinds of excellence needed for success in the most defensibly described present-day liberal educations have every right to be. I myself have met bright people and dumb people of both sexes and every race and ethnic group that I know. The one surety that teachers such as me come to is that only a student's actual work is the proper measure of his or her academic success. Compared to the actual exams and papers that the student produces, SAT scores and all the rest are quite secondary. Always, the proof is in the pudding. On the other hand, until we develop better predictors, based on better correlations between the actual work that students do in their college courses and the performances that their diagnostic test scores led us to expect, we have no alternative but to use, gingerly yet courageously, the predictors that we now have. We should use these predictors honestly, and not try, dishonestly, to dumb our canons of academic excellence down to what an ignorant but vociferous lobby for political correctness would prefer to be the governing criteria.

I want teachers in Christian colleges to be free exemplarily to voice opinions such as this and act upon them. I want the debate about these issues to be civil, humorous, and ongoing. Seldom is there any educator's experience that cannot generate a useful contribution to this debate. Almost always when professors speak from what they have found actually occurring with their students, "excellence" starts to fill out to the full figure, the ideal roundness, that the term ought to carry. I agree that it is more important that teachers pursue excellence day by day in their classrooms than that they debate about it endlessly. Thomas à Kempis's observation about the greater value of feeling compunction than knowing its definition is germane. But if a certain amount of debate is necessary to reestablish the rightness of giving top priority to a traditionally rigorous understanding of intellectual excellence, then college professors have no moral alternative to engaging in it. The issue is too crucial to let know-nothings determine it by default. For the same reason, we have to keep lobbyists for various outside interests at their proper distance. It is a gross disorder when big donors get to say who will receive the honorary degrees or founders' medals that express the college's sense of human excellence. The first order of business in a college that knows what it is about is fostering the pure desire to know. Most of the rest should be commentary — how to support this central operation. Academic freedom boils down to assuring as best we can the exterior and interior conditions necessary for pursuing the pure desire to know and honoring intellectual excellence. The proper work of the Christian college is to polish bright minds so that one day they can become silver with knowledge, golden with wisdom, and apt candidates for a beatifying vision of God. The community that does not appreciate the value of this work does not deserve a good college. Indeed, it forces me to think evangelical thoughts about the futility of tossing pearls before swine.

Arts and Sciences

I have no quarrel with practical, applied, professional education, as long as it does not attempt to usurp the undergraduate curriculum. The old model that the old American families with the old money followed was ideal: a good prep school, a liberal arts education, and then specialization in law school or business school or medical school, or perhaps even a Ph.D. in something like political science, history, or economics, if the expectation was that the scion would go into public service. The prep school and the liberal arts education were foundational: to develop the young person's mind, attune his (to a lesser extent her — the finishing school was not a full education) sensibilities. The graduate studies were specialized and practical, designed to give the new A.B. or, less frequently, B.S. a competence prized in the world of commerce or government. On occasion engineering could become the undergraduate concentration, but the old model resisted this move. It thought it better to have an undergraduate major in mathematics or physics or chemistry than to have him plunge right into applied studies. In the beginning was the general, what could nourish and free the overall mind. Later could come the specific, after the young person had learned to think at large, had been stretched by the classics.

So the arts and sciences have been the backbone of the traditionally ideal American collegiate experience, and their curricula have simply updated the medieval trivium and quadrivium, or the counterreformational Jesuit *Ratio Studiorum*, as new fields of knowledge emerged. First the physical sciences and then the social sciences forced reconsiderations of the old hegemony of philosophy and theology. But into the late 1950s and early 1960s Jesuit schools continued to require full minors in philosophy of all under-graduates. (It is telltale that philosophy merited this attention but theology did not. The late pre–Vatican II church lived by natural law more than Scripture.) Even though one may lament the actual content of curricular requirements such as these, the instinct be-hind them remains admirable, at least in my view. All students, in virtue of their plain humanity, ought to gain what J. H. Newman called "the habit of philosophy." That is an ability to put prob-lems in context and analyze them in a disciplined fashion. While we should debate how a given college with a given professorate and student body can achieve this goal best, there should be no debate about the desirability of the goal itself. If we do not still have the ambition of teaching our undergraduates to think well and, in the Christian context, to know well the overall contours of God's creation, then we ought to turn in our sheepskin and go run a kiosk.

The arts and sciences therefore have dominated the model cur-riculum that I have developed to make specific my Christian theological sense of how higher education ought to shape itself nowadays. The arts, or humanities, arise from cultural and politi-cal contexts, but they are the place in our curricula where personal reality receives its richest attention. Certainly, some studies in other realms of reality (notably, social psychology and theology) have important things to say about the self, but literature and philos-ophy remain the great sources of reflection on personal human experience. Others better aware than I of what studies in mu-sic or painting or dance tend to develop will have to explain the sense of "arts" that is most apt there. Often I have found myself sad that collegiate life, specifically the professorate, seems regularly to deal with drama or music or painting badly, under-appreciating it and trying to fit it to a wooden framework for measuring tenurability in terms of written publications. That may be fine for art history or musical criticism but it seems to dena-ture what the performing arts are about and so have to offer to undergraduates.

The social sciences, including at least portions of history, have been responsible for the traditional student's gaining a realistic sense of how human beings tend to live together politically. En-riched nowadays by studies of ritual and communications, these political investigations continue to offer students rich vicarious experiences of the ways of the worlds of foreign policy, economics, and social life in such disparate situations as tribal villages and emergency wards. The physical sciences have given students their essential exposures to the natural world, and in the best colleges such sciences have been humanistic — as concerned to impart a sense of what the reflective biologist thinks about the world and how such a scientist works as to impart factual information about miosis and mitosis.

Last, studies of divinity, generally underrepresented in even Christian colleges, ought to deal with the ultimate realities that define all people's human situation and the prime sources, scriptural and sacramental, that the religions have developed from and for dealing with ultimate, sacred reality. Since the dawn of modernity in the Enlightenment, theology has been on the defensive, pressured by modern rationalism to declare itself something emotional or credulous (fideistic) and so at best marginal to the intellectual enterprise institutionalized in the university. I have spent an entire chapter trying to show the poverty of this attitude and pressuring, so I shall not repeat myself here. Suffice it to say, on the precisely Christian theological grounds of this book, that a college that does not give divinity curricular status equal to that given the humanities, the social sciences, and the natural sciences is in my mind dominated by a woeful, extremely deleterious ignorance.

It is clear that I am open to the charge of special pleading in this matter, since I am the chair of a department of religious studies at a Catholic university. It may be that there is merit in that charge, and I have scant expectation that by the year 2000 the majority of American Christian colleges will have adopted a curricular layout such as the one that I have proposed here. Indeed, I count my own college relatively wise and fortunate to have retained a requirement of three courses in religious studies. But you readers should note the objective grounds for the fourfold layout that I have proposed, and test it out on Christian theological grounds.

If you believe in God — the real thing, not a cultural museum piece — then "divinity" has to bulk large in your estimates of "reality." Indeed, you may need to study well the historical roots of Christian humanism to avoid a theological imperialism and appreciate why the humanities, the social sciences, and the physical sciences should be equally important in the Christian educational scheme of things. Whether or not this appreciation comes to you easily, however, I shall be surprised if you are not hard put to argue against the balance and generality that I have proposed from a Christian theological analysis of what the most desirable undergraduate education would be.

The theological grounds for making the undergraduate curriculum humanistic (determined by the arts and sciences) boil down to the primacy of developing the capacities of the student, who ultimately is an image of God. The theological grounds for speaking of reality as possessing four irreducible zones come to me by way of Eric Voegelin, who spent a long lifetime puzzling about the nature of history. Voegelin's conclusion was that the moments that ought to direct our estimates of the shape of the whole were the "leaps in being" where human vision became clearest. In such leaps as that of the Israelite prophets, which lead to "revelation," and that of the Greek philosophers, which lead to "reason," the way to periodize time became as clear as it would ever get.

The later Voegelin rejected the notion that one could arrange the history of the most important leaps in being along a straight time line, coming in the fourth volume of his *Order and History* to a sophisticated sense of the simultaneity of many relevant developments and the importance of what he thought of as the equivalence of historical (human) experience. Thus people who experienced reality predominantly in terms of a cosmological mythopoeia tended to deal compactly with the whole that I have described in relatively differentiated fashion as the four distinct yet related realms that the humanities, the social sciences, the natural sciences, and divinity studies ought to investigate. Though they suffered the impact of all the major forces in reality just as did people in more differentiated cultures, people dominated by the cosmological myth (by storied forms of the conviction that nature is alive, and that nature includes the range of all that is) did not have at their disposal the increasing sophistication about the workings and structure of the human mind that the classical Greek movement from the Presocratics to Aristotle developed.

This noetic differentiation had its pneumatic parallel in the biblical materials, both those of the Hebrew Bible and those of the New Testament, but in Voegelin's view the clearest sense of human rationality developed among the Greeks, and so from the Greeks came the most precious tools for understanding history.

(For Voegelin Plato broke through the cosmological myth and understood that the divine is a trans-cosmic "beyond.") Interestingly, Greek historiography or historiogenesis itself was less linear than biblical sacred history, which set a genesis in the beginning and looked forward to a parousiac if not apocalyptic consummation. But the sharpest tools for appreciating our human synthetic character and position in the world came from Hellenism, first pagan and then Christian.

Modernity offered some useful correctives to the classical anthropology, especially regarding the historicity and cultural conditionedness of all human living, and in the modern centuries natural science rightly became cause for great pride in human potential. But the gnosticism to which I referred previously when retailing Voegelin's theories caused as much grief as the further differentiations that modernity sponsored caused joy. In Voegelin's view the horrors of Nazism and Marxism-Leninism are fully legitimate children of the stereotypical aberrations of the modern mind (recall Buber's "eclipse of reason"). As a college professor, I see a reformed, criticized, renovated traditional collegiate education dominated by studies in the arts and sciences as the best way to stimulate the debate between modern (and postmodern) intellectual developments and traditional (theological) ones that I would like all my students to enjoy as a fine way to experience the excitement, indeed the deadly seriousness, of the intellectual life. Plato versus Machiavelli, Jesus versus the Grand Inquisitor — these are antagonisms that have tried modern people's souls. The arts and sciences come alive in them.

The Heart of the Educational Matter

In a collegiate context, the heart of the educational matter is a variant of the conviction of Irenaeus of Lyons that the glory of God is human beings fully alive. When an interesting pedagogue such as Jonathan Z. Smith, a former Dean of the College at the University of Chicago (where the ghost of Robert Hutchins still stalks at midnight), discourses on method in introducing college students to religious studies, his advice is to try to do a few things well, by concentrating on getting one's students to think more critically, to analyze and reason more cogently, to write more clearly than they could when they began. The specific few things that one has one's students study and the given exercises in analysis or writing matter less than a clear sense of the goal. The goal is virtually the same as what I described when glossing Newman's term, "the habit of philosophy." The goal is turning out students who know how to think.

Now, bright students will almost always think better than dull ones, regardless of what we teachers do, so when we consider our role in students' development we ought to be modest. Here I recall Lonergan's dry *obiter dictum* about insight: Insight is an act that occurs frequently among the intelligent and rarely among the stupid. Still, granted a certain level of talent, students can gain through the tutelage of us professors more than enough progress, improvement, to justify our salaries. For example, many bright students are fuzzy about the transcendental precepts. They have yet to come to appreciate the need for patient, unprecipitous, unprejudiced attention to what they are studying. Generally they are good at being intelligent, because they have strong minds, but even in the realm of insight proper we can help them by underscoring the need for good images by recalling the Aristotelian notion that understanding comes from grasping in phantasm the form organizing a given matter.

Third, and often most importantly, bright students frequently need help to appreciate the crucial distinction between insight and judgment. Where insight is direct, judgment is reflective. Where insight concerns what may be so, judgment concerns what is so — what has been verified or falsified. Finally, where insight tends to be the measure of raw intelligence, judgment is the measure of wisdom and maturity. For Lonergan, insights are a dime a dozen, judgments are the cognitional crux. And whereas many people complain about their memory, few complain about their judgment (confess themselves to be fools). All those credulous people who lose their shirts in the stock market, who get taken in by hawkers of laetrile, who succumb again to druggos with a glib tongue — all such people have bad judgment, though many of them are quite bright.

Finally, there are in Lonergan's fourth and fifth transcendental precepts (be responsible, be loving) parallel lessons awaiting elaboration by sound teachers. Once we have determined as best we can what is so, we have to ask, What therefore ought we to do about this (how reshape our theory of nuclear particles, or of the mechanisms of myeloma, or of the ways that our boyfriends get back into drinking)? And at the end of the elevation and deepening of consciousness that comes as we move from experiencing through understanding and judging to deciding, we have to deal with the significance of the overall drift, undertow, tidal movement that we find in these dynamics of our minds. Ideally, at this end we come to see that our vocation moves us toward a love of being, of what is so, that is unrestricted, universal, capable of being satisfied only by God.

However one prefers to exemplify the process of sharpening students' sense of how to analyze and think well, whatever the phrase one favors ("the habit of philosophy," "the examined life," "the mind trained to rigor"), the point is generally the same. To paraphrase the crochety professor of the old television show *The Paper Chase* when he would meet his first-year law students on opening day: "You come to me with your minds full of mush. I try to make you think like lawyers" — or physicists, or psychologists, or poets, or theologians. The mush is common. The way of introducing rigor varies from discipline to discipline. But all mature ways of studying involve paying attention, sharpening one's wits, realizing what questions one still has to answer before passing judgment, and then, at the point where life raises questions beyond those with which an academic discipline may rest content, deciding what one's responsibilities are and setting one's decision in the context of one's overall spiritual movement, one's foundational Platonic *zetesis,* toward the divine beyond.

Let a student of decent talent simply get involved with a worthy problem, one sufficiently important yet also sufficiently delimited to suit the student's present capability, and the process of learning can begin with a realism, an authenticity, that shows directly, without any need for extrinsic preaching, how inextricable good thinking is from good living. Certainly, just as people with right order in their souls do not live to eat but rather eat to live, so people with right order in their souls do not live to think but rather think to live. Nonetheless, thinking is at least as central and pleasurable as eating. How we think, and what we choose to make the major preoccupations of our minds throughout our lives, determine a great deal of what we become.

There is no responsible disjunction of thinking from feeling or loving. The same eros that takes us out of ourselves in response to an elegant mathematical equation or a profound theologoumenon takes us out of ourselves in response to a handsome face or figure. The delight of the mind in learning, clearest usually in children digging abstractedly at the beach or working puzzles at Montessori school, is a natural sign of our human vocation. To recall Aristotle again, all human beings by nature desire to know. Indeed, research, study, and education in general will soon appear to be natural, will quickly show their connatural rightness, if we can lead students to experience through such occupations that they are becoming themselves more and more.

Yes, it is hard to overestimate the laziness of many students, the swiftness with which they turn traitor when spring brings the first warm days of sun. And it is hard to fight the cynical pragmatism afoot everywhere, grumbling that metaphysics never made anyone a dime. On the teacher's side, though, is the basic mechanism of the human makeup. We human beings have to know, if we are to survive. It is as natural for the infant to explore the world, probe the significance of her toes and stick her splayed fingers into her daddy's beard, as it is for her to eat and sleep and fill her diaper. The theological correlative is the hope, perhaps even the optimism, to which Christian faith binds us: "Where sin abounded, grace has abounded the more," and "Grace builds on nature." No place is not a presence of God. God has abandoned no human mind or heart. God wants the life of the sinner, not his death. God wants us to leave our simple ways and work hard for wisdom. At the most discouraging times of the academic calendar, when the grind and the flu have gotten all parties down, it is well to remember this positive Christian slant encouraging the process.

What we do in higher education is congruous with what we are as human beings. Our work at learning befits how we have been made. Though, as Shakespeare saw, knowledge makes a bloody entrance and, as Aeschylus saw, madness is rife, the difficulties of gaining wisdom — realism, mental health — do not take away the joys. Thus from the beginning of the Psalter we learn that the just person delights in meditating on the law of God day and night — that the Torah is congenial. Thus, as Deuteronomy is sure, the behavioral ways that God has stipulated in the covenant are not far above us and beyond our reach. They are near, easy, attractive.

The good spirit moves our souls so that we can taste and see the goodness of the Lord. Wisdom is savory, tasting good down to the depths of our souls. We are made for the light, despite all the darkness in us and around us. Higher education is a small yet precious portion of the maturation that can bring us to the point where we make these traditional positive views of our human potential our own.

Wherever we begin, whatever curricular content we impose on our students, some such goal as facilitating the intellectual portion of such a maturation ought to remain canonical. In the Christian theology behind my analysis of higher education, the full maturation of any person involves feelings and actions as well as thoughts, but no responsible teachers despise thoughts — ideas, the development of their students' capacities for insight and judgment. In other sections, I have stressed the objective range of reality to which I would have undergraduates be exposed. As well, in developing that point I have added the judgment that students ought to learn not only how current cosmology sketches the natural world, or how current historical studies view the place of Alexander the Great, but also how astrophysicists think and work, how historians go about their revisions and reevaluations. Here I have stressed the second sort of enrichment: education in how professionals think that the mind works best in their field. But I do not mean to retract my prior emphasis on the four irreducible realms of reality to which I think all students ought to be exposed, in the study of which I think all ought to be exercised.

Rather, my ideal is a curriculum that sharpens the student's mind precisely through setting up for the student an experience of how the mind works best when studying chemistry or literature or anthropology. If I have added a transcendental perspective (the precepts that apply to all knowing), the new content that this new perspective places before the student is minimal. The goal of knowing what knowing is, a main ambition of modern philosophy, remains a fine hope around which to organize one's critical evaluations of the methodological aspects of an undergraduate education, but the requisites for achieving this goal are less new courses in epistemology or cognitional theory than a heightened and broadened awareness of what actually goes on as good scientists, politicians, painters, and Scripture scholars or ethicists do their work.

The Creative Moratorium

In the traditional Hindu schema for the ideal life cycle, the first phase is studying with a guru. The objective in this phase is a deep immersion in the (Vedic) tradition. The second phase returns the disciple to the world to marry, raise children, work in business and government — in a word, contribute to keeping secular life going. Third, however, the mature person, seeing his grandchildren and the whiteness of his hair, will retire from secular business to contemplate what time ought to have taught him. In this process, he will return to the lessons he learned as a student but could not appreciate fully then, for want of practical experience. Last, if the retired contemplative is fortunate and comes to enlightenment, he can wander the world as a free spirit, giving testimony to the rightness of the traditional wisdom.

In the beginning, then, of an ideal march toward wisdom is a time of freedom from practical concerns. One can study what the best authorities of the past had to say about a given problem and learn the language involved. The full significance of any of the revered precepts depends on an experience that young people seldom have, but just by learning the traditional language, getting into their systems the key notions, they can make a good start. The old Christian pedagogues who urged memorizing key prayers, the Creed, and answers from the catechism knew that much later the words memorized in youth could return, giving the person in adult trouble good ways to focus her hurts and hopes.

The masters of prayer who counseled staying with meditation until it no longer gave satisfaction had a similar end in view. People would only be the better for having gotten a firm grasp of the intellectual content of the doctrines, images, and precepts expressing their tradition. When the Spirit moved them away from these matters, asking them to leave the upper regions of the mind and move to the regions of the heart, where love means more than knowledge, they ought to respond generously, without fear. But a John of the Cross knew that good spiritual directors were learned as well as experienced — were people who both knew the tradition and themselves tried to pray well.

Erik Erikson, the prime recent theoretician of the life cycle in American culture, made finding one's identity the principal psychological work of youth. Then, with a sense of who one was, one could form attachments to other people and start to shoulder the tasks of adulthood, which meant focusing on "generativity": the secular fruitfulness and responsibility that the Hindu schema placed in the second *ashrama* ("householdership"). For Erikson wisdom was the proper preoccupation of the final stage, but wisdom depended on one's having acquired the necessary prior virtues. Certainly, one could speak of wisdom at the stage of youth, as one could speak of identity at the stage of old age, but the proportions tended to vary. What youth could contribute to a successful old age, a happy ending of one's passage through personal time, was a solid formation in who one was as Jane Doe, who any Sally X or Tony Y was as a human being.

What I find common in these slightly different schemata for thinking about an ideal maturation is the implication if not explicit request that youth be allowed some freedom from practical concerns, so as to explore what lies ahead of it and what the most revered authorities have said about the best ways to proceed. From time to time all human beings can profit from sabbaticals (periods when they are free from ordinary work), and so the traditional Chinese tried to build in a sabbatical time parallel to that which India put in the third *ashrama* (forest-dwelling) by requiring that adult children mourn for three years at the death of their parents. The death of one's parents is a natural time for contemplating one's own end and progress. Freed of ordinary social obligations, the truly filial child would mourn at length in order to get deep into his or her marrow the sure end of all human flesh.

Granted, these schemata have something idyllic about them, and we should never forget the millions of children who have been set to work as soon as their little fingers could weave or stack or gather. Indeed, they are with us to this day in many third world countries. Nonetheless, when we can we should honor the kinder and wiser tradition of leaving children free for at least ten years after they reach the age of reason, so that they can study the traditions that form their particular culture. It may help if we remember that traditional Jewish boys studied the Talmud intensively, as traditional Islamic boys worked on the Koran. In the process they picked up many of the tricks of memorizing and analyzing, of how to place a text in context and sift through the traditional interpretations for the one currently most apt, that would serve them well later, in their work and their parenting. Indeed, whatever they did later, Jewish men tended to be haunted by these early years and the ideal of becoming wise about Torah. Thus Tevye the Dairyman mused rather mournfully that if he were a rich man he would study at leisure. Thus perhaps the most touching expression of misogynism in traditional Jewish culture was the prohibition on girls' studying Torah (a prohibition with poignant analogues in traditional Hindu, Muslim, and Christian cultures).

Take what lessons you will from this anecdotal support that I would adduce for making what for us Americans are the traditional college years (ages seventeen to twenty-two) free for liberal studies. What generations of poor immigrants to America took as the most crucial lesson was the value of working hard at unattractive jobs so that their children might study and do better. Yes, often this parental ambition and motivation was practical, in that "doing better" meant becoming qualified in medicine or law or some other competence that held good prospects for wealth and prestige. But mixed in was often a reverence for more contemplative learning, which helped to make parents willing to let sons go into the rabbinate or the priesthood. Joined with the prestige that these occupations (and, *mutatis mutandis*, religious life for women) carried as holy, as thought to be bearing more directly on God than did secular occupations, was the prestige that they carried as entailing higher studies — refinements befitting gentlemen. The prospect of having a child become a scholar pleased many lower- and middle-class immigrants, even though it did not prevent them from mocking the impracticality that the prospective scholar might display on occasion.

The prospective scholar, in turn, tended to feel some pressure from the sacrifice of his or her parents — pressure to appreciate what they had paid, in various ways, so that this opportunity for study could come about. Yet such young scholars also tended to find, often to their pain, that their higher studies took them away from the commonsensical worldview that had served their parents, both well and ill, even in the areas of religion. Callow students could for some years look down on the peasant ways of their parents, but as experience brought maturation a more nuanced judgment tended to emerge. What Lonergan has called "intellectual conversion" does tend to separate those who experience it through higher studies from people who remain limited to common sense. In its final stages, however, such a conversion brings us to the unknowability of God, and so it is quite humbling, and so it tends ultimately to make us appreciate better any of our elders who have survived with grace. Still, at intermediate points intellectual conversion to the transcendental precepts, especially those concerning judgment, may make us feel like outsiders, strangers, even in familial places where but a few years ago we felt completely at home.

Students who are going to become significantly informed, possessed of reflective appreciation, and articulate about the conditions for wisdom and the substance that must go into it need a rich experience of precisely this feeling of estrangement or alienation. Between unreflective common sense and enlightenment comes a time of unease, of feeling that the world has turned over and rocks are no longer rocks. Old ways, accepted unthinkingly from childhood, have fallen apart. New ways, capable of taking one across the stream of experience to wisdom, have yet to make a full appearance or fully take hold. The result is a soreness of soul, at times even a panic of mind, reminiscent of the dark night of the senses that John of the Cross describes. What we used to rely on has let us down. We know that the unexamined life of the cave, as Plato pictures it in the *Republic*, is not worth living, but we have yet to understand why, yet to see our way clear to a better human being. If we persevere, we shall almost always begin to get such a clearer vision — find our channel, sail into a harbor that promises to provide for us well. But sensitive teachers realize that the creative moratorium that college ought to provide can be extremely painful for good students. Far from being a time to laze out and guzzle beer at the frat house, it ought frequently to amount to major surgery on the student's soul.

One ought not to undergo major surgery lightly, nor perform it at the flick of a wrist. Equally, one ought to be warned that the healing process can be lengthy. Perhaps the humanities are the most perilous courses, along with some aspects of theology (I am thinking of J. B. Metz's "dangerous memory" of Jesus), because they are the ones that bring students face to face with themselves most abruptly. Perhaps in those parts of the curriculum courses should carry warning labels: "Buyer beware," or "Caution: Drinking this liquor can be dangerous to your worldly health."

The Contemplative Colony

Higher education ought to provide not just youthful students but also the culture at large with the fruits that only grow in contemplative moratoria. This aspect of higher education is clearest on the graduate level, where research, investigations holding the promise of developing new knowledge, hold sway. Certainly, what collegiate teachers do in laboring for the intellectual conversion of their students contributes significantly to the overall quotient of reflectiveness, contemplative awareness, and potential wisdom that a given culture possesses. But the more advanced cultures, those with the greatest resources available to support expensive ventures in government, commerce, scientific research, and fine arts, tend to depend on full-time researchers, many of whom dwell in universities.

What teaching such full-time researchers do tends to take the form of directing graduate students and be rather informal. It is by working in revered Professor X's lab that the fledgling biochemist learns her craft. It is by participating in Professor Y's famous seminar and writing a serious paper that the fledgling history scholar passes from undergraduate work to the doctoral level. The young medievalist portrayed in Frank Conroy's novel *Body and Soul* shows us the excitement that this transformation can generate. Once she was living an unhappy life as a spoiled little rich girl. Now she is lean but happy, poor but convinced that her work more than justifies her poverty.

When the intellectual life first captivates our souls, we can enjoy transports of joy. This is what we were made for. This can give us a beautiful reason to be. We may eventually decide that we want to be teachers more than pure researchers — people who form the next generation more than people who push back the borders of present knowledge. But in the best of cases this decision will not diminish our love of the intellectual life. For what we will see ourselves offering our students is precisely an initiation into the life of the mind that has made all the difference in our own cases.

The contemplative colony housed in higher education is the cluster of researchers and teachers who provide one of the clearest foci for the life of the mind. Any society or culture in which such a colony abides without appreciation is woefully Philistine. Certainly, much good research goes on outside the groves of academe, especially in the applied sciences. And, also certainly, many supposed contemplatives within academe are teachers and researchers deficient in joy. For a variety of possible reasons, the life of the mind has lost its allure. The romance has died, with no certainty that it will be reborn again. Teachers can burn out, especially if they are asked to teach staggering loads. Researchers can be frustrated by failures in their projects or squabbles over funding. The contemplative colony housed in the university is more beholden to the world than is that tucked away in a monastery. Granted, even monasteries have their practical needs and internecine problems. But monasteries have an easier job of justifying their existence than do academic contemplatives. Monks have only to point to the existence of a God who more than justifies their paying her attention full time. It is enough therefore that they sing their offices well and not pester the laity unduly. Academic researchers have to justify their being in front of an unreligious, pragmatic audience which tends to think in terms of practical fruits. Thus Bell Labs and Merck Pharmaceuticals have employed thousands of Ph.D.s, but archeologists and modern dancers often have to scrape and bow for support.

Just as the heart of the undergraduate educational matter is not practical (preparing Johnny to become a C.E.O.), so the heart of research in either the arts or the sciences is not results that will translate into new, profitable products. In both dimensions of a healthy higher education, the heart of the matter is the pure desire to know. Even after we have made all the requisite nods to the financial, societal, and simply human factors involved, the fact remains that the core of a healthy higher education is nonprofit: a contemplation pursued for its own sake. Art is for its own sake, which is beauty. Science is for its own sake, which is knowing better the natural world. Social science can be for its own sake, which is knowing better the political realm. Theology is for its own sake, which is knowing God. When a Congress is so small-souled that it does not see the wisdom of supporting pure work in the arts and sciences as a fundamental contribution to the common good, the people whom that Congress ought to serve are in trouble. As Scripture says, without contemplation the people perish. As Jesus says, people do not live by bread alone.

In virtue of the Incarnation, Christians ought to have a clear sense of the twofoldness of their hopes and responsibilities. They ought to hope for daily bread and summer roses. They ought to feel obliged to get the poor food, shelter, medical care, education, and the other necessities of a decent human life. They also ought to feel obliged to support the arts, fund the basic sciences, appreciate the work of think tanks focused on government, and desire in their church a robust cadre of free theologians. It is not a matter of either/or. An incarnational faith seldom lets it be so simplistic. It is a matter of honoring two sets of debts, of fostering two sets of hopes.

On another occasion I should like to develop the theme that simplicity, "poverty" in the sense praised by the Matthean Jesus in the beatitudes, can make a huge contribution on both sides of this ledger. The simpler our lifestyles materially, the more compatible with the carrying capacity of the earth and a just distribution of the resources of the earth, the better our chances of fulfilling what is entailed in asking our Father for daily bread. The simpler our lifestyles materially, the less that things take up our time and squat on our attention, the better our chances of not living by bread alone. One can have a full life possessing only a garret room, a perky space heater, and two sets of clothes. One has to eat, but bread, water, and vegetables continue to be relatively cheap. For twenty-five dollars one can purchase hours of wonderful recorded music playable on inexpensive equipment. For less than that one can get first-rate sheet music for one's little flute. In many cities for five dollars one can spend a day among masterpieces of art. Some natural science entails high expense, but some mathematics continues to require only a pencil and paper. The same for virtually all poetry. And prayer (religious rather than academic contemplation)? Prayer doesn't need beautiful chapels, though many people who pray love to haunt them. Prayer can make do with any scene worth contemplating: the sun or the rain, the bum on the corner or the grand lady showing sable.

In the crucial showdown between time and money, contemplatives are wont to choose time. Indeed, a measure of their purity is their inclination to love the process of their work more than its products. Finished, a great writer such as Patrick White often can barely stomach his book, though later it may cheer him from time to time. He writes because he has to — because of what he finds, what happens to him, in the doing. The same for the dancer or the musician or the runner of rats who burns to know why they can get through his maze.

So late nights and early mornings, when the bustle tends to be low and quiet invites the mind to clarity for purer work, are the times beloved in the contemplative colony. This can make for little sleep, or for writing off the noonday as time for the devil — the cleaning, the shopping, the work on committees, the nap. The great contemplative need is for psychic space and leisure. Josef Pieper's thesis that leisure is the basis of culture remains persuasive. For all that contemplatives can profit from rubbing elbows with the hoi polloi, the gist of contemplative creativity remains lonely, leisurely thinking.

In the contemplative colony, creative work is both the justification and the therapy. Shamans who do not shamanize tend to sicken. Painters who do not paint, poets who do not write, monks who do not pray tend to drink. The scientist who hates her lab is in trouble. The teacher who turns up his nose at the classroom has lost it. Good work, the kind that we wish for all our friends, is a blessing and a healing. Because of it we have better things to do than surf the net for pornography. We do not care about making a killing on Wall Street. Granted food and shelter for those in our care, we want only to be left free to do what challenges us, what calls forth our best talent, what gives us our most defensible satisfactions. If diagnosis is our great gift, we want most to study puzzling patients. If administration is our talent, we want most the chance to whip a worthy group into shape. The forms of good work in which we exercise ultimately intuitive gifts are more numerous than the kinds of laboratories in the science building or the labels on carrels in the library. But common to all creative works is an itch, an inner potential, that we see best when we reflect quietly late at night.

Like the examination of conscience essential in the religious life, a more general reflection at bedtime or sunrise can tell any creative worker how to get back on course. More broadly, for any society as a whole the contemplative colony ought to serve as an esteemed monitor and conscience. Where would we be ecologically, had we not been forced to heed the voices of Rachel Carson and others studying the state of our lands, our waters, our air? Where would we be politically, if no Cesar Chavez or Martin Luther King, Jr., or Elie Wiesel, or Nadine Gordimer had cried out from the throes of a ruthless contemplation of the people's perishing? Where we are ecologically and politically is far from ideal, but at least we are not fully deadened in conscience. At least we have a minimal scientific, historical, and moral awareness of the consequences of the choices that we have been making. So whereas the academic contemplative colony as such is not directly prophetic, any clear-eyed, detached, uncoopted view of the health or sickness of our human performances in any of the four zones of reality calls the people to account. As the relationship between Lonergan's third and fourth precepts has it, after having been reasonable we all have to be responsible. After judgment comes decision.

Administration

Administrators in higher education ought to see themselves as the facilitators of the prosecution of the vision compelling their institution. If the vision comes from Christian theology, they ought to see themselves as the servants of the servants of Christian intellectualism. Teachers are servants of intellectualism, for that is what we should want them to foster in their students. Researchers are servants of intellectualism, for that is what their research boils down to. Administrators are those charged with smoothing the way for teachers to teach and researchers to work at the edge of old knowledge, in the nursery of new knowledge. This can be a thankless charge, when professors are churlish snobs all but snapping their fingers for the *garçon* to replenish their water. It can be a rewarding charge when a department or a college starts to hum like a good machine, when all the pieces start to work together harmoniously.

The best educational administrators are people who might have succeeded as full-time teachers or researchers. In the best of cases, they have agreed to work as administrators because they can see such work as facilitating the common good. As well, often they are intrigued by the relatively mild version of politics that tends to develop on college campuses. As one wag has put it, the battles are so intense because the stakes are so small. But even when the stakes are small in material terms, professors can feel that they are debating matters of considerable spiritual moment. And even when professors are wrong as well as petty, they make interesting studies in human nature. For like many students, professors tend to be bright and idealistic. And, like many alumni, over the years they can become savvy, especially if their studies have focused on the ways of the world. So trying to get professors to cooperate, compromise, and keep their eye on the ball can be a fascinating business. Despite the 10 percent who create 90 percent of the problems, the professorate can furnish a good field for managerial skills.

As I have stated, I believe that the best polity in local affairs is a consultative monarchy. By "local affairs" I mean a political unit small enough to allow leaders to know their constituents yet large enough to generate an estimable impact. The "consultative" part of my best polity is an effort to assure the most desirable aspects of democracy: the full contribution of the gifts of all involved, the full representation of the needs of all involved. The "monarchical" part is an effort to provide for decisiveness: a clear locus of adequate authority. Many good collaborative projects die aborning for want of an adequate execution. Some ill-advised projects come into being through lack of a properly consultative birth control, but others continue on respirators because no one has the authority or the guts to pull the plug. I want an administrative situation in which the two sides of this equation balance. So have wanted all the educational administrators I hold before myself as models.

It helps an administrator to be good with numbers. It helps even more for her to have a drift, a habit of mind, toward trying constantly though peacefully to improve the conditions for her charges' flourishing. In the case of a department head in a college, the charges are both faculty members and students. The courses that the department offers have overall to reflect the objective contours of the discipline and the subjective needs of both the teachers and the students. Usually the result is a compromise. There are other courses that the department would offer, in an ideal world. There is a better expression of the professors' talents and a better meeting of the students' legitimate interests. But with a decent exercise of consultative monarchism a respectable curriculum usually results. Those consulted provide both input and feedback. The monarch adjudicates disputes and looks out for the good of the whole. As well, he or she finally bites the bullet and decrees the end of the time for debate, the advent of the time for voting and executing.

Administrators tend to be the ones who represent the college or university to the "outside" world. To them fall the tasks of raising funds, generating good publicity, recruiting students, deciding on projects of community service, maintaining the loyalty of alumni, and so forth. If college athletics come to stink of irregularity, even criminality, the administrators in charge are most to blame, including the college presidents. If the public at large is unwilling to support the college, what blame attaches to the college itself becomes a burden to administrators more than others. Teachers ought first to teach. Researchers ought first to do research. Students ought first to study. Each has some political responsibilities, and so some political rights, but the first responsibility in each case is for the given workers to do well their given works. When professors lust to be politicos rather than stars in the contemplative colony, disorder gathers on the horizon like a dark cloud. The same for when students spend more time at demonstrations than at their books. Occasionally the times require an outpouring of political representation. Arguably, moments during the Vietnam War or the Civil Rights movement were such times. But if agitation, demonstration, becomes business as usual, a college is wobbling. (Equally, if serenity stems from inertness rather than passionate concern for study, the college is wobbling.)

The advantage of espying all this from the administrator's crow's nest is the chance to take in the whole scene. Administrators can get a fuller picture than any of the other players. They can gather a better appreciation of all the twists and turns. No political entity is without its pulls and counterpulls, its factions warring benignly or bitterly. Virtually by definition a "political entity," a body social, embraces enough differences to guarantee conflicts. The task of the administrator is to make such conflicts as constructive as possible. Frequently putting the opposing parties together in the same room can bring about a dialectical progress. The old guard gets the chance to display the wisdoms in its conservatism. The young turks get the chance to make their case that the times they are achanging. Those who feel that the rights of the discipline are in peril can try to show how or why that is so. Those who feel that the needs of the students are being ignored can also try to show how or why that is so. More often than not, the result of such meetings is better understanding all the way around. More often than not, when all the major issues have reached the table, the group can adjust its policies so as to take account of a new, better representation of the realities in question.

Administration at its best offers those trying to practice it a fine school in realism. Teachers may not have to concern themselves with fundraising, in fact, should not concern themselves greatly, but administrators generally do. Teachers can wait for students to show up and fill their classrooms — because administrators have recruited them. Yes, teachers can, should be able to, say that their fine work gives the recruiters a good product to sell, but without sufficient sales the college will go under. Properly understood, the bottom line offers a solid dose of realism. Similarly, the place of the administrator at the crossroads of several operational lines tends to give her a good view of all the traffic. Interestingly, for all the equality of their right to teach in the core curriculum, humanists, social scientists, natural scientists, and theologians come from different angles and may as groups have distinctive personalities. There are no hard and fast rules in this matter, just as there are no sureties that surgeons will be choleric and psychiatrists will be flaky. But social scientists often speak the worst jargon, while professors of English and history have been the worst politicians on several campuses where I have worked. The high salaries paid to professors in law or business, compared to those paid professors in the liberal arts, let alone to the salaries paid to staff members, tend to cause considerable resentment. As in Orwell's *Animal Farm*, all animals are equal but some are more equal than others — doublespeak with a vengeance.

The (relatively) high salaries paid to administrators call for a justification in terms of their making the whole operation profitable in several senses. Administrators have more to say about the marketing of the educational product than do workers in the classroom. They also have more to say about the atmosphere of the workplace as a whole. They take more guff, develop more ulcers, and have to develop tougher hides. Academics often have tongues sharper than their consciences. The gossip can be dismissive and bilious. Administrators bear a greater brunt of this nastiness than do professors' academic peers.

However, the dyspepsia sometimes signal in the professorate is simply a potential ready to hand and hard to stomach in all human gatherings. The saints are few, and few sinners appreciate us as we think they should. The upside of being an administrator is (1) coming home at night with fewer illusions than some of one's colleagues and (2) enjoying the chance to help other people flourish. The generativity that I mentioned above, when reflecting on Erik Erikson's sense of the tasks of middle age, finds a good outlet in administration. There one has the chance to care for an enterprise for which one feels a great affection, even a great sense of debt. (This same motivation can work wonders in ecclesiastical administration.) Working from that affection and sense of debt, it is easy to remember that the name of the good administrative game is not power for self-aggrandizement. The name of the good administrative game is a tough, realistic, yet kindly service.

Conclusion

The Problem of Vision

We are rounding the corner and heading for home, Cigar demolishing the field in the Belmont. Our task has been to elaborate a Christian theological essay on higher education. After introducing the project, we have ruminated our way through four major realms of reality, all of them begging representation in a solid, humanistic undergraduate curriculum. Then, in the prior chapter, we took a second theological look at education — the project we had outlined in our introductory reflections. Now the task is to conclude, by dealing with some of the questions that I hope have become clearer through our expository work to this point. This first of these questions concerns vision — the pertinence of a theology (or a philosophy) of higher education.

We may consider the "problem" of vision from two perspectives. The first is practical, a matter of common sense. The second is theoretical, a matter of critical understanding. Concerning the first perspective, the practical, I must say that at many colleges the rhetoric in the catalogue is both fine-sounding and ignored. It is a fine thing to speak of offering students a well-rounded education and developing their capacity to think critically. It is quite another thing to accomplish these goals by moving students through a curriculum structured precisely to achieve them.

Concerning the second, theoretical perspective, my experience is not that colleges are too idealistic. My experience is that most don't know what they are doing, don't have a firm grasp of what "educated" ought to mean. So, in the persons of their administrative leaders, colleges waffle and posture and slink away to "management" models developed for corporate businesses. For example, few college presidents or chairmen of the board of trustees will say frankly that the community is cutting off its nose to spite its face if it refuses to fund basic research. Few college presidents will act on their knowledge that the football team is a financial

198

and moral liability. Few such leaders really believe that classics or theology or abstract art ought to have a place in a humanistic curriculum regardless of its pragmatic, cash value. Increasingly, boards of trustees are composed of people from business who think of educational administrators as managers. Increasingly, the blind are leading the blind and both are veering toward the pit.

Vision, a clear sense of what we want to do, is the *sine qua non* of a collegiate venture. Unless those collaborating in the venture know the final cause of their common work, they are bound to feel that they are stabbing in the dark. The proper final cause, in my view, is producing students educated well, which I take to mean educated liberally, through their concentrating on the arts and sciences. Whatever conduces to this end ought to enjoy a positive prejudice, which is not the same as a carte blanche. Whatever we cannot defend in view of this end ought to be put on the defensive, thought likely to disappear soon.

What we teach and how we teach it ought to square with where we think we are going, with what we think we are trying to achieve. My argument that we ought to teach students the basic contours of objective reality and expose them to the main modes of critical investigation that researchers in each realm of objective reality report are most apt follows from a vision of the whole of human experience and divine creation.

If you want responsibly to propose a curriculum radically different from the one that I have proposed, you will have to expose and defend a radically different vision. Unless you are not a Christian, you will, I think, be hard pressed to do this. And if you are not a Christian, and so are inclined to propose a curriculum that excludes divinity (in virtue of your not thinking this fourth realm credible), you will still have to make your case rationally, against all the shamans, prophets, and sages down the ages who have said that your view is bunk — less a faithful report of what is so than a commentary on your own inadequacies.

Thus discussions of "vision," are not always mild and genteel. Debating about vision can provoke a war of worlds, a clash of faiths, that can hire apocalyptic imagery. Because of differences in their visions that now strike many theologians as minute, Protestants and Catholics slaughtered one another by the thousands during the Hundred Years War. Because of differences in their visions of slavery and a common willingness to let slavery become the overriding symbol of their wider disagreements, northern and southern citizens of the United States killed millions and nearly destroyed the union of which they had been so proud after the Revolution. So vision, what we see or believe that we see, can be all important. From defective intellectual vision, as I see it, fundamentalists the world over live in what is objectively, but not necessarily subjectively, bad faith — in ignorance that easily strikes the liberally educated believer as willful and so culpable. For want of vision, most colleges originally Christian but now de facto secular have failed to see that they were losing their heritage by forfeiting their fealty to the Creed. (Other colleges, of course, have failed to see the changes that modernity has been right to demand of them, and so have become religious ghettos.)

The sadness that I feel at this point stems from watching the capitulation of good schools, both Christian and secular, to the pragmatism of recent times and noting their concomitant loss of a persuasive vision of their enterprise. Few deans or provosts have had the wit or guts to force showdowns over what the curricula in their schools ought to be intending. More often than not, the situation on the ground, in the trenches, is that the generals do not know where they are going. As a result, their trumpet is uncertain. The desirable alternative is not a tyrannical voluntarism, big daddy saying do what I say because I say it. The desirable alternative is establishing as leaders, those with the crucial say, people who are visionary because they are themselves well educated.

Correlatively, it would be a blessing were people who are not well educated, who do not have a grasp of the whole that is broad and deep, humble enough to refuse to assume positions of crucial responsibility. It would also be a blessing were people who are well educated to realize in their mature years that generativity may require them to assume positions of leadership and responsibility. In due time, the best and the brightest have to let themselves be offered as candidates for key positions, have to allow themselves to be made bishops by acclamation. Ambrose of Milan acceded to the will of the local people in this way, becoming the spiritual father of Augustine. Astute members of boards of trustees in colleges would think up analogous ways of consulting the faithful in matters of educational leadership.

My vision of higher education depends on my Christian theology, which I understand traditionally to be my faith seeking understanding. My faith considers Jesus to be as Schillebeeckx has described him: the (nonpareil) sacrament of our encounter with God. In virtue of this consideration my theology comes quickly to an incarnational view of reality that differentiates itself into the four realms that I have worked over repeatedly. Inasmuch as a Christian version of the classical Greek *paideia* can see education as the development of the potential that Christ has revealed our human makeup to possess, I think that we Christian educators can set our students to their humanistic, political, scientific, and theological studies with confidence that we are showing them the full range of God's reality.

As well, I think that we Christian educators can claim as our own the classical goal of coming to consider nothing human foreign to us. Certainly, the history of ideas suggests that after modernity we must deal explicitly with constantly reformed versions of the critical questions developed in the Enlightenment. Especially relevant still are: How do we know, and how do we know that our knowing is trustworthy? In my view, we answer both of these "critical" (Kantian) questions best by intellectual doing. I would have us educators not let our students get lost in detached debates about how to bridge the gap between subject and object but rather observe carefully, participatively, how bright people make their way in the theoretical and practical worlds.

For example, our physicists do know the atomic world, well enough at least to have been able to detonate atomic bombs and devastate Japanese cities, so they, we, can know the atomic world. We human beings overall do know other people well enough, at least now and then, to become successful friends, lovers, parents, bosses. Therefore, we can know other people adequately. The same form of argument reminds us that saints have come to know God well enough to have been made holy, so human beings can know God sufficiently to become holy.

When we take on the modern burden of epistemology, therefore, we need not capitulate to skepticism from the outset. If we do know in some circumstance, we can know. *Ab esse ad posse valet illatio.* The oracle at Delphi challenged all supplicants to know themselves. Through the mercy of God many addicts have answered this challenge and reformed their lives. Therefore, a significant self-knowledge is possible, and the oracle was not setting us an impossible task. In the process of accomplishing it, numerous people have become well educated, coming to see that to know themselves they had to know God and the world that God has made. Therefore, a successful education is possible — we can realize our visions.

This lesson, so obvious as to be embarrassing, leads me to suggest that we ought to pay more attention to our successes than usually we do. It ought to be a high priority for us to identify biographically the kinds of intellectuals we want to produce. Is the late Lewis Thomas a worthy model of a well-educated person who happened to specialize successfully in biomedical research, specifically immunology? If so, then why do we not analyze how he got to be that way and make our analysis into a first draft, a beginning model, for when we take up the task of educating well biologists coming along two generations after him? Did a Karl Rahner or an Yves Congar or a Raymond Brown develop into an admirable theologian by accident, or was there something replicable in his education, a lesson for all places and times? How did Barbara Mikulski move from being my classmate at the Institute of Notre Dame in Baltimore to being a U.S. Senator? What is the lesson for aspirant politicians there? If these questions make sense in specific contexts, why don't we educators gather them together so as to formulate a more general sense of what in the world we want to achieve? It is not enough to content ourselves with platitudes about critical thinking. It is incumbent on us to spell out, nail down, what we want to achieve — in my view, students who become Christian intellectuals — and how we are going to structure curricula that do this.

The educational vision that I seek is therefore both theoretical and practical. It opens before us a vista of what we should want to explore and a catalogue of ways and means to do our exploring. I do not see why it is rare to find a college unified around a vision of the comprehensive reality that it ought to have students investigate, of the methods of inquiry in which it ought to exercise students, and of how it ought to let competent faculty members in each curricular realm go about deciding the specific requirements best suited to their accomplishing their part of the educational task. These do not seem to me bits of esoteric wisdom, arcane insights known only to a gnostic few. They seem to me just simple precepts of common sense combined with an adult grasp of the intellectual significance of Christian revelation. So I have to ask, at what point does our apparent blindness become at least a suggestion, perhaps even an accusation, that we have mired Christian higher education in sin — loss of faith and courage?

Social Support

To raise the question of how to find or garner sufficient social support for a humanistic Christian theological enterprise in higher education is to unsheath a two-edged sword. Along one side runs the cutting matter of whether the counterculturalism of authentic Christianity condemns it to being marginal. Karl Rahner faced this issue by wondering whether in the future Christians would not find themselves in new diaspora. Along the other side runs an equally sharp challenge to elaborate an intellectual version of the good news that will honor the natural fit between Christian faith and the human soul ("the soul is naturally Christian," many of the Hellenistic fathers thought). In that case, lack of response may indicate that we have done our job badly, not showing as we should have how beautiful is the mind that our Christian higher education would develop.

Seeking social support, educators tend to receive a sobering set of lessons. Many alumni who have prospered financially have become conservative politically and religiously. Many other potential supporters have been breathing the air of pragmatism so long that they cough when exposed to Christian idealism. Educators therefore hear few nay-sayings when they propose developing schools of law or engineering. When they propose developing contemplative colonies focused on the arts and sciences, they may see many faces go blank. This is not to say that there are no longer patrons for the arts or lovers of good theology. It is only to face up to the obvious. In the wake of Ronald Reagan, intellectualism has a hard time of it in American culture.

All the more so is this the case when one's intellectualism makes one allergic to ideology, averse to joining a partisan camp. I have been over some of this ground before. Suffice it to say here, where the issue is how to present what we educators are doing to the wider public whose support we need, that sometimes we face a difficult problem. It would be much eased if we could be simplistic, paint the world in black and white. But we cannot be simplistic, must insist on maintaining some nuance, because that is reality as we contemplate it. For instance, in many church circles I find myself having to defend feminism, while in many feminist circles I find myself having to defend religion. For further instance, I suspect that some readers of this book will think my educational proposals very conservative while others will think them radically idealistic. From the regularity of finding myself in cross-cut situations such as these, I've come to think that while sometimes it is a badge of honor to be accounted one who calls for a plague on both erring houses, other times it may well be a sign that one has become idiosyncratic.

Voegelin's sense of "ideology" consigned it to "secondary reality." As he saw it, philosophy (the traditional Socratic love of wisdom), is concerned with primary reality (the four irreducible zones that Voegelin elaborated and I have described). Philosophy, or honest intellectualism in general, therefore could not be ideological. Always it had to give primacy to what people actually experience, to how reality actually presents itself, rather than to any theory — Christian as well as Marxist or Pragmatist or Capitalist — of how reality has to be.

In the case of Christian ideologues, usually ranged on the right, occasionally on the left, the problem that Voegelin saw often was a reification of biblical or creedal symbols. Christian ideologues tended to tear formulas or tropes from their original evocative contexts of faith and try to make them into propositions that "orthodox" thinkers could manipulate in a supposedly scientific game. This led to proof-texting and the exaltation of an extrinsic magisterial authority. A theological positivism entered in, due to a loss of the influence of the mystics. An impoverished form of scholasticism and a growing influence of canon law made outsiders come to consider "dogma" a dirty word. All of this (I have elaborated beyond Voegelin's own reflections on reification) devolution in the Christian sensitivity to religious symbols has made theology vulnerable to being coopted, or rejected out of hand, by a modern mind dominated by empiricism and rationalism. Michael Buckley's studies of the rise of atheism from the sterility of modern Christian theology make the same point. Theology lost its nerve and began to try to square God's circle.

At any rate, the right-wing Christian groups who want to police lectures and articles, reading everywhere violations of orthodoxy, seem to me but ironic and painful counterparts to the leftist groups who monitor political correctness. I do not understand why adults would not be embarrassed to let themselves be bullied by such people, whose grasp of the spiritual life obviously is tenuous. For you cannot know much about the spiritual life and not be taken away by its mysteriousness. You cannot deal with a real God and not come to a great respect for negative theology. I have heard right-wing young priests say that we should make no distinction between God and the church. How is that not a violation of the first commandment? How is that not a flunking of the penny catechism? Equally, however, I have heard in faculty lounges village atheists blathering on as though it were unquestionable that God is dead and life has no great significance. That there are data suggesting that many understandings of "God" are dead and that the question of afterlife is moot on the grounds of reason—these seem to me clear. But that contemporary intellectuals are crazy to pay any mind to theology—that seems to me just stupid.

If any of this nonideological moderateness is persuasive as a mark of the well-educated Christian, then you can see the sophistication that becomes requisite when educators venture off their campuses in search of support from the wider community. What we do in a properly Christian higher education makes us frown on new age spiritualities, thinking them all imagination and no critical judgment. It also makes us frown on purely pragmatic extrapolations from "what works"—brings a higher return on one's investments. If the cross of Christ does not remain at the center of our theological vision, one day we shall stand before God accused of having denied our Lord. Yet some versions of liberation theology abuse the cross of Christ, canonizing the poor as though they were bound to be holy and wise. I sympathize greatly with leaders who must face all this complexity when trying to raise funds and explain what their college is trying to do. Although more than once I have found myself criticizing such leaders for tending to err on side of accommodation to worldly values, I have no great confidence that I would do their job better.

All the more so is this the case when educators face opposition from church officials as well as, or in league with, captains of industry. Christian higher education cannot become the captive of *any* power group, *any* ideology, without starting to feel like a whore. Nor is this an idle danger. There are good reasons why some critics think that the term "Christian higher education" is an oxymoron. Usually such critics argue that faith requires a sacrifice of the intellect that is not moral. In other words, they think that one cannot honestly be both a believer and a scholar (one free to follow the evidence wherever it leads.) At other times such critics argue a reversed version of the same thesis: The modern university has become intrinsically secular; therefore, to preserve faith one has to abjure the canons of the humanistic, or social scientific, or natural scientific disciplines.

In both cases, the proper counterproof lies less in rhetoric than in providing living examples to the contrary. If many Christian believers are in fact first-rate intellectuals, then the claim that Christian intellectualism is impossible is bogus. So I would stress that our solicitations of outside support create occasions when we should actually demonstrate Christian intellectualism to those we are wooing. If we set up occasions when our best professors can explain their work, our best students can explain their enthusiasms, we shall be both telling the truth and putting our best foot forward. Beyond nostalgia lies an appeal to alumni and other potential patrons of Christian higher education that spotlights the distinctiveness of the Christian vision. Such an appeal could, for example, show the Christian reasons why people in our midst love to study the Milky Way or the court portraits of Goya or Beethoven's late quartets. They love to do works such as these because at the end of the day they can feel that they have been contemplating luminaries of God's creation. They count nothing human foreign to them because everything human bears to them a message from the God they find disclosed most beautifully and adequately in Jesus the Christ.

Lifelong Learning

Such a presentation would be in effect a gentle seminar on lifelong learning. We would be reminding our potential supporters of the resources we have for turning students on to an entire way of life. If our teachers count nothing human foreign to them because their Christian intellectualism has made them feel at home in the whole wide world, then many of our graduates may come to feel this way, not closing their books with a bang on graduation day but looking forward to reading new ones. We have succeeded with our students when we have helped them to fall in love with learning. Our most honest pitch to our potential supporters is that we are good at doing this — making this match, setting up this love. Our job is to show the beauty of the beloved suitable for our students: the world as come from God. If we can do this and equip our charges with the gifts for making their way to this beloved, we can count ourselves a success. Dante spending his life trying to measure up to Beatrice is a relevant symbol. Augustine spending his life responding to the voice from heaven that bid him "pick it [the Bible] up and read" is another. On first looking into Chapman's Homer, or first coming to appreciate Aquinas on grace, or first watching an excellent surgeon at work one's mind can be charged for the rest of one's life.

In my province of the curriculum, the intrigue is to try to bring students to realize why Jesus or the Buddha or Muhammad or Confucius was so alluring to his contemporaries. Why did those who heard them think that no one had ever spoken so persuasively, so graciously, as they? For traditional Muslims the eloquence of the Koran is a major proof of its divinity. For traditional Christians, the parables of Jesus reveal depths of humanity that one can find on no other tours. Traditional Buddhists take refuge in the Buddha, the Dharma (Teaching), and the Sangha (Community), because these are three "jewels" available nowhere else. Confucius became *the* authority in traditional China because his words mediated the teachings of the prehistoric sages better than any others.

There is an intrigue in all these great deposits of religious wisdom, and also in the psychodynamics of how they come to be recanonized generation after generation. So it has not been enough for Jewish rabbis to say that the highest task is studying Torah (Talmud). Unless each generation found such study self-justifying, a love radiant in its own life and times, the saying would soon ring hollow. Analogously, why does Jesus never go out of fashion among serious Christians? How does the centrality of Jesus in the Christian message create the hermeneutical circle that justifies faith in him at the beginning and rewards it tenfold at the end? And what does this centrality, which is also an inexhaustible riches (in Paul's view), mean for a lifelong Christian intellectualism? How does the love of understanding one's faith open vistas with which we are never bored, contemplating which we always find more to study than we have time or energy to pursue?

The key, I think, is mystery — the surplus of meaning that both excites our minds and defeats them — so that we can abandon ourselves to the divine mercy. And the special selling point for a Christian higher education is that no one does mystery better than we do, no doctrine of God is more gripping or sophisticated. In virtue of the Incarnation, the unique Christian doctrine, the Christian mind takes on a character, at once analogical, dialectical, and mystical (or mystagogical), as I have said, that is quite distinctive. All flesh is grass, even the flowers thereof, yet all flesh is also anointed for divine gladness. Flesh itself is how God has made his, her, its foremost dwelling among us. The Word of God took flesh and dwelt among us, full of grace and truth. Jesus became (sinful) flesh, identifying God with us utterly intrinsically. Therefore, we have the right to believe, which sometimes turns into the most daunting challenge, that nothing can separate us from the love of God in Christ Jesus our Lord. Therefore, we can meet our need to believe, which sometimes turns into the most wonderful joy, that God loves us unconditionally, because of God's own goodness, not our works or merits.

There is nothing in our experience foreign to God, nothing that Jesus our high priest did not learn, often painfully. Our flesh, which often we sully, and our minds, which every day show us limits and cracks, and even our hearts, which occasionally condemn us, are not our final measure. Even when our hearts do condemn us, God is greater. Always, God is greater, so always there are grounds for hope. And, with grounds for hope, we can always try to pick ourselves up, stop our whining, get on with it again. Neither death nor life nor angels nor principalities nor things past nor things yet to come is greater than God. Only God is God. What a wonderful mystery!

The learning that we can launch in Christian higher education takes aim at the beatific vision of the always mysterious God central in the traditional Catholic view of heaven. In technical scholastic terms, we find our fulfillment through contemplating the first cause of the reality that we have been exploring our whole lives. This first cause, of course, is God. The efficiency that makes the world, and the finality that moves the world forward, and the formality that we focus upon when asking what creation is all occur adequately only in God. God is the sole sufficient reason for the world, as faith interprets our human experience. So to contemplate God, see God face to face, is to find the force, the mind, the love that we have been seeking in all our inquiries, no matter how piecemeal their fashion.

The funny kicker is that there is no end in God, and so no rest in heaven. The quest goes on, giving us wonderfully full employment. We shall never exhaust the splendid intelligibility of God, nor shall we ever stop finding new reasons for loving God's goodness, new glimpses of the divine beauty that ravish our hearts. If God is as the Christian tradition has tended to depict divinity and if we human beings are as crucially made for God as this same tradition has depicted us, then heaven is a nuptials without ending — a perfecting mating of cause and capacity that will bring us endless delight. Theologians are swinging at the end of their tethers, of course, when they speculate about the being of God and the share in that being that makes our heaven. But their speculations are so encouraging that we should forgive them their enthusiasms. Indeed, their speculations are virtual doxologies — songs of the soul praising God.

The "life" in the "lifelong learning" that we Christian educators should want to champion therefore does not finish at the grave. Certainly, we may hope to have helped our students to become properly sober, appreciating the force of human ignorance, mortality, and sin, but we may also hope to have helped them to hope for the resurrection of their bodies and their participating in the life of the world to come. I find myself wondering lately whether I do not hear far too little appropriate talk about the ultimate end of being human, as Christian faith understands it. I wonder whether we Christian intellectuals have not let ourselves become ashamed of our creedal hopes, abusing a proper movement to underscore Christian responsibility for the world by turning it into a neglect of the otherworldliness without which our faith cannot be what it has been down the centuries. This would be almost comically stupid, because it is so obvious that no human reforms, no matter how right and effective, are ever going to quiet our restless hearts, ever going to replace heaven. The Marxist critique of pie in the sky is only half right. Divinity has made us for itself. We have here no lasting city. The incarnate beauty of Christ bids us make earth as fair as we can, make the children of earth as wise as we can, but always with the proviso that we not forget the end of Christ himself, his death and resurrection, his ascension to the right hand of his Father for his fulfillment, his sending of his Spirit as a down payment on our own eternal life. The perspective of the New Testament forbids our being this-worldly in an exclusive sense. It insists that the following of our Lord make us citizens of two worlds, denizens of both now and then. As a result, our best learning both makes this world congenial and shows us why at his end Aquinas thought that all his writings were straw.

Education and Church Control

As a saint and a great intellectual, Aquinas resides in the public domain. The Christian church has no exclusive rights to him, holds no exclusive copyright. The same with other geniuses who have shaped high Christian culture: Dante, Michelangelo, Vivaldi, Mendel. This location of high Christian culture outside the controls of the church, in the public domain or commons, suggests a protocol for the conduct of Christian higher education. If by "the church" we mean Christian believers (more or less fervent, more of less orthodox, but nonetheless Christian in their bones — for example, James Joyce), then certainly the church is bound to exercise the sorts of controls that go into the making of high Christian culture. These controls, however, are almost without exception internal, intrinsic to the processes of art and science and theology that create high Christian culture. There is little in them of heteronomy, extrinsic police work. The control comes from the inspiration, which is that of Christian faith, hope, and love. The control comes from the Christian God, personified traditionally in the workings of the Holy Spirit and tending regularly to make Jesus the archetype of human achievement.

Christian education can learn most of what it needs to know to do its job well by contemplating the most illustrative achievements of high Christian culture. Parallel to the contemplating of exemplary recent figures (Cesar Chavez, Eric Voegelin, Rigoberta Menchú, Rosemary Haughton) who can stimulate precious reflections on what we ought to consider the models for our end products, our students, thirty years down the road stands a contemplating of figures at a greater distance who became great benefactors of their times by mining their Christian faith. We Christians should invite any educators or common people interested in contemplating the genius of a Cervantes or a Shakespeare to do so with ardor, just as we should consider our modest own the example of a Buddha, a Nagarjuna, an al Ghazali, a Newton, an Einstein, a Max Planck, a Mohandas Gandhi, a Jackson Pollock, a Georgia O'Keeffe, a Mary Cassatt, a Toni Morrison.

These are all public figures reminding us of great achievements displayed out on the commons, the green sward that delights us all. We cannot control this commons, in any restrictive sense. We cannot control education, if we let the term denote lifelong learning. And, in virtue of our own incarnational faith, we Christians should not want to. In virtue of our own incarnational faith, we Christians should believe that Christ has made us free for free art, free science, free political service, and, understood in Augustine's sense, free love. The climate and condition and effect of the Spirit of Christ is freedom. Any defensible control of education in things of moment for eternal life has to justify itself in terms of its serving freedom, its helping the free children of God enjoy their liberty more and more fully.

Getting down to the case of institutions of higher education run under Christian auspices, I find little changing. The analysis seems to me to hold as firmly for a Santa Clara University or a University of Notre Dame or a College of the Holy Cross or a College of Notre Dame of Maryland as for education and high Christian culture at large. Nothing human ought to be foreign to an institution of higher education run under Christian auspices, in virtue of the anthropology (understanding of human nature) foundational in the Christian creed. Nothing beautiful or wise or salvific produced by an institution of higher education run under Christian auspices, or by any other sort of institution run under Christian auspices, for example, an office of Catholic Charities or an office of the American Friends Service Committee, ought to be withheld from the commons, the public domain.

The intellectual life, as we find it housed in our universities, has as one of its glories a commitment to publication — making what scholars discover available to all. The contemplative colony is not a gnostic circle, in the sense of a group closed to outsiders who want to learn but are deemed unworthy because of some characteristic secondary to their humanity (age, race, sex, nationality, religion).

The coin of the realm in a healthy college or university is intellectual acumen, demonstrated intellectual competence. The value of the realm is the new knowledge that it generates, the old wisdom that it repristinates, and the traditioning that it accomplishes by initiating a new generation of intellectuals.

It is both foolish and vain to try to control this intellectualist process from outside. It is foolish: the coin of the realm makes outside controls counterfeit. It is vain: It will not work, the people involved would rather return to barter. The only effective ecclesiastical influence, shaping, or guidance of higher education is one that offers encouragement, financial support, and theological backing. Just as parents have to believe in their children and friends have to believe in their friends or love affairs go down the whirlpool for want of trust, so church leaders have to believe in higher education and trust that Christian intellectuals will take care of their own, for the sake of the common good.

This is an instance where the principle of subsidiarity developed in the history of Christian political reflection ought to come home to roost. We should try to solve problems at the most local level, empowering the leaders responsible so that they can do their jobs. We should not forget the principles of ecology and thereby isolate any local church or school or social office, but we should trust that the people involved there are the ones best equipped to deal with the problems and develop the potential in question. Otherwise, we are almost certain to commit several blunders. The first is issuing edicts when we do not possess the information necessary to make them wise and practical — which information includes a great deal of local common sense, a feel for the often largely tacit local dynamics. The second is puffing ourselves up through inflated estimates of the charismata of office in the church and taking two or three steps down the road to pharisaism.

The Pharisees whom we meet in the New Testament thought that they knew, that they were the wise guys, because they had the (largely self-conferred) degrees and status that set them up as the overseers of their times. Even prescinding from the lack of good faith that Jesus found in them, we can say that in the New Testament the Pharisees tend to be pompous asses. It should not have been their business to badger the man born blind or the woman taken in adultery, out of a fussy concern for the letter of the law. Their concern, like that of their priestly contemporaries, should have been the free, happy flourishing of the people's faith, of the life of the synagogue.

Equally, it should not be the concern of present-day church leaders to snoop into nooks and crannies of our Christian colleges, as though they knew better what the details of our curricula or our liturgies or our policies for hiring and firing ought to be than do we who work there every day. To their credit, the American Catholic bishops have largely agreed with this point of view, not intruding themselves into higher education and supporting it with few strings attached. For this, though, lately they have been taking some Roman flak, getting some Vatican grief. So we should offer them our helpful sympathy. They are suffering from a lack of wisdom in the leaders hierarchically above them, an abeyance of the principles of subsidiarity and collegiality. The good news is that this can make them less inclined to make such errors themselves.

In the next section I shall take up the issue of theology and church control, having in mind such recent cases as those of Charles Curran, Edward Schillebeeckx, Hans Küng, and Gustavo Gutiérrez — *causes célèbres*. In this section I have already alluded to the principle of subsidiarity. Let me conclude by musing about the principle of collegiality.

What comes to mind first is the tradition of the Eastern Orthodox churches, which opted historically not to place themselves under Roman primacy but to function as a concerto of bishops. Second comes to my mind the supposed completion at Vatican II of the ecclesiastical business begun at Vatican I. At Vatican I the spotlight fell on the rights and services of the papacy, culminating in the definition of papal infallibility. At Vatican II the spotlight fell on the bishops, supposedly constructing the proper setting for the Petrine office, which was for the bishop of Rome to be first among a college of equals. Concern for the church universal falls to the whole college. Oversight belongs to the entire episcopate, indeed, in humbler fashion, to every Christian. Collegiality therefore is arguably at the heart of ecclesiology. The consultative monarchy that I have described as desirable at local levels loses none of its twofoldness when we consider how government may function best at the higher levels of the Roman Catholic Church, where the Petrine office is most honored.

For the more restricted part of the flourishing of the Christian community that falls to higher educators, the principles of subsidiarity and collegiality imply as an ideal a great freedom and a small oversight, in the context of a warm, mutually supportive collegiality. Educators ought to have all the support and power ("portfolio") that they require to do their jobs well. Ecclesiastical overseers ought to trust what these educators are doing, be grateful for their hard labors, and meet with them in a spirit of brother-and-sisterhood to discuss how something already good might become still better.

As American Catholic educators keep reporting to Rome, apparently without having yet gotten their message across, cultural context is crucial. One cannot think usefully about the future flourishing of a university such as Georgetown or Notre Dame or Boston College without appreciating the history of higher education, both general and Catholic, in the United States and the implications of our current American cultural pluralism. The United States is not Italy or Spain or India or Argentina or Malaysia. Just as we should not try to fit Christian higher education in those countries to an American bed, so we should not try to fit Christian higher education in the United States to any of their beds, or to some cot thought to be universally Christian. Procrusteanism is foolish wherever we practice it. We can not dissolve the dialectical tension between the one and the many by a single canonical code.

The one and the many in the church, which is universal and which varies from locale to locale, ought to stand in a creative tension, and by and large they do. In necessary things (which are few, if we take our view of Christian faith from the simple creed), we should be one. In doubtful things (which are most, due to human beings' historical and geographical variety), we should all be free. And in all things, we should love one another as we love ourselves, giving one another the benefit of the doubt, speaking fully honestly and encouraging others to answer completely without guile.

This is collegiality expanded to the proportions it requires if the church today is to enjoy simultaneously the power and the benefits implied in two of its traditional notes: oneness and catholicity. Without agreement on the creed, we cannot be a community sufficiently united to function honestly and well as the people of Christ. Without freedom to preach the gospel to all nations, baptizing every child of woman that we can in the name of our trinitarian God, we cannot be catholic. By extension, we cannot be catholic without assuming that any native culture has a soul naturally Christian and making ourselves the servants of the healthy emergence of this natural Christianity in a given time and place. By extension, we cannot be one unless we can all love and respect the offices, such as the Petrine and the episcopal, that serve us the great good of being in fact a community that hangs together because we have taken to heart the cross and triumph of Jesus.

Opinions can vary about what needs to be done to move Christians closer to an ideal balancing of unity and catholicity, through a wiser and more loving collegiality. What cannot vary, in my view, is a commitment to honor both sides of the equation — to keep the seesaw level. In Christian higher education, the seesaw is moving away from a time when religious communities controlled most of the play to a time when lay people ought to shoulder more of this responsibility. In my view, however, the typical Catholic college also needs to move the angle of its articulate theology up and the angle of its tolerance for secular self-definitions down.

Finally, none of us should fear or resent inquiries from any sector of the public we serve about what we are doing presently. Specifically, if people in Christian higher education fear discussions with ecclesiastical leaders, American bishops themselves or their representatives, then there is work to be done on both sides. Good leaders do not want to excite worry or fear. It is only tyrants who think that the pagan emperor ("Let them hate me as long as they fear me") was an admirable example. Faithful disciples desire a communal discernment of spirits, examination and manifestation of conscience, and representation to their superiors of how things are going in their pursuit of the common good. When the church, all of us lay Christians and our hierarchical leaders together, thinks about higher education, it is this communal discernment that I would urge, because it offers the best promise of making us all fully aware that we all are simply (sinful) people whose lives are short, who have never become God's privy counselors.

Theology and Church Control

The only aspect of the question of how church leaders ought to deal with theologians that falls to me by right, by the design of this essay, is the academic one. When I survey the orbit of concerns entailed by this Christian theological reflection on higher education I find one significant work to be that of academic theologians — professors in colleges or universities who deal with the zone of divinity from a commitment of Christian faith. They are not professors of religious studies, who in my distinction between religious studies and theology are not obligated to believe in the faith that they are explaining. Rather academic Christian theologians are professors who (1) accept the traditional Christian notion that theology is faith seeking understanding and (2) offer to the Christian community as a whole the service of their often excellent training in making the various articles of the Christian creed as intelligible as they can be in view of the intrinsic mysteriousness of God. What would the leaders of the church who feel themselves empowered and held to exercise responsibility for the teaching (*magisterium*) of the Christian faith think of, do with, academic theologians, were such leaders optimally dextrous and wise? That is the question I want to pursue here.

Granted what has gone before this section, the reader will not be surprised to find that I think that optimally dextrous, wise church officials would think well of academic theologians and would treat them well, mainly by trusting their integrity and leaving them free to exercise their presumable charism of explicating Christian faith creatively and faithfully. Just as there is no substitute in art for the artist's self-criticism, which in times of being ignored by the critics and the public has to become a touching auto-cheerleading but in times of fame has to become a keen nose for bullshit, so there is no substituting for the theologian's own conscience, her own love of the faith that she is exposing and deep desire to serve it well.

It is stupid, crude, and insulting all in one for people who are not trained theologians to set themselves up as arbiters of work on the front lines. It is an embarrassing hubris or simple lack of self-knowledge for bishops who have not themselves cracked a demanding book in twenty years to say that genius like that of Rahner or Lonergan has stepped over the line. The charism of office does not convey any immediate boost of one's IQ to cover the fifty-point spread separating one from a genius like Lonergan. There is no substitute for either natural talent or long years of studious work. It is as astounding as it is naive and prideful for a church leader to think that, simply by having been anointed into a given office, he has become holy, or wise, or learned. God save us from the dumb and the proud — above all, from the dumb who are also proud.

What ought to happen is that theologians should work in conditions that give them the maximal freedom and then maximal responsibility should be asked of them. They then publish the fruits of their researches (historical, biblical, doctrinal, ethical) and let the chips fall where they may. If those responsible for guiding the church as a whole judge that a given formulation of the faith threatens to do more harm than good to the simple laity, they have the duty and so the right to counter such a formulation and discourage its promulgation among the Christian masses. In other words, they ought to say, simply and, one would hope, after consultation with the troublesome author, that Rahner's view of "anonymous Christians," or Curran's view of the supremacy of the individual conscience in the matter of contraception, or Schillebeeckx's view of the divinity of Jesus, or Gutiérrez's view of the political entailments of the gospel presents problems of sufficient moment to trouble those holding care for the soundness of doctrine in the church. Rahner, Curran, Schillebeeckx, and Gutiérrez (and Boff and de Lubac and J. C. Murray, and all the others, recent or long past, who have run afoul of the Holy Office/Congregation for the Doctrine of the Faith) ought to be left free, indeed ought to be supported in their intellectual freedom, so that they might be as ruthlessly scholarly (honest) and creative as possible. They ought to be left free, indeed encouraged, to say exactly what they think, on the basis of painstaking research, and then expected to say, "So be it," if those responsible for the faith of the church universal find their findings problematic, especially pastorally.

What should not happen is that theological scholars feel pressure from church authorities to tailor their researches to the cloth of the bishops, the cardinals, even the popes involved. In the conscience of any genuine scholar lives a far higher authority, the one holy God. What the institutional leaders of the Catholic church have often chosen not to understand is the rightness of the critique and genius of the Protestant Reformers. The church is not God — cannot be, without promoting itself as an idol. The conscience of the individual believer has an unmediated connection to God, as well as a mediated one, and this unmediated connection ought to be inviolable.

The understanding of loyalty to the church expressed in the famous dictum of Ignatius Loyola that "what I see as white, I will believe to be black if the hierarchical church thus determines it" will not pass muster nowadays. If one thinks nowadays, after the Enlightenment, about what intellectuals owe to the church and about what church leaders ought to want of intellectuals, to say the least one has to enter more nuance. If I see something as white, and after being told that it is black still see it as white, I have to keep saying that to me it seems white. I can say that my superiors tell me that it is black. But I cannot say that their telling me this has changed what I see, if in fact it has not. In most cases I can leave to them the responsibility for acting on what I take to be an error; I cannot only if such a leaving would be sinful — likely to produce serious practical harm. I can be prudent about my disagreement with them, so as not to undercut their rightful authority. But I cannot lie to them or for them. If they do not like what I have to say, that's their problem. My problem is to keep faith with the truth, which includes both what I see and their rightful interest in my vision.

The leadership of the church has no right, indeed if it knew its business would never want to claim the right, to bully our consciences, our judgments speculative or practical, so as to pressure us to call black white, or white black, or purgatory a scriptural doctrine, or celibacy for priests a scriptural doctrine, or the ordination of women a contradiction of the will of Jesus, or — on and on and on. Such would be a scandalous state of affairs, meaning by that precisely the church's leadership putting in the way of our faith a large, unnecessary stumbling block.

We have to keep faith with what we know to be the case for us through our most honest assessments of conscience. If in such assessments we find, again and again, that God has made us lesbian or gay, then that is what we are, regardless of what some church officials say we ought to be. If in such assessments we find that we have to limit our family and that church-approved practical interpretations of "natural" contraception just do not allow us to meet our obligation to limit our family, then we have to conduct our marital relations on the basis of this most conscientious decision. A healthy teaching authority in the church would rejoice to see us doing so.

Healthy teachers want their students to mature and flourish, even if this means that the students come to criticize the teachers sharply. Healthy parents want their kids to become independent, even if the price is some years when the kids are mouthy. The church cannot be what it is and should be, a community of free adults, unless it truly wants the independent loyalty of its members. Jesus was not in the business of compulsion. The loyalty that he sought was not the kind canonized in the military or many business corporations, let alone in the mafia. Jesus was willing to let his deeds be the proof of his mission. He was willing to rest his case on the assumption that fair-minded people would find him credible. As the New Testament presents things, his denunciation of the Pharisees who came to plot his death focused on their foul-mindedness. They did not judge justly. They brought prejudices, unnegotiable agendas, that blinded them to the truth.

The deepest reach of the irony dripping through John 9, the story of the man born blind, is that the Pharisees claim to see but do not — will not admit the evidence of their senses because of their ideology. They find it intolerable that Jesus should be the messiah, let alone the Son of God. Therefore, the deeds that proclaim Jesus to be the messiah cannot have happened. The fallacy is as gross as that. The lesson is as simple: Judge theologians by their whole service to the church; judge individual Christians by the overall conscientiousness of their behavior. In both cases, assume competence and good will until the evidence no longer allows that assumption. Do not think of yourself as a watchdog, a policeman of correctness. Think of yourself as a senior partner in a dialogue about what faith can mean and how best to render it for the good living of the life of Christian discipleship — the good living of the free, joyous children of God.

Wisdom and Dying

Recently I looked through a series of studies published in the 1994 volume of *Theological Studies* (pp. 706–38). Back to back, continuously, ran a note on the ordination of women and an exchange about the infallibility of the ordinary magisterium. The note called into serious question the scholarship behind such Vatican statements as Pope John Paul II's *Ordinatio Sacerdotalis* of May 30, 1994, and the Sacred Congregation for the Doctrine of the Faith's *Inter Insigniores* of October 15, 1976. The conclusion was that theologians want intrinsic reasons for official interpretations of faith, and that these documents do not give them. The intrinsic reasons cited from the medieval authorities used to bolster the documents boil down to the natural inferiority of women to men. Even the Vatican pauses nowadays before basing its views of who is eligible for ordination on such a reason.

The exchange between Germain Grisez and Francis A. Sullivan over the infallibility of the ordinary magisterium has in the background an article that Grisez and John C. Ford published in *Theological Studies* in 1978 arguing for the infallibility of the church's teaching about contraception. As the distinctions mounted, I lost heart, finding it enough to agree with Sullivan that it is hard to call infallible a position not commanding a consensus among professional theologians.

The first piece, the note on the ordination of women, struck me as scholasticism at its best — and not simply because I could cheer the result that emerged: a demonstration that the official position to date does not provide intrinsic reasons why women cannot be ordained. The three pieces constituting the exchange about the infallibility of the ordinary magisterium struck me as scholasticism at its worst — and not simply because I disliked the notion of breaking infallibility free of the strict conditions imposed on it by many theologians, which tend to limit the infallible pronouncements of the popes to two: the declaration of the immaculate conception of Mary and the declaration of her bodily assumption into heaven. Grisez and Sullivan whittled down the substance of the issue between them to so thin a difference that I could hear Nero fiddling. I realize that the issue itself could bear enormous implications, as Bernard Cooke's fine popular series of articles on the papacy imply (see the *National Catholic Reporter*, February and March 1995). But the form in which these two professional theologians were casting their argument made me call into question the wisdom of all such ventures. At some point talmudists and koranic lawyers and Christian canonists and scholastic theologians ought to realize that they are abusing the faith they ought to be serving. At some point it ought to be manifest even to them that their slicing away kills the living body and turns their classroom into a morgue.

I want Christian higher education to operate from a vision, with a mentality, that makes faith come alive more fully — that is wise in the ways of the truly liberated mind. This means, I find, that my students need some schooling in how best to listen to the authorities who are proposing to mediate the Christian tradition to them (which on occasion includes me). On the one hand, they ought to be docile — teachable, willing to let their minds be led by accurate references to venerable authorities and clear expositions of intrinsic reasons, which, in theology, obviously have their limits, due to the mysteriousness of God. On the other hand, they ought also to be critical — inclined to ask whether the rendition of the venerable authorities is fair, to ask what changes when one takes into account the differences between the times of such past authorities and our present times, and to ask finally whether the reasons brought forward for the official position are in fact persuasive. In the case of the ordination of women, if the times have changed significantly since the days of either Jesus or the medievals, and if the main intrinsic reason adduced for the nonordainability of women to the priesthood is the natural unfitness of women for the ruling station that orders imply in a hierarchical church or, alternatively, is women's lack of the physical resemblance to the male Jesus that officiating sacramentally *in persona Christi* requires, then I hope that my students will find themselves puzzled, unpersuaded, and skeptical.

Wisdom involves a maturation of mind and heart, of imagination, reason, and will, that leads to a lovely balance between credulity and skepticism, between flaccid openness and hard closedness. It involves trying to hear accurately, understand clearly what one has heard, sift both one's hearing and one's understanding judiciously, and then move calmly into an action consonant with one's judgments. Wisdom is humble but also courageous. It knows that one may be only a child, a novice, concerning the matter in question, but it will not let one say that the emperor has clothes if it sees him buck naked and shivering.

Occasionally we come to divides, differences of opinion entailing crucial decisions, that yawn like grand canyons. Fortunately these are few and far between. Normally the position of the Vatican about the ordainability of women is sufficiently marginal to the overall goodness of maintaining one's Christian faith by living in the Catholic Church that the position need not lead one into a crisis of conscience and a shift of church allegiance. However, I now see every month signs that many women are seriously disaffected from their natal Catholic faith, and in some of these cases the estrangement is very painful. On the whole the women are wise enough to realize that the church is quite different from God, and that all the other churches have their problems. But a kinder, gentler, wiser church leadership would provoke much less estrangement. Indeed, a truly wise church would, in my opinion, encourage all its people to take themselves less seriously, beginning dramatically at the top.

What is the link between this sort of savvyness, this quite political wisdom, and death — the link that the heading of this section implies? The link is that because we all die, all of us have built-in the rudiments of the wisdom of not taking ourselves too seriously. For the purposes of this essay, the point is that we educators have going for us the sad but not grim reality that no one human has yet defeated death — that even kings and cardinals and Gilgameshes die. For Christians, the sadness of death is not grim, but only because of Jesus. No king or pope or professor can cause death not to be grim. Only the resurrected Christ can do this.

If we do not set our educational ventures against the backdrop of human mortality, they will not be realistic. That was a major argument I tried to make early in this essay. It is equally true, however, that if we do not make the resurrected Christ our decisive hermeneutic in assessing the significance of human existence, our educational ventures will not be Christian. We may claim that they are Christian. We may advertise them as Christian. But their substance, their intellectual vision, their wisdom will not in fact be Christian. And so, they will not in fact, by right, counter the grimness that human existence without faith in the resurrected Christ is bound to carry. They will not elaborate the heights and depths of a news that is good through the grave and beyond.

Unless one thinks that God is not good as Jesus depicted him to be, dying in Christian faith is a comforting prospect. Educators should indeed prepare their students to make their way well in the world, but an all-important factor in this preparation is laying out the significance of death. For Christian educators, the significance of death is penultimate. By the paradigm of Jesus, the use of Jesus as their privileged point of entry, Christian intellectuals can think thoughts about the world and human destiny that suggest how to live in time with grace. They can speak practically of a balance between commitment and detachment that reflects the work, death, and resurrection of Jesus. This balance can hold good prospects for helping students be present to the moments constituting their days without getting submerged in them and so losing their grace. Educators can also speak speculatively of a similar grace of the mind, a similar balance in one's worldview, that comes from appreciating the divine dimension of reality through the lens of Jesus, the Incarnate Word of God.

Jesus, the Incarnate Word of God, suggests that the world comes from God, and so is both holy and important. He also suggests that the world is not God and so is not the most holy or important reality that human beings deal with. Reality is twofold, and so the minds that deal with reality best, the hearts that love reality best, balance two allegiances. Jesus is fully human, and so should we disciples of Jesus try to be. Jesus is fully divine, and so we disciples of Jesus should worship and pray that his Spirit will accomplish our divinization through faith in him.

The same Ignatius whose rule for thinking with the church I criticized earlier brought forth another dictum that I revere. We should work as though everything depended on God, and we should pray as though everything depended on ourselves. Translated for its speculative equivalents, I think that this Ignatian dictum means that we should think of God as the first mover, the most significant agent, in all that we do, and so be neither indolent nor workaholic. At the same time, we should also recognize our finitude, mortality, ignorance, and sinfulness, all of which threaten to mottle our work, our being, to the point where most of what we do miscarries, and this recognition should lead us to fall on our knees in profound prayer, aware that God must help us if we are to do any good or gain our salvation.

The two parts of the dictum loop together to form a single insight. God is always primary — everything good is always a grace. Before they come to us, our students ought to be able to understand the bare denotations of these words. In the midst of their time with us, we should try to make the words turn over, explode, blow out the windows to show brave new worlds. At the end of their lives, we can hope, our students may be able to bless us for having started them on an intellectual process that has ended with their being able to embrace the proposition that everything is grace and so that all matter of things can end well. That is precisely how I want my Christian theology of higher education to end.

Index